LEGENDS OF FLIGHT

WITH THE NATIONAL AVIATION HALL OF FAME

FOREWORD BY FRANK BORMAN

BILL YENNE

CONSULTANTS:

MICHAEL E. JACKSON, EXECUTIVE DIRECTOR, NATIONAL AVIATION HALL OF FAME

WALTER J. BOYNE

PUBLICATIONS INTERNATIONAL, LTD.

Bill Yenne has authored over two dozen books and is a member of the American Society of Journalists & Authors and the American Aviation Historical Society. Among his works on aviation are *U.S. Air Power, The History of the U.S. Air Force, The Pictorial History of American Aircraft,* and *The Pictorial History of World Spacecraft.*

Michael E. Jackson is on the Board of Directors of the National Aeronautic Association and is a member of State of Ohio's Committee on Aviation Education. With over 4,000 hours of flying time in various military and civilian aircraft, he has been awarded 21 different American and foreign decorations.

Walter J. Boyne is a retired colonel in the United States Air Force and a prominent military and aviation consultant and author. Mr. Boyne is former director of the National Air and Space Museum and the author of *The Smithsonian Book of Flight, Classic Aircraft,* as well as a host of other military and aviation titles.

Additional research and editorial assistance provided by C.V. Glines, a retired colonel in the United States Air Force, award-winning author, and curator with the History of Aviation Collection Department at the University of Texas, Dallas.

Special thanks to Kristine Kaske and David Bergiven of the Smithsonian Institution's Office of Printing and Photographic Services and to Rick Ruhman of the American Society of Aviation Artists for their generous assistance with this book.

FOR THOUSANDS OF YEARS, the sky has motivated humankind to reach for the limits. The literature and religions of the ancient Egyptians, Greeks, and Romans reflected their desire to take wing and fly. It was only a matter of time until humankind would find a way to meet this destiny. Once the Wright brothers and others of their time "broke the code," there was no stopping them. In less than a hundred years, humankind has not only overcome the forces that bound us to the earth but has ventured far into space and returned safely. What tremendous progress has been made in such a relatively short time!

The National Aviation Hall of Fame (NAHF) was founded in 1962 to honor America's air and space pioneers. In 1964, President Johnson signed an Act of the U.S. Congress officially chartering the National Aviation Hall of Fame as the nation's way of recognizing United States citizens who have made significant contributions to aviation and aerospace.

The first NAHF enshrinees were, appropriately, Orville and Wilbur Wright—the first to fly a powered, heavier-than-air aircraft. Since the first ceremony in 1962, over 150 aviation greats have been enshrined into the National Aviation Hall of Fame. These enshrinees cover the entire spectrum of aviation accomplishment. The National Aviation Hall of Fame enshrines military and civilian pilots and astronauts, but induction is not limited to pilots only. The organization welcomes inventors, record setters, business leaders, and major contributors to the advancement of all areas of aviation.

One could write at length about what the mission of the National Aviation Hall of Fame strives to accomplish. The NAHF perpetuates the memory of aviation greats, honors their accomplishments, and promotes their achievements; but, in the final analysis, the National Aviation Hall of Fame is about two things: people and aviation. It represents the continuing story of people who faced seemingly insurmountable obstacles and found a way to overcome the problems and advance mankind into the air and into space. One might argue whether the story began at Huffman Prairie near Dayton, Ohio, or in Kittyhawk, North Carolina, or even earlier, but no one can predict where it will lead.

While all of the individuals included in this book are not enshrinees in the National Aviation Hall of Fame, they share common characteristics the NAHF honors: a sense of adventure, the willingness to take risks, curiosity, dedication, and a love of flight. That is what makes these people legends of flight and what the National Aviation Hall of Fame honors through its enshrinees and in the spirit of flight throughout the world—and beyond.

Michael E. Jackson
Executive Director
National Aviation Hall of Fame

CONTENTS

PREFACE ★ 3

FOREWORD ★ 6

INTRODUCTION ★ 8

CHAPTER 1
THE WRIGHTS LEAD THE WAY ★ 12

Wright Flyers I, II, III, and Model A
Curtiss *Reims Racer*
Blériot XI
A.V. Roe Triplane *Avroplane*

CHAPTER 2
AMERICA FALLS BEHIND ★ 32

Royal Aircraft Factory S.E.5a
Sopwith Camel
Glenn Martin Bombers
de Havilland DH-4
Nieuport 11 and 17
Spad XIII
Fokker E.III, Dr.I, and D. VII
Curtiss JN-4

CHAPTER 3
THE GOLDEN AGE OF FLIGHT ★ 58

Lockheed Vega
Ryan NYP *Spirit of St. Louis*
Douglas World Cruisers
Boeing P-26 Peashooter
Boeing 247
Curtiss Schneider Trophy Racers
Piper Cub
Douglas DC-2 and DC-3

CHAPTER 4
WORLD WAR II ★ 92

Curtiss P-40 Warhawk
North American P-51 Mustang
Boeing B-17 Flying Fortress
Grumman F6F Hellcat
Mitsubishi A6M Reisen Zero
Supermarine Spitfire
Messerschmitt Bf109
Boeing B-29 Superfortress

CHAPTER 5
THE COLD WAR ★ 128

Lockheed P-80/F-80 Shooting Star
North American F-86 Sabre
Boeing B-52 Stratofortress
McDonnell Douglas F-4 Phantom II
McDonnell Douglas F-15 Eagle
Boeing KC-135 Stratotanker
Lockheed C-5 Galaxy
Lockheed SR-71 Blackbird
Lockheed F-117 Nighthawk
Northrop B-2 Spirit

CHAPTER 6
THE JET AGE INTO SPACE ★ 168

Douglas DC-6
Beechcraft Bonanaza
Bell X-1
Learjet
Boeing 707 and 747
North American X-15
British Aerospace/Aérospatiale Concorde
Rutan Voyager
Rockwell Space Shuttle Orbiting Vehicle

APPENDIX ★ 204

INDEX ★ 212

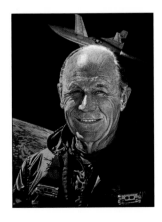

THE 20TH CENTURY will be remembered as the era of aviation. Compressed into a historically short period of time, an industry was born and flourished. But it is inaccurate to describe aviation merely as an industry. It is far more than that. The men, women, and machines that followed the Wright brothers' pioneering efforts in North Carolina literally changed our civilization. The change came rapidly. It is still hard for me to believe that I was circling the moon only 64 years after the first manned flight.

This remarkable book chronicles the aviation century, from 1900 to present day. Throughout this span of time, we find that the individuals were as different—and legendary—as the airplanes.

Astronaut Frank Borman accomplished a great deal during his NASA career. He was the mission commander for the Apollo 8 mission, which was the first time humans orbited the moon. During the Gemini 7 mission, Borman and Jim Lovell set an endurance record of 13 days 18 hours 35 minutes in orbit, which was the longest of all Gemini flights.

In December 1968, one day before the launch of Apollo 8, Jim Lovell, Bill Anders, and I had lunch with Charles and Anne Morrow Lindbergh. The introverted man who did more to popularize aviation than any other human was enthralled by the prospect of a lunar flight. The lunch lasted till almost dinner as we were able to turn the focus of the conversation from Apollo 8 to his historic flight to Paris. He remembered to the ounce the fuel burn of his Wright engine and other detailed parameters of

his voyage. His inquisitive mind calculated how far the fuel carried aboard the *Spirit of St. Louis* would carry Apollo 8 toward the moon (not very far). He obviously possessed a scientist's searching intellect. Lindbergh's natural shyness evaporated as he recounted his other aviation interests, including his association with Dr. Goddard and the early days of rocketry. His passion for flight and exploration was almost tangible.

To other pioneers in aviation, the airplane was not an instrument for scientific exploration but a machine for commerce or for defending freedom.

I remember a dinner I had with Captain Eddie Rickenbacker when I was with Eastern, trying to preserve the airline he built almost singlehandedly. His message was much more pragmatic than Lindbergh's. Safety, economy, modern aircraft, and hard work were words that flowed from his mouth. Words that flowed with the same passion Lindbergh had displayed. Rickenbacker was fond of talking about his civil airline experiences, including his near bout with death in a DC-3 crash, but he almost never referred to his World War I fighter exploits.

If I were to choose the one individual who contributed more to aviation than any other person in its first century, it would be a man who combined Lindbergh's intellect and inquisitiveness with Rickenbacker's drive and leadership. That man was Jimmy Doolittle. His accomplishments include the first flight totally dependent on instruments, the development of high-octane gasoline, the first raid on Tokyo, and wartime general and leader of the U.S. Strategic Bombing of Germany. All of this from a small, self-effacing man who never lost his zest for aviation. I listened intently one day at Wright-Patterson Air Force Base as he described his Thompson Trophy victory in the Gee Bee racer. Though he disliked the aircraft, he flew it very carefully to victory and then he never flew it again. As a matter of fact, he quit air racing because he thought the risk-to-reward ratio was too heavily weighted toward risk.

When I asked him about his many close calls, he assured me that he never took an uncalculated risk. His whole approach to aviation had been very conservative. He attributed his survival to that conservativeness—and a great deal of luck!

In the pages of this book you will be introduced to many legendary aircraft—the wonderful machines that allowed humanity to be unleashed from its earthly home. You will also find the story not only of Lindbergh, Rickenbacker, and Doolittle but of many other men and women who embraced this new medium with the enthusiasm that led to great achievements and great sacrifice.

Perhaps even more importantly, you will be able to capture that sense of fascination and wonder that led us to this calling. This desire that never seems to weaken our dream to spread our wings and fly!

People often ask me what was it like to fly to the moon. After a brief description, I tell them that the lasting memory I have of Apollo 8 was viewing the earth from the moon. I was filled with awe, wonder, and humility. I will never forget that moment. I will also never forget that wonderful moment 53 years ago when I sailed over a row of trees and brought a 65-horsepower Taylorcraft to a safe landing on my solo flight. The feeling of fascination was the same on both flights.

Frank Borman

Colonel Frank Borman
Astronaut, Gemini 7
Commander, Apollo 8

FROM THE STORY OF DAEDALUS and Icarus to the Wright brothers to Chuck Yeager, humankind has been fascinated with the ability to fly and the yearning to go faster, farther, and higher. Early artworks and paintings depict winged heroes and birdlike gods flying with ease and grace. Our fascination with flight inspired many experimenters and adventurers to explore the realm of the skies by creating all types of flying "machines."

We imagined that our science and our ability to engineer wonderful machines would allow us to conquer the skies. Even Leonardo da Vinci—who dreamed of human flight in the 15th century—had written that "a bird is an instrument working according to mathematical law…which it is within the capacity of man to reproduce with all its movements but not with a corresponding degree of strength, though it is deficient only in the power of maintaining equilibrium."

Believing that the flight of birds was merely a matter of mathematics and an exercise in engineering, da Vinci felt that humankind's superior ability to comprehend abstract reasoning would overcome our innate clumsiness to allow us to soar among the clouds. He was right, but it would take us a mere four centuries to get off the ground.

The chronicle of human flight started with the explorers who created the flying machines. Trying to imitate birds, adventurers created flapping wings, called ornithopters, to soar through

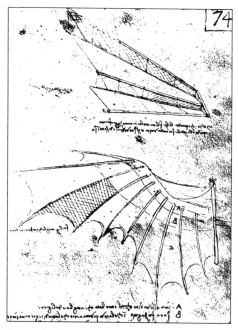

Leonardo da Vinci believed that humankind could achieve flight by emulating birds. His sketches of flying machines were based on his study of bird wings.

the air. From as early as the year 1010, experimenters tried—and failed—to fly with these devices. While the ornithopters were not successful, the study of their wings provided valuable information for the inventors of the 1800s. The result of their research led to the development of the glider.

Inventors, researchers, and engineers such as George Cayley, Otto Lilienthal, and Octave Chanute attained the dream of flying with their glider experiments. Cayley achieved a major breakthrough in heavier-than-air flight with his understanding of wing shape and lift. He developed several gliders with fixed, curved wings; his coachman became the first person to glide successfully in the air with one of Cayley's models.

With gliders, it seemed that humankind had achieved the "effortless" goal of flying through the skies like a bird. Even though glider flights were successful, humankind could not imagine a flight by a powered, piloted aircraft. When the explorers and pioneers of aviation finally did achieve powered flight, it was not as effortless as it was for birds—it was a challenge, and it was an adventure.

Throughout the history of humankind's experience in the air, there has always been adventures and adventurers. There are Lindberghs among us, and there are many of us who admire them for their spirit and for their yearning to go faster, farther, and higher. This book is about the adventures, the adventurers,

In 1783, lighter-than-air flight was achieved when the Montgolfier brothers from France invented the hot-air balloon. By November of that year, the first human flight was accomplished when the Marquis d'Arlandes and J. F. Pilâtre de Rozier floated over Paris in a Montgolfier balloon.

and the wonderful machines that made it all possible. This book is about them—the legends of flight.

The history of flight, as told through the legendary milestones chosen for this book, is a story of human achievement through technology and determination. It all began in 1903 at a place called Kill Devil Hill. "Only those who are acquainted with practical aeronautics can appreciate the difficulties of attempting the first trials of a flying machine in a twenty-five-mile gale," wrote Wilbur and Orville Wright. "As winter was already approaching, we should have postponed our trials to a more favorable season, but for the fact that we were determined, before returning home, to know whether this machine possessed sufficient power to fly, sufficient strength to withstand the shock of landing, and sufficient capacity of control to make flight safe in boisterous winds, as well as in calm air. When these points had been definitely established, we at once packed our goods and returned home, knowing that the age of the flying machine had come at last."

In their statement, which was the world's first aviation press release, the Wright brothers set out the same principles that have continued to be on the minds of every test pilot from their day to ours: Does it have sufficient power to fly? Does it have sufficient strength to withstand the shock of landing? Does it have sufficient capacity of control to make flight safe in boisterous winds, as well as in calm air?

Indeed the age of the powered flying machine had arrived with the Wright flight in 1903. The dream of da Vinci and other adventurers was fulfilled on a windy hill, but tomorrow would be, as it always is, another day. It would be a new day with new dreams and new challenges. The Wright brothers had their checklist, but as Louis Mouillard had asked in the latter 19th century, once humans had reproduced all "gaits of the bird," would we not want to challenge the possibilities beyond them?

And we would. First there was distance. Aircraft flew across the English Channel, then across the Atlantic, then around the world. In 1927, Charles Lindbergh flew nonstop across the Atlantic alone. In 1986, Jeana Yeager and Dick Rutan flew around the world nonstop. Then there was speed. Within ten years of the first flight, France's Maurice Prevost had broken the 100 miles per hour barrier, but within a generation, whole classes of aircraft would routinely fly faster than 400 miles per hour and would push the envelope of sonic flight, buffeted by the boisterous wind of the sound barrier.

When Chuck Yeager set out to break through the edge of that envelope in 1947, he asked of the Bell X-1 the same questions that the Wright brothers had asked of their Flyer I over four decades before. In the love affair with technology that characterized the era of Yeager's first supersonic flight, people asked themselves whether there were possibilities beyond their own achievement and imagined those possibilities to be infinite. Only 12 years after Yeager, when Scott Crossfield settled into the cockpit for the first flight of the North American Aviation X-15, he knew that this aircraft was mandated not simply to fly safely and land safely but to fly six times the speed of sound and to fly altitudes above 225,000 feet, nudging the edge of the envelope that separated safe landing from the realm of outer space.

Pilots have flown faster, farther, and higher, and they have experienced the solitude of solo night flight and peace among the clouds. They have also experienced the glory, gallantry, and sheer terror of aerial combat in every war fought in the 20th century. The first combat pilots took to the sky in World War I in cumbersome, boxy Fokkers and Sopwiths painted in bright colors, clattering through the sky at two miles a minute. Over the coming decades, aircraft designers modified the angular form of aircraft, coining the word "aerodynamic" to describe their sleek and fluid lines of the planes that evolved in the 1930s. By the time of World War II, the average speed of a combat aircraft had doubled—and doubled again.

The need for speed in aerial combat also hastened the development of jet engines. In the years leading up to the Second World War, jet propulsion attracted some attention but little investment. Indeed, it was not until the last year of the war, when Germany's amazing Messerschmitt Me262 proved itself in battle, that jets were embraced with enthusiasm. After the war, piston-engined combat aircraft were abandoned en masse in favor of fast jets. Though it would take about 15 years, jets also replaced their piston sisters on the commercial airways. The jets revolutionized air travel, shortening distances and cutting travel times. Within a generation, trips we accepted as a long and virtually unthinkable journey had come to be perceived as a routine vacation.

But pilots fly for reasons other than faster, farther, and higher. "The sun at twilight from up there," wrote Jacqueline Cochran, the first woman to fly faster than the speed of sound, "seems twice as bright and warm while rolling over the horizon with a smiling good night. The stars seem to hold their distance by only a mile or two.... I have chased many a rainbow through the heavens and I have also chased a moonbow."

As Cochran suggests, pilots also inhabit another world. In 1933, Peter Supf wrote in his book *Airman's World*, "The airman has to renounce many of the delights of the traveler on the ground. The scents and sounds of the earth are not for him. He cannot see the thousand tiny beauties of the summer day, the open cups of flowers, gleaming beetles, and flaunting butterflies; he cannot hear the wind in the leaves or the twittering of birds. But he is compensated by charms of a different sort. He delights in the ever-changing patchwork of light and shadow on the earth's surface, the toylike aspect of everything beneath, the wonderful patterns which roads, rivers, valleys, forests and hedgerows provide in unbroken succession.... The loveliest play of colors I ever saw was on arriving over Venice. Suddenly the sea shimmered a silken grey between white clouds. Then the clouds were behind us and the sea was blue, flecked with four, five, six rows of white combers.... In the midst of all this, the island city of Venice, and smaller islands set in shining emerald green.... I never knew Venice until I had seen it from the air."

Have we as a species conquered the air? Did da Vinci believe—when he imagined people emulating birds—that we would or could conquer the air? Did Mouillard have it in mind when he dreamed of challenging the possibilities beyond the capabilities of the birds? We don't know what they imagined, but in fact, we have not conquered the air. The air cannot be vanquished and that is why, for us, flight will always be an adventure.

The pilot is always in awe of those unconquerable skies. John Gillespie Magee, Jr., was an American who enlisted in the Royal Canadian Air Force in October 1940 and was sent to England to fly Spitfires. Magee was killed in action in a dogfight on December 11, 1941. He was 19. The sonnet "High Flight," composed shortly before Magee's death, eloquently expresses the wonder and beauty of the skies.

> Oh, I have slipped the surly bonds of earth
> And danced the skies on laughter-silvered wings;
> Sunward I've climbed, and joined the tumbling mirth
> Of sun-split clouds—and done a hundred things
> you have not dreamed of—wheeled and soared and swung
> high in the sunlit silence. Hov'ring there,
> I've chased the shouting wind along, and flung
> My eager craft through footless halls of air.
> Up, up the long, delirious, burning blue
> I've topped the windswept heights with easy grace
> where never lark, or even eagle flew.
> And, while with silent, lifting mind I've trod
> the high untrespassed sanctity of space,
> put out my hand, and touched the face of God.

THE WRIGHTS LEAD THE WAY

HUMANS HAVE LONG dreamed of emulating the flight of birds. In Italy at the end of the 15th century, two men, Leonardo da Vinci and Giovanni Battista Danti, designed machines for "mechanical flight" that were close to workable. In 1781, Jean-Pierre Blanchard in France designed a "Flying Chariot" in which the pilot sat at the center of a giant rotating fan. It might have worked, but the fan couldn't turn fast enough to get the vehicle off the ground. The need for a power source that could move a propeller faster than a human could with arms or legs was the critical stumbling

With Wilbur Wright looking on, Orville Wright sputters down the launch rail and lifts into the air in humankind's first powered flight on December 17, 1903.

block to heavier-than-air flight. By the early years of the 19th century there were steam engines capable of doing this, but these engines were too heavy to lift their own weight. It would take an internal combustion engine and the genius of two bicycle shop owners from Ohio to get the idea of heavier-than-air flight off the ground.

Lighter-than-air flight was another matter. By the end of the 18th century, scientists made two important discoveries: gases expand when heated, and warm gases rise since they are thinner. Theoretically then, if warm gases could be contained within an envelope, the envelope and lighter objects attached to it would also rise. In 1783, another pair of brothers, the Frenchmen

While the French led the way in sponsoring air meets, the Germans were also enthusiastic supporters of the new sport. Berlin promoters put up 150,000 marks and invited pilots from all over the world.

Joseph Michel Montgolfier and Jacques Etienne Montgolfier, invented the hot-air balloon based on that theory. In September of that year, the Montgolfiers held a demonstration before King Louis XVI and Queen Marie Antoinette. The first passengers to make the historic flight were a duck, a rooster, and a sheep. Then on November 21, 1783, the Marquis d'Arlandes and J. F. Pilâtre de Rozier floated over Paris in the first manned lighter-than-air balloon. Two years later, Jean-Pierre Blanchard, the same inventor who tried to build a heavier-than-air machine, was the first to fly the English Channel in a balloon.

While lighter-than-air technology advanced during the 19th century, heavier-than-air technology remained out of reach. In England during the 1840s, Sir George Cayley, England's "father of aeronautics," and also William Samuel Henson each designed several human- and steam-powered aircraft but none of those planes could get a human being off the ground in sustained flight; the steam engines were still too heavy. Cayley's work did a great deal to advance our understanding of aerodynamics and of how wings achieve lift. He built several successful model gliders, and his concepts of lift, propulsion, and control were developed by others.

Although the German inventor Otto Lilienthal successfully flew a small steam engine-powered model in 1877, it wasn't until 1891 when

In the years leading up to World War I, European aviation enthusiasts held numerous air races. The one held in Lyon, France, in May 1910 offered 200,000 francs in prize money.

he finally succeeded in building a glider that carried a human being. Lilienthal made over 2,000 flights in his gliders, covering distances up to 820 feet, before he was killed in a crash in 1896. It was during this same year that Samuel Langley successfully flew a model powered by a tiny steam engine.

Langley knew that steam technology could never be used in a heavier-than-air craft large enough to carry a person, and he was already looking at the new gasoline engines. What he did not know was that there were two researchers in Ohio who were also building gliders and exploring the use of gasoline engines. Thus the stage was set for the final dash to powered heavier-than-air flight.

THE FIRST POWERED heavier-than-air craft to successfully transport a human being, the Flyer I evolved from gliders that were designed and flown by Wilbur and Orville Wright between 1900 and 1902. Like the gliders, the Wright Flyer was a biplane with a framework constructed of spruce and ash that was covered with unpainted linen fabric. It had a wingspan of 40 feet 4 inches, a wing area of 510 square feet, and a length of 21 feet 1 inch. It was 8 feet high from the bottom of its landing skids to the top of the upper wing, and it weighed 750 pounds.

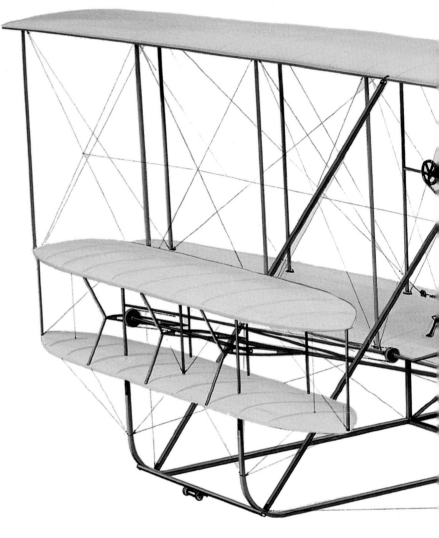

The idea of powering an enlarged version of a Wright glider evolved in October 1902 during conversations between the Wright brothers and their friend, engineer Octave Chanute. Based in Chicago, Chanute was also a glider-builder, and he was actively advising and encouraging the Wrights since 1900. Chanute came to North Carolina, where the testing was taking place, and after observing the excellent airworthiness of the gliders, he suggested that the Wrights were ready to try powered flight.

The Wright Flyer I was powered by a 12-horsepower gasoline engine with four in-line cylinders designed by the Wright brothers and built by their only employee, Charles E. Taylor. The first flight took place at Kill Devil Hill near Kitty Hawk, North Carolina, on December 17, 1903. Orville took off into a 27 miles per hour headwind and covered 120 feet in 12 seconds. The longest flight that occurred on the first day of trials was 852 feet in 57 seconds.

The Wright Flyer II was first flown from the Wrights' Simms Station airfield at Huffman Prairie near Dayton, Ohio, on May 23, 1904. The primary difference between it and its predecessor was that it was powered by a 16-horsepower engine.

However, both the Flyer I and Flyer II exhibited control problems when turning, so the Wright brothers went back to the drawing board. On September 20, 1904, the Flyer II became the first aircraft flown in a complete circle. Wilbur Wright's demonstration was important because it demonstrated the maneuverability of the aircraft.

Flyer III was similar to the first two in its overall appearance, but its design took into account many of the lessons

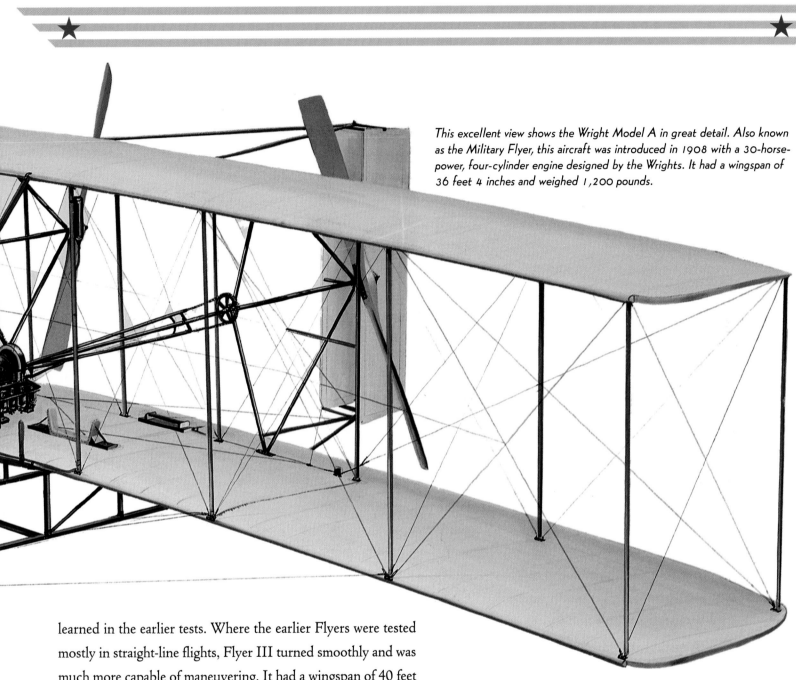

This excellent view shows the Wright Model A in great detail. Also known as the Military Flyer, this aircraft was introduced in 1908 with a 30-horse-power, four-cylinder engine designed by the Wrights. It had a wingspan of 36 feet 4 inches and weighed 1,200 pounds.

learned in the earlier tests. Where the earlier Flyers were tested mostly in straight-line flights, Flyer III turned smoothly and was much more capable of maneuvering. It had a wingspan of 40 feet 6 inches, a wing area of 503 square feet, and a length of 28 feet. Like the earlier Flyers, it was 8 feet high from the bottom of its landing skids to the top of the upper wing. Flyer III weighed 855 pounds, which was 14 percent more than Flyer I. The first flight test of Flyer III occurred on June 23, 1905, and it was in this aircraft that Wilbur Wright set a 1905 endurance record of 39 minutes 23 seconds.

In the meantime, there was a strong contingent in France, led by Ernest Archdeacon of the Aero Club, that refused to believe the Wrights had actually achieved heavier-than-air flight.

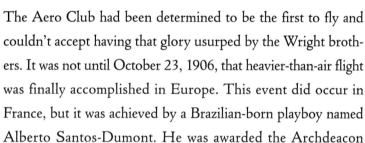

The Aero Club had been determined to be the first to fly and couldn't accept having that glory usurped by the Wright brothers. It was not until October 23, 1906, that heavier-than-air flight was finally accomplished in Europe. This event did occur in France, but it was achieved by a Brazilian-born playboy named Alberto Santos-Dumont. He was awarded the Archdeacon Prize and 3,000 French francs for having made the first Aero Club-recognized flight to exceed 812 feet—an accomplishment attained by the Wrights three years earlier.

Over the next two years, France became a center of aviation. Charles Voisin, Henri Farman, and Louis Blériot all achieved powered flight, and Santos-Dumont flew a monoplane. The

(Above left) *Before they achieved their legendary powered flight, Wilbur and Orville Wright conducted extensive tests with man-carrying gliders. Here, Orville is airborne on a North Carolina sand dune in their 1902 glider.* (Above right) *The history of aviation began at 10:35 on the morning of December 17, 1903, when Orville Wright lifted off for a 12-second flight over the dunes of the Kill Devil Hills. Wilbur watched with intense interest and then took a turn himself.* (Right) *The Wright brothers stand in front of their hangar at Simms Station on Huffman Prairie near Dayton, Ohio. Their Flyer, on its track, is ready for a test flight.*

In the fall of 1903, if a person had been called to wager upon who would lead the first project to achieve heavier-than-air flight, that person would have wagered on Samuel Pierpont Langley. He had the technical background and the effectively unlimited support of the Smithsonian Institution and the U.S. War Department. And he had an aircraft that was almost ready to fly—almost.

Born in Roxbury, Massachusetts, Langley was educated in Boston's public schools. Rather than attend college, Langley chose to teach himself and studied engineering. He held the chair in astronomy at the Western University of Pennsylvania (later the University of Pittsburgh) from 1867 to 1886. He also headed the Allegheny Observatory, where he studied sunspots, invented the bolometer to measure the distribution of heat in the solar spectrum, and developed a method to determine the solar constant of radiation. He was appointed assistant secretary in 1887 and secretary in 1891 of the Smithsonian Institution in Washington, where he established the Astrophysical Observatory.

Langley became interested in aviation and obsessed with the notion of heavier-than-air flight. In 1896, he successfully flew a 25-pound model airplane powered by a 1-horsepower steam engine. This test, performed in the presence of government officials and such notables as telephone-inventor Alexander Graham Bell, inspired a great deal of official interest.

Shortly before he was assassinated, President William McKinley earmarked the considerable sum of $50,000 from the War Department budget to finance Smithsonian secretary Langley in an official effort to build a heavier-than-air vehicle. Langley knew that steam propulsion was a thing of the past so he first turned to Stephen Balzer who designed and built an air-cooled rotary radial engine. Later, Charles Manly became involved with the project. He improved upon Balzer's design, creating the first successful internal combustion gasoline engine. Quarter-scale models of both Langley's aircraft and the Balzer-Manly engine were produced and successfully test flown in 1901 without a human pilot aboard.

The Aerodrome, as Langley dubbed his machine, was completed and ready for flight test in the autumn of 1903, even as the Wrights were putting the finishing touches on their Flyer. While the Wrights would use the lifting power of wings to get their airplane into the air, Langley's plan was to launch the Aerodrome from a catapult constructed on the roof of a houseboat anchored in the Potomac River.

The first flight test was scheduled for October 7, with Charles Manly at the controls. Everyone held their breath as the Aerodrome shot forward on the catapult, and everyone gasped as it crashed into the river. Not even a hint of lift had been achieved by the airplane, which now floated, badly damaged, in the Potomac. Amazingly, Manly survived the crash.

Langley and his large, competent Smithsonian/War Department crew rebuilt the Aerodrome and set up to try again. The date was set for December 8. This time, the rear wing failed on launch, and Manly was nearly killed as the disintegrating craft fell into the cold, dark waters. Langley issued an official statement that the Aerodrome project was over. Nine days later came the news that the boys from Dayton had flown their airplane at Kitty Hawk.

In 1914, Glenn Hammond Curtiss built an airplane that was similar to Samuel Pierpont Langley's 1903 Aerodrome.

Langley died in 1906, less than three years later. His successor as the Smithsonian secretary, Dr. Charles Walcott, later supplied the original Aerodrome to Glenn Curtiss, who would use the plane in his attempts to beat the patent-infringement lawsuit directed at him by the Wright brothers.

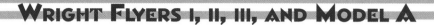

This photograph from around 1910 shows a good view of the Wright Flyer A making its way along its launch rail at Simms Station. In a moment it would be airborne and cruise over Huffman Prairie.

diehards still refused to believe the Wright Flyer could fly. Finally, in August 1908, Wilbur Wright went to France to put the issue to rest once and for all.

The demonstration was held at the Hunaudières racetrack near the city of LeMans. On the afternoon of August 8, hundreds of spectators gathered to watch the Wright's Flyer fly. The machine was lined up on the take-off rail mechanism. Wilbur climbed aboard and flexed the wing-warping mechanism that the Wrights used to control the wings. The engine came to life and suddenly the Flyer was airborne. Wilbur made a wide circle over the field, flying 2,500 feet in 105 seconds and landing to a wave of applause from the observers.

The French appreciated not only the fact of the flight but also its style. Wright's circle was observed as far smoother than that accomplished by Henri Farman when he flew Europe's first circular flight in January 1908. Archdeacon observed, "For too long a time the Wright brothers have been accused in Europe of bluff. They are today hallowed in France."

The flight at Hunaudières did more than prove that the Wrights were not bluffing, it led to financial gain for the Wright brothers since Flyers were soon produced in France.

The first Wright aircraft actually sold to a customer, however, was the Wright aircraft designated as the Military Flyer or the 1908 Flyer, which was also known as the Wright Model A. It was with this Flyer that the Wrights "sold" the public on the idea of flight. This aircraft was similar to its sisters in general appearance, but it was somewhat smaller and heavier. It had a wingspan of 36 feet 4 inches, a wing area of 415 square feet, and a length of 28 feet. The Model A weighed 1,200 pounds and was powered by a 30-horsepower, four-cylinder engine that provided a top speed of 44 miles per hour.

A month after Wilbur went to Le Mans, Orville Wright took the Model A to Fort Meyer, Virginia, to put on a demonstration for the U.S. Army Signal Corps. The Signal Corps was responsible for observation and reconnaissance for the Army, and they envisioned a useful role for airplanes in accomplishing this task. But before the Signal Corps accepted the plane, they required a series of trials for speed and duration of flight. The first flight on September 9 drew praise from the assembled Army brass, and on his second flight, Orville took Lieutenant Frank Lahm up in the air. Lahm became the first Army officer to fly in a heavier-than-air machine.

Over the coming week, Orville continued to make demonstration flights for the Signal Corps. All of these flights went smoothly until September 17. Wright took off with Lieutenant Thomas Selfridge. They made three circles at an altitude of 150 feet when suddenly there was a loud crack and the propeller spun off. The plane began to fall, and Orville struggled to maintain control. His efforts were to no avail, and the airplane crashed into the field. Selfridge struck his head in the crash and died that night—aviation's first fatality. Even though Wright was unable to walk away from the crash, he recovered to fly again.

The following summer, once Orville was well enough to fly, he resumed the trials of the Model A Flyer. On July 12, 1909, he took Lieutenant Frank Lahm as his passenger and flew the aircraft for more than an hour, demonstrating one of the Signal Corps' requirements for their Flyer. After the series of successful summer trials, the Signal Corps ordered their first Wright Military Flyer. The Flyers would continued to play an important role in the world of aviation for the next several years, but after Wilbur's death in 1912, the name was never again associated with an important aircraft.

(Right) *This artist's conception shows Orville Wright and a uniformed U.S. Army officer in flight over the verdant Virginia countryside in a Wright Model A.* (Below left) *This view provides a good look at the four-cylinder engine of the Model A Flyer. The engine was built by Charley Taylor and designed by the Wright brothers.* (Below right) *Pilot Calbraith Rodgers takes off in his Wright Model EX, bound for California in September 1911 on the first transcontinental flight. The aircraft bore the brand name of his sponsor, Vin Fiz Grape Drink.*

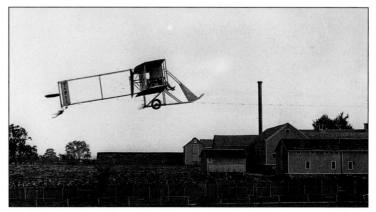

Wilbur Wright was born in Millville, Indiana, and his brother Orville was born in Dayton, Ohio, where they later opened a small bicycle manufacturing shop. In 1896, the same year Otto Lilienthal died and Samuel Langley first flew his powered model glider, the Wrights began seriously working on kites and gliders with an eye toward one day building a flying machine capable of carrying a person.

In 1900, the failure of their glider led the Wright brothers to build their first aeronautical wind tunnel so they could carefully study the flow of air over wings. Armed with this information, and with some engineering input from their friend, glider-builder Octave Chanute, the Wrights constructed the first of three biplane gliders. They also used U.S. Weather Bureau data to locate a place with strong, steady winds suitable for testing a glider. This led them to a place called Kill Devil Hills on North Carolina's Outer Banks near the town of Kitty Hawk.

Wilbur first went to Kitty Hawk in September 1900, and Orville followed three weeks later. The brothers returned to Kill Devil Hills each autumn for three years and made numerous flights. By October 1902, they made glider flights over 622 feet and were ready to try powered flight.

Late in 1903, Wilbur and Orville returned to Kill Devil Hills with their Flyer I biplane, which was driven by the Wrights' own 12-horsepower engine connected to two contra-rotating propellers with bicycle chains. They waited several days for the right combination of wind speed and direction, but on December 14, when Wilbur took the first turn, he suc-

Wilbur Wright tests the wind speed with his pocket anemometer in preparation for a demonstration flight in 1909. By this time, the brothers were at the peak of their success.

ceeded only in nosing the Flyer into a dune. Three days later, at 10:35 on the morning of December 17, Orville Wright lay down prone across the bottom wing and grasped the controls. With the small engine sputtering noisily, he coaxed the machine into the air.

The first powered flight of a heavier-than-air machine carrying a person lasted only 12 seconds, with Orville covering 120 feet. By the end of the day, each of the brothers had made two successful flights, with Wilbur covering 852 feet in his last turn at the controls. The telegram they wired home to Dayton closed with the simple phrase "Inform press, home Christmas."

Even before they left North Carolina to be with the rest of the Wright clan for the holidays, the news of their success had circulated throughout the world. The French expressed disbelief, the British Army sent a colonel from their balloon factory at Farnborough, and Samuel Langley fumed.

The Wright brothers set up their new Simms Station "test center" and airfield at Huffman Prairie near Dayton, Ohio. Now that they had moved from gliders to powered flight, they no longer needed the unique wind conditions of the Outer Banks. In May of 1904, their Flyer II made a number of successful flights, and the press was invited to watch. Like the original Flyer, however, it manifested a tendency to stall in turns, and the Wrights went back to the drawing board. The result was the larger Flyer III, which was a more reliable airplane and was able to successfully fly a distance of 24 miles. On October 5, 1905, it set an endurance record of 38 minutes aloft.

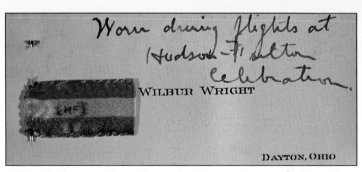

Wilbur Wright pinned his calling card with a special piece of ribbon. This ribbon was originally pinned to his lapel when he flew in the celebration commemorating Henry Hudson's sail up the Hudson River in 1809 and Robert Fulton's voyage by steam boat in 1809.

Their success with Flyer III gave the Wrights the confidence to start soliciting orders, but the governments of Britain, France, and the United States all rejected the idea of acquiring military Wright Flyers. It was not until 1908 when the U.S. Army finally ordered one, and by that time, several European inventors had successfully tested heavier-than-air machines.

The brothers made numerous demonstration flights in Europe and the United States. While Orville stayed in the United States to prepare for War Department tests, Wilbur traveled to Europe in 1908. On August 8, 1908, he made his first public flight at Le Mans, France. The French, who had accused the Wrights of bluffing, were greatly impressed. Wilbur continued making several flights in France, and Orville joined his brother there in

The two bicycle shop owners from Ohio, Orville (left) and Wilbur Wright.

1909. In countries where the governments had previously turned down military versions of the Flyer, there was now interest from private parties; the Wrights issued licenses for firms in Britain, France, and Germany to build their aircraft. In 1909, they founded the American Wright Company, and in 1910, they started a flying school in Montgomery, Alabama.

By 1909, however, only six short years after the triumph at Kill Devil Hills, the tide was running out for the brothers. For centuries, humans had dreamed of flight but were unable to construct the machine to make it possible. But now that the aviation genie was out

of the bottle, he was working double time. Aircraft manufacturers throughout the world were building successful airplanes. In France, Louis Blériot had built an airplane with which to cross the English Channel; in England, Alliot Verdon Roe built a triplane; and in the United States, the energetic Glenn Curtiss had transformed himself into the foremost American planemaker. When the French city of Reims held the first major aviation meet in August 1909, Curtiss's airplane placed first in the big race, with Blériot in second place. There were a half dozen Wright airplanes in the field, but they finished in the back of the pack.

The Wrights sued Curtiss for patent infringement and won some early rulings, but the case was stalled when the government pooled patents as an emergency measure during World War I. The case was never reopened after the war. It seemed that these aviation pioneers from Ohio were not destined to be captains of the industry.

Wilbur Wright died of typhoid fever in 1912, and Orville sold his interest in the American Wright Company (later the Wright Aeronautical Corporation) in 1915 to devote himself to his work as director of the Wright Aeronautical Laboratory in Dayton, Ohio. Over the years, he continued his research and was also appointed to the National Advisory Committee for Aeronautics, but for the most part, he maintained a low profile as a quiet observer of the aeronautical revolution that he had helped to spark.

THE FIRST AIRPLANE successfully designed and built specifically to win an international air race was the *Reims Racer*, also known as the Reims Machine. This plane was a modified variation of the Curtiss No. 1, or *Golden Flyer*, which was the first airplane developed by Glenn Curtiss after Alexander Graham Bell's Aerial Experiment Association (AEA) was dissolved.

In 1909, Glenn Curtiss went to France to take home a $5,000 air race prize offered by the American newspaper tycoon and sports promotor James Gordon Bennett.

Curtiss produced several aircraft for the AEA, notably the *June Bug*, which flew in June 1908. Only a month after the *June Bug* made its first flight, the Aeronautic Society of New York was formed to promote heavier-than-air flight. The Aeronautic Society was actually a spin-off of the Aero Club, which favored lighter-than-air flight, formed in 1905. One of the first steps taken by the Aeronautic Society was to approach Glenn Curtiss to build an airplane for the express purpose of teaching members to be pilots.

As winter came in 1908, the Aerial Experiment Association was on its last legs. Curtiss was doing work for the Aeronautic Society, and another important AEA member, U.S. Army Lieutenant Thomas Selfridge, was killed in the September crash of a Wright Flyer at Fort Meyer, Virginia. On March 31, 1909, Alexander Graham Bell abruptly announced that the AEA had accomplished its goals for research into heavier-than-air flight, and it would be disbanded. Curtiss now had more than enough incentive to throw himself into his work on the Aeronautic Society machine.

The *Golden Flyer* made its debut on May 29, 1909, at the Morris Park racetrack in the Bronx in New York City. Glenn Curtiss made the first airplane flight within the city limits of New York. The *Golden Flyer* had a wingspan of 28 feet 9 inches, a length of 33 feet 6 inches, and weighed 550 pounds. The *Golden Flyer* was powered by a 25-horsepower, four-cylinder in-line engine, built by Curtiss, which provided a top speed of 45 miles per hour. It was constructed of wood and bamboo and covered with rubberized silk. In its design, Curtiss made use of ailerons as control surfaces rather than the wing-warping mechanism the Wrights favored for control and maneuvering.

By this time, word was circulating about an international air race known as La Grande Semaine d'Aviation (The Grand Week of Aviation). This great race was to be held at Reims, France, in August 1909. It was the first major international air show, and four major prizes were awarded, including one from the expatriate American newspaper tycoon and sports promotor James Gordon Bennett. He offered a prize of $5,000 and a trophy to the fastest aviator.

(Above) *Glenn Curtiss prepares his Reims Racer for the 1909 Reims race. He went on to win the race, beating out England's George Cockburn and the legendary Louis Blériot, France's aviation hero.*
(Left) *Glenn Curtiss entered the Grande Semaine d'Aviation (The Grand Week of Aviation) at Reims in August 1909 using an aircraft based on the Golden Flyer, which he had built for the Aero Club of America.*

The Curtiss Reims Racer *was built by Glenn Curtiss specifically to win the Grande Semaine d'Aviation (The Grand Week of Aviation), an air meet held at Reims, France.*

Glenn Curtiss saw the race as an opportunity for good publicity. The Aeronautic Society was so pleased with the work he'd done for them, they readily agreed to help sponsor him. He also secured the endorsement of the Aero Club of America. Curtiss was the only American competing. There were several Wright-designed aircraft present, but the brothers did not attend. The original idea was to enter the *Golden Flyer*, but it was damaged in the previous month, so Curtiss decided to build a replacement at the same time the original was being repaired.

Though it was largely similar, the *Reims Racer* differed from its predecessor in that it was powered by a 51.2-horsepower V-8 rather than a straight four-cylinder engine. The engine weighed an additional 150 pounds, bringing the total weight to 700 pounds, but the increased power was worth the additional weight. Curtiss also had a hunch that the reduced wing area would decrease drag and increase speed, so he test flew the new aircraft leaving the fabric off the wing tips. It worked, so he trimmed the wings to 26 feet 3 inches. The length was 33 feet 6 inches—the same as the *Golden Flyer*.

The big day of the Gordon Bennett Race was August 28, 1909. The competitors were comprised of England's George B. Cockburn, three Frenchmen, including the great Louis Blériot, and Curtiss. Almost from the start, Curtiss amazed the crowd with his speed, edging out the second-place Blériot on the 40-kilometer course with a speed of 47.06 miles per hour to take the grand prize. The following day, Curtiss took first again to win the 30-kilometer Prix de la Vitesse.

Promoters throughout Europe begged Curtiss to bring the *Reims Racer* to their air shows, and he immediately accepted an invitation to Brescia in Italy where he won the Grand Prize, the Altitude Prize, and $7,600. It was a good summer for Glenn Curtiss.

Back in the United States, Curtiss demonstrated the *Reims Racer* in Los Angeles in January 1910 before leasing it to Charles Hamilton.

Born in Hammondsport, New York, Glenn Curtiss was enthralled by the excitement of motorcycle racing, and as his tinkering turned to building, Curtiss was soon building motorcycle engines. His interest in motorcycles turned to racing, and in 1907, he established a world's motorcycle speed record of one mile in 46 seconds.

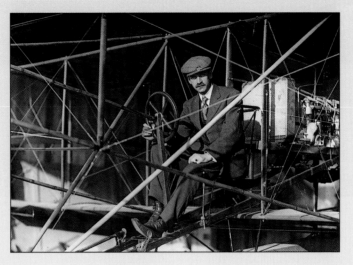

During the first decade of the 20th century, the news of the Wright brothers success had gotten a lot of young experimenters interested in aviation, and Curtiss was no exception. Late in 1907, he joined Alexander Graham Bell's Aerial Experiment Association (AEA), and soon he became the organization's star designer. On July 4, 1908, the AEA's third aircraft, the *June Bug* flown by Curtiss, won the Scientific American Silver Trophy for the first flight to exceed one kilometer. The *June Bug* was powered by a 40-horsepower air-cooled V-8 designed by Curtiss and Charles Kirkham.

In 1909, after Bell disbanded the AEA, Curtiss formed his own company. In August 1909, he took a version of the *Golden Flyer*, his first post-AEA airplane, to the first international aviation meet in Reims, France. Before a crowd of 150,000, he beat Louis Blériot by about six seconds to win the meet's 20-kilometer final race.

On May 29, 1910, Curtiss flew the *Hudson Flyer* from Albany to New York City in just under three hours to take a $10,000 prize offered by *The New York World*. Later in the year, Eugene Ely, one of Curtiss' company pilots, took off from the deck of the U.S. Navy's cruiser USS *Birmingham* in the same aircraft. This first-ever feat prompted the Navy into buying two Curtiss airplanes.

Though he was grabbing headlines and taking big prizes with his racing efforts, Curtiss was also busy on the design and innovation front. In 1911, he began building hydroplanes, or seaplanes, and in 1912, he won the Robert Collier Trophy for his development of the "hydroaeroplane." This led, in turn, to more orders from the U.S.

Navy, which allowed Curtiss's company to grow and prosper.

Meanwhile, the successful Glenn Curtiss was facing difficulties on another front. His company had eclipsed the Wright's as the United States' foremost aircraft and engine manufacturer, and the Wrights, who held many important patents, sued for infringement. The suit wound its way through legal corridors until 1914. By this time, Curtiss felt forced into a brazen and still-controversial stunt. In an effort to render the Wright patents void, he attempted to prove that Samuel Langley's Aerodrome, which had preceded the Wright Flyer I's flight by nine days, had really been a viable machine. In order to do so, Curtiss built and successfully flew an aircraft he touted to be an exact replica of the Aerodrome. It wasn't. It weighed twice as much, had a better distribution of weight, and the wings were configured differently. Even still, it couldn't stay in the air longer than five seconds. The case was never finally decided. During World War I, the patents were pooled in a wartime emergency and by 1919, none of the principals of the two firms were still in control.

In 1915, Curtiss, along with banker Clement Keys and John North Willys of the Willys-Overland Automobile Company, formed the publicly traded Curtiss Aeroplane & Motor Company, Ltd. During World War I, the Curtiss Aeroplane & Motor Company developed the famous JN series of training aircraft, known as "Jennies." This series of planes was the most widely mass-produced American aircraft in the first 15 years of aviation history. The company also continued to build and develop flying boats for the U.S. Navy, including the NC-4, which was used in 1919 for the first successful airplane crossing of the Atlantic Ocean. In 1929, shortly before Glenn Curtiss died, the Curtiss Aeroplane & Motor Company, Ltd., merged with the Wright Aeronautical Corporation to form the Curtiss-Wright Corporation.

THE AIRCRAFT USED by Louis Blériot for his historic first flight across the English Channel was the Blériot Type XI, a monoplane with a wingspan of 25 feet 7 inches and a length of 26 feet 3 inches. Designed by Louis Blériot, the Type XI was his fourth successful monoplane. It made its first flight on January 23, 1909, under the power of a 30-horsepower REP engine, but that power plant was later replaced by the 25-horsepower Anzani 3 engine.

Louis Blériot's cross-Channel flight in the Type XI came on July 25, 1909, when he took off from Les Barraques near Sangatte, France, and flew toward Dover in Kent. He flew the aircraft at an altitude of between 150 and 300 feet with his average speed being 45 miles per hour. The XI was not equipped with a compass, and Blériot drifted off course to the east. When he was finally able to see the English coast ahead through the fog, Blériot realized his mistake and turned to follow ships that he assumed were headed for Dover. He landed in a field near Dover Castle at 5:12 a.m., 37 minutes after takeoff.

Louis Blériot's success resulted in numerous orders for the Type XI, and it was sold to both military and civilian customers. Harriet Quimby, the first woman to fly the English Channel, also flew a Blériot XI. The Blériot XI also has the distinction of being the first airplane used in war, serving with Italy in its 1911 war with Turkey. On October 22, 1911, a Blériot XI became the first aircraft ever to conduct an aerial reconnaissance of enemy troops in wartime, and on November 1, 1911, a Blériot XI became the first aircraft to drop bombs on enemy positions.

Later, the Blériot XII was created as a direct development of the Blériot XI. This new Blériot first flew on June 12, 1909, and later became the first aircraft to fly with two passengers.

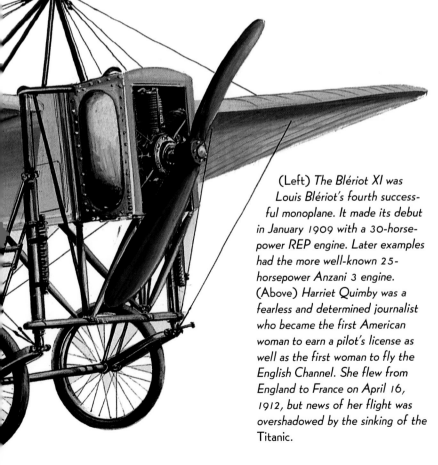

The designer of the first successful monoplane and the first pilot to fly across the English Channel, Louis Blériot was born in Cambrai, France, and studied engineering in Paris. In 1900, he built a motor-powered machine, called an ornithopter, intended to fly by flapping its wings. This experiment failed, but the undaunted Blériot continued his work toward a practical airplane.

During 1903, as Langley and the Wrights were at work in the United States, Blériot teamed up with Gabriel Voisin to build a floatplane glider, which flew during 1905. Blériot experimented with the design and construction of several biplanes before turning to the development of what would evolve into the world's first successful monoplane, the Blériot V, which got off the ground in 1907.

Blériot continued to build and develop both monoplanes and biplanes, while eyeing the £1,000 prize being offered by the London *Daily Mail* for the first successful flight across the English Channel. For this attempt, Blériot developed the Blériot XI monoplane, probably the most advanced aircraft of its era. Blériot took off from Les Barraques, near Sangatte, France, on the morning of July 25, 1909, and headed north into history.

Turning his attention to aeronautical design and engineering, Blériot became president of the aircraft company Société pour les Appareils Deperdussin in 1914. He renamed the company Société Pour Aviation et ses Derives (SPAD) and turned a floundering manufacturer of racing planes into one of France's leading manufacturers of combat aircraft. During World War I, SPAD built over 5,600 aircraft for France and exported some to Britain and other countries.

(Left) *The Blériot XI was Louis Blériot's fourth successful monoplane. It made its debut in January 1909 with a 30-horsepower REP engine. Later examples had the more well-known 25-horsepower Anzani 3 engine.*
(Above) *Harriet Quimby was a fearless and determined journalist who became the first American woman to earn a pilot's license as well as the first woman to fly the English Channel. She flew from England to France on April 16, 1912, but news of her flight was overshadowed by the sinking of the Titanic.*

IN THE HISTORY of British aviation, few aircraft builders have earned the prestige and reputation equal to that of the firm founded in 1910 by Sir Alliott Verdon Roe. Originally he called it the A.V. Roe Company, but he soon succumbed to the curse of a one-syllable surname and the company was renamed as, simply, Avro.

Roe's aviation career began,

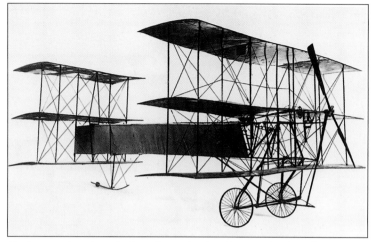

Roe's second triplane, built with metal rather than wood tubing for its frame, was first flown in 1910. He ultimately built two, one for demonstrations and one to sell to W. G. Windham.

as did many such careers in those days, with flying models. In 1907, he entered an aircraft design contest sponsored by London's *Daily Mail*, and he later built a full-size biplane in which he taxied and "hopped" but never actually flew. Roe's "hop" of June 8, 1908, was long considered to be the first powered heavier-than-air flight in British history, but in 1928, credit was officially transferred to J.T.C. Moore-Brabazon who achieved sustained flight on May 2, 1909, in a French Voison airplane.

Heavier-than-air flight was born in the United States but nurtured in France. During the first few years, Britain lagged behind, but by 1908, there were several interesting players in the field. Besides Roe, other aviation designers included a 27-year-old bus designer named Geoffrey de Havilland and an American named Samuel F. Cody. A flamboyant self-promotor, Cody capitalized on the name recognition of William F. "Buffalo Bill" Cody, who was of no relation, by wearing a handlebar mustache and a wide-brimmed cowboy hat.

Cody came to England in 1901 to promote his man-carrying "war kites" and took up powered heavier-than-air flight. His first powered flight took place in October 1908 at Farnborough in a self-designed biplane with a 52-foot wingspan. If Roe's June "hop" was allowed and if Cody did not crash after a flight of 1,391 feet, their attempts would have been Britain's first two flights.

De Havilland built his first airplane in 1909, but it crashed on his first attempt. His first successful flight came in September 1910, and, as the case with Roe, it was considered the first milestone in the history of a successful British aircraft builder.

For all practical purposes, Roe's triplane—known as the Roe I or *Avroplane*—is where Avro began. The triplane was constructed of pine, spruce, and ash, supported by steel tubing, and covered with muslin-backed paper. It had a wingspan of 20 feet, a wing area of 285 square feet, and a length of 23 feet. It was originally powered by a 9-horsepower, two-cylinder JAP engine but was later replaced by a 24-horsepower Antoinette.

On June 5, 1909, Roe towed the 300-pound *Avroplane* out of its birthplace to a level area on the Lea Marshs. He cranked up the engine, and the small aircraft lifted tentatively into the air. He made several short flights over the next few weeks, and on July 23, he made a voyage of 899 feet. For Avro specifically and for British aviation in general, it was only the beginning.

(Above) *The A.V. Roe Triplane II is readied for flight. Like its predecessors, it was constructed in a shed under a railway bridge over the River Lea in Walthamstow, Essex.* (Left) *The A.V. Roe Triplane II is airborne, circa 1910. It was the first of his craft for which there would be a paying customer. Like all of Roe's triplanes, it was constructed of pine, spruce, and ash.*

AMERICA FALLS BEHIND

THE FIRST WORLD WAR was the first aviation war. Although balloons had been used for observation in various conflicts of the 19th century and airplanes had been used in Italy's war with Turkey in 1911, World War I was the first war in which airplanes became an integral part of battlefield action. The necessities of combat led to innovations and advances in aeronautical engineering and engine design that may not have developed so quickly if not for the war. Planes became faster and more efficient, and advancing developments emerged from wartime emergency.

When the war started, aircraft were mostly the same flimsy machines that they'd been in 1910, and they were used primarily for observation. Soon, however, pilots started to carry handguns to fire at other planes, and steel darts were dropped on ground troops—the airplane had given birth to the warplane.

(Above) *Shown here is a wasp-waisted tunic worn by a British Royal Flying Corps aviator during the early days of World War I.* (Opposite page) *The Red Baron closes in on the Sopwith Camel of Canadian Lieutenant Wilfred May. Suddenly, Captain Roy Brown slides into position behind the Red Baron and opens fire.*

Technically, the warplane was born with the adaptation of the machine gun to the airplane. In the beginning, the guns were placed in the rear of two cockpits and fired backward or sideways by the observer while the pilot flew the plane. Shortly thereafter, it became apparent that forward-firing machine guns would make the warplane a much more effective weapon. The only problem with that idea was the engine was typically in the front of the airplane, and a forward-firing machine gun fired through the rotating propeller.

In April 1915, French ace Roland Garros attached metal plates to protect his propeller from forward-firing machine guns, but this resulted in deflected bullets flying every which way at a high velocity. Later the same month, Anthony Fokker and Heinrich Luebbe developed a system of synchronization in which the machine gun could be made to fire through the arc of the turning propeller only when the blades were not in the way. The system was installed on a Fokker Eindecker, and suddenly the German Air Force seemed virtually invincible.

For nearly a year, the British and French pilots were at a distinct disadvantage. Their planes were nearly swept from the skies by a combination of synchronized German guns and skilled, fearless German pilots such as Oswald Boelke and Max Immelman. By mid-1915, German pilots in their Fokker Eindecker planes had become known as the "Fokker Scourge."

By early 1916, however, the Allies responded by introducing a new generation of aircraft that were not only faster and more maneuverable than the early Fokkers, they also had synchronized guns. The balance of power shifted to the Allies but then returned to the Germans with the introduction of the Albatros biplanes.

In 1917, the British Sopwith Camel and the French SPAD XIII gave the Allies the advantage once more and set the stage for the most intense period of aerial combat. For his part, Fokker developed the legendary Dr.I triplane in 1916 and the great D.VII biplane in 1917. While Fokker selected a rotary engine to power his Dr.I, in-line engines built in 1917 such as the Rolls Royce V-12, the French-built Hispano-Suiza V-8, and the American V-12 Liberty came into favor with the Allies. There were excellent aircraft on both sides, but ultimately, air supremacy over the battlefields and trenches of World War I was a function of quantity. The Allies outproduced the Germans four to one.

Often overshadowed by the fast single-engine fighters were the larger, multiengine aircraft. Aircraft builders such as Handley-Page in Britain and Gotha in Germany produced notable large twin-engine bombers, but the largest and most advanced aircraft of the war included those produced by Count Gianni Caproni in Italy and Igor Sikorsky in Russia. Indeed, the Sikorsky four-engine Ilya Mourometz bombers were the largest aircraft of the era.

Meanwhile, the United States lagged behind. When the United States entered the war, the aviation section of the U.S. Army Signal Corps had less than 100 flyable military aircraft. None of these was suitable for combat, and no practical American-designed warplane was any-where near production. When General William Mitchell formed his combat squadrons in Europe in 1917 and 1918, they were equipped with French Nieuports and SPADs. The British-designed de Havilland DH-4 was the only air-craft built in the United States that actually served in combat.

The best American-designed and American-built aircraft at that time was the Curtiss JN-4 Jenny. While the Jenny was no combat aircraft, it was a reliable trainer. Curtiss built these planes fast enough and in sufficient quantities so that American airmen were thoroughly prepared to take their place alongside Europe's best pilots.

IN THE FIRST TWO years of the war, the British aircraft industry languished behind the French and the Germans. The Royal Aircraft Factory's Henri Farman–designed F.E. series of pusher biplanes were clearly not state of the art and suffered dramatically in the "Fokker Scourge" of 1915. Indeed, it was this crisis that led the team of H.P. Folland, J. Kenworthy, and Frank Goodden to develop the S.E.5. The designation stood for "Scouting, Experimental," though in service, it is remembered for neither of these descriptions.

Unfortunately, a crash during a flight test in January 1917 cost Goodden his life, delaying the production of the new aircraft. It was not until later in 1917 that the Royal Aircraft Factory began production of the S.E.5, which was soon replaced on the assembly line by the S.E.5a. In service with the Royal Flying Corps, the S.E.5a was used by aces such as Major Edward C. Mannock, who scored 73 aerial victories, and the great Canadian pilot William Bishop, who scored 72 victories.

The S.E.5 had a wingspan of 26 feet 7.5 inches and a length of 21 feet 4 inches. It weighed 1,940 pounds and was powered by a 150-horsepower, air-cooled Hispano-Suiza V-8 engine that provided a top speed in excess of 120 miles per hour. The similar yet more compact S.E.5a had a wingspan of 26 feet 7.5 inches and a length of 20 feet 11 inches. It weighed 1,940 pounds and was powered by a British-built 200-horsepower, Wolseley V-8 engine that provided a top speed in excess of 138 miles per hour, with a ceiling of 22,000 feet and an endurance of 2 hours 30 minutes. The S.E.5a's armament included a movable Lewis machine gun, which had the ability to move upward to facilitate attacking from below.

The Royal Aircraft Factory S.E.5 and S.E.5a were among the most important aircraft to serve with the British Royal Flying Corps during the early years of the First World War.

(Above) *A Royal Flying Corps pilot in an S.E.5, at right, cranks up his 200-horsepower, Wolseley V-8 engine as squadron mates look on. In the background are a row of French-made Bessoneau cloth-covered portable hangars.* (Left) *In this remarkable picture, two British S.E.5s are seen escorting a captured German Fokker Dr.I triplane, flown by a British pilot. The Dr.I could easily outmaneuver the older S.E.5s.*

PERHAPS THE SINGLE most famous—and certainly the most successful—British aircraft of World War I, the Sopwith Camel was the creation of the Sopwith Aviation Company. Thomas Sopwith, the founder of this company, had designed his first airplane, the Tabloid, in 1912.

The first of 5,490 Sopwith Camels entered service with the Royal Flying Corps and the Royal Navy Air Service in 1917 as part of the new generation of British aircraft to take to the air in the wake of the "Fokker Scourge" disaster. Eventually, Camels also served with both the American Expeditionary Force's Air Service and with the Belgian Royal Air Force.

The Camel had a wingspan of 28 feet and a length of 18 feet 9 inches. It weighed 1,422 pounds and was powered by various air-cooled engines throughout its illustrious career. These included the 130-horsepower, nine cylinder Clerget, the 110-horsepower Le Rhône, and the British-made 150-horse-power Bentley B.R.1. The Camel's performance depended on the choice of engine, but it's top speed was in the range of 115 miles per hour, with a ceiling of 19,000 feet.

The Sopwith Camel is credited with 1,294 enemy aircraft destroyed. The most notable aerial victory—according to some historians—came on April 21, 1918, when the Baron Manfred von Richthofen was reportedly shot down. On that date, Canadian Captain Roy Brown and his squadron were flying a combat air patrol over LeHamel, France, when they encountered the dreaded "Flying Circus" led by the great ace Richthofen, better known as "The Red Baron." Rookie pilot Lieutenant Wilfred May's guns jammed just as he came

into combat with Richthofen. Just as May was about to become the Red Baron's 81st victory, Captain Brown jumped the German from behind and, in moments, Richthofen was no more.

Despite the Camel's wartime success, it cost many lives in training accidents. It had a limited postwar career and was replaced by its larger sister, the Sopwith 7F.1 Snipe. Introduced in 1918, during the war's closing months, the Snipe had a wingspan of 30 feet and a length of 19 feet 10 inches. It weighed 2,020 pounds and was "handmade" by Herbert Smith to incorporate the new 230-horsepower, nine-cylinder Bentley B.R.2,

which gave the Snipe a top speed of 121 miles per hour and a ceiling of 19,500 feet.

The Snipe may have been the best warplane to serve in the war, but it was available in only limited numbers until the last months before the November 11, 1918, Armistice. Eventually, 1,500 planes were built since the Snipe was the standard Royal Air Force fighter in the years immediately after World War I. The Snipe also served in Iraq until 1922 with British forces policing that country in the wake of the dissolution of the Turkish Ottoman Empire.

The Sopwith F.1 Camel was the most important British fighter of the First World War. It first saw combat in 1917 and continued in service until the Armistice, flying with the Americans and Belgians as well as the British.

SIR THOMAS OCTAVE MURDOCH SOPWITH

The man whose surname is synonymous with the most successful British aircraft of World War I, Thomas Sopwith learned to fly in 1911 and soon developed a good reputation as a racing pilot. In 1912, he set up his own manufacturing firm. Although Sopwith Aviation Company, Ltd., was known mostly for landplanes, the first plane off the assembly line was the "Bat Boat," which was one of the world's first amphibious airplanes.

Sopwith produced many new aircraft types over the next several years, including the Pup, an important pursuit aircraft in the early years of World War I. In 1914, a modified floatplane version of the Sopwith Tabloid won the Schneider Cup race, and later the same year, a Tabloid landplane was used on a daring and successful raid against the big German Zeppelin sheds at Dusseldorf. A year later, Sopwith's Triplane was considered to be one of the first major British aircraft of World War I and was the inspiration for Anthony Fokker's legendary Dr.I. The Sopwith Camel was one of the best British scouting or pursuit aircraft of the war, and its successor, the Sopwith Snipe, was the standard Royal Air Force fighter well into the 1920s.

The First World War was the glory period for Sopwith Aviation, but its fortunes slumped in the soft postwar airplane market. Sopwith dissolved the company in 1920. He then formed the Hawker Engineering Company with test pilot Harry Hawker. Soon after the new company was formed, Hawker was killed in a crash in 1921. Later, the Hawker Engineering Company was renamed the Hawker Siddeley Group, and Sopwith became a director.

HEN THE UNITED States entered World War I, neither the Army nor the Navy possessed any aircraft suitable for combat operations in Europe. The most glaring need for single-engine pursuit aircraft was addressed primarily through the acquisition of French Nieuports and SPADs. In order to satisfy the requirement for large, multiengine aircraft to carry large bomb loads over rela-

When it first flew in August 1918, the MB-1 was a proud accomplishment for the U.S. Army's fledgling Air Service.

tively long distances, the U.S. Army focused its attention on types that were developed in Britain and Italy.

A serious controversy ensued in the summer of 1917 over whether the British twin-engine Handley-Page O/100 or the Italian trimotor Caproni Ca33 should be selected as standard equipment. The controversy came to a head in November when a contract issued to Curtiss in September to build 500 Capronis was canceled. In January 1918, a deal was reached whereby Handley-Page would build 500 bombers in England using American-made parts and Liberty engines. Ultimately and ironically, both the U.S. Navy and the U.S. Army Air Service flew borrowed Italian Capronis, but neither service flew many long-range bombing missions.

By January 1918, as the Caproni-Handley-Page dispute unfolded, the U.S. Army realized the necessity for an indigenously designed and produced multiengine bomber, and a

contract was issued to the aircraft company founded in 1909 by Glenn L. Martin. He was asked to develop a twin-engine, long-range observation and bombing aircraft loosely based on the two European models. The initial designation was GMB (Glenn Martin Bomber), but in service it was known as the MB-1 (Martin Bomber, First).

The GMB was first flown on August 17, 1918, but the war ended three months later and it was never used in combat. The GMB would have been part of a major air offensive against German industrial centers that was planned for early 1919 but was obviated by the Armistice on November 11, 1918.

The Glenn Martin Bomber, America's first aircraft of its size and type, was similar to the Handley-Page, though slightly smaller. The GMB had a wingspan of 71 feet 5 inches and a length of 46 feet 10 inches. It weighed 10,225 pounds with a full load and a crew of four. It was powered by two 400-horsepower Liberty 12A engines that gave it a cruising speed of 92 miles per hour, a range of 390 miles, and a service ceiling of 10,300 feet. The GMB/MB-1 was armed with five .30 caliber machine guns as defensive armament, and it carried a bomb load of 1,040 pounds.

There were 50 GMB/MB-1 bombers ordered, but the contract was cut to ten when the war ended. A plan for an enclosed-cockpit commercial transport version of the aircraft never came

(Above left) After building the MB-1 and MB-2 for the U.S. Army, Martin produced in-line-engined torpedo bombers for the U.S. Navy. These included the MT-1, which was later redesignated as the TM-1 under the 1923 nomenclature. (Above right) Powered by a Pratt & Whitney R-1690 Hornet radial engine, the Martin T3M-3 was a landplane torpedo bomber produced for the U.S. Navy. The torpedo is visible, slung under the fuselage. (Below) Although the Martin MB-1 bomber was the first American-designed bomber, it was not extensively used during World War I since it was not produced until 1918.

GLENN LUTHER MARTIN

Born in Macksburg, Iowa, Glenn Martin became interested in the notion of human flight at an early age and was an avid kite builder. He was still a teenager when the Wright brothers accomplished their first flight at Kitty Hawk, and this event inspired him to pursue a career in the new field of aviation.

Martin taught himself to fly in 1909, using a pusher biplane he designed and built himself. Having learned to fly, he was awarded the 56th American pilot's license. He formed his own company and divided his time between exhibition flying and designing aircraft. In 1912, he accomplished a round-trip flight between Newport Beach, California, and Santa Catalina Island.

Before the First World War, the Glenn Martin Company built the Model TT, the first tractor biplane delivered to the U.S. Army. During the war, Martin received the order for the army's first twin-engine bomber under the simple designation GMB for Glenn Martin Bomber. Martin's reputation for twin-engine bombers continued to grow. The company produced the B-10, for which Glenn Martin earned the 1932 Collier Trophy; the B-26 Marauder, produced in larger numbers than any other Martin airplane and one of the weapons that helped win World War II; and the B-57 Canberra, a twin-jet bomber that had a notable service career spanning more than two decades.

In 1960, five years after Glenn Martin's death, the company ceased to build aircraft in order to concentrate on the Titan missile, which was used both as an intercontinental ballistic missile (ICBM) and as a launch vehicle for manned and unmanned spacecraft. In 1995, Martin merged with Lockheed.

U.S. Army Captain Roy N. Francis planned a cross-continental flight in 1919. Before he was to begin the flight, a hurricane destroyed the hangar in which the plane was housed. The wings of the plane were damaged to such an extent the Army abandoned the proposed flight.

to fruition, but in 1920, the U.S. Army ordered a successor aircraft. Originally designated MB-2, the new, larger aircraft entered service as the NBS-1 (Night Bomber, Short Distance). The MB-2/NBS-1 had a wingspan of 74 feet 2 inches and a length of 42 feet 8 inches. It had a gross weight of 12,027 pounds and was powered by two 420-horsepower Liberty 12A engines. Turbo-superchargers were fitted experimentally but didn't work out. Even still, the NBS-1 had a top speed of 98 miles per hour and a service ceiling of 7,700 feet, lower than the MB-1 because of greater gross weight. The range was 400 miles—apparently the basis of the "Short Distance" designation—with a one-ton bomb load.

The Martin bombers equipped all eight U.S. Army Air Service bomber squadrons through the mid-1920s and had a moment of glory in July 1921 when they sank three captured German warships—including a battleship—in a demonstration of the effectiveness of aerial attacks against warships.

A soldier in campaign hat and riding boots poses in front of a Martin MB-1. The Glenn Martin Bomber, as it was known, was based on a similar aircraft that was built by Handley-Page for Britain's Royal Air Force.

WILLIAM "BILLY" MITCHELL

One of the early advocates of strategic air power, Billy Mitchell was born in France and raised in Milwaukee, Wisconsin. He learned to fly at a civilian school in Virginia and began his military career as a private in the infantry during the Spanish-American War. After the war, Mitchell received a commission as a second lieutenant in the signal corps.

In 1915, he was assigned to the aviation section of the Signal Corps, and during World War I, he became a U.S. combat air commander. In September 1918, he commanded a French-U.S. air squadron of almost 1,500 planes. He returned to the United States in 1919 and was appointed assistant chief of the air service. A strategic thinker, Mitchell was the first to plan and execute massive air attacks behind enemy lines, a doctrine that was followed successfully by the U.S. Air Force from World War II to the Persian Gulf War.

In 1921, General Mitchell organized a series of demonstrations to show that aircraft were an effective weapon against battleships, which were then assumed to be the ultimate long-range defense of the United States. In July, Mitchell's bombers sank the captured German battleship *Ostfriesland* as well as two other warships, and in September, they sank the retired U.S. Navy battleship *Alabama*. The U.S. Navy was both embarrassed and enraged.

Mitchell did not go away quietly. He continued to speak out about the importance of air power and was considered insubordinate in doing so. He was court-martialed in 1925 and demoted. He died before his theories were proven during World War II. A special medal in his honor was authorized by Congress and approved by President Truman on August 8, 1946. It was presented to his son in 1948 by the Chief of Staff of the newly created U.S. Air Force.

DESIGNED IN BRITAIN in 1916 by Geoffrey de Havilland, the DH-4 not only served on every front where the Royal Flying Corps was engaged, but it was also built in the United States for the American Expeditionary Force Air Service. In fact, it was the only aircraft built in the United States to see combat in World War I.

Though designed in 1916, the DH-4's entry into service was delayed until 1917 by the search for an ideal engine. This turned out to be the Rolls Royce Eagle VII, which was a water-cooled V-12 delivering 375 horsepower. As both an observation aircraft and a bomber, the DH-4 was widely used by the British. When the Americans entered the war in April 1917, it was pressed into service by the American Expeditionary Force and selected for production in the United States.

The American production of the DH-4 was undertaken by Dayton-Wright, a new company formed by automobile executives from General Motors, Hudson, and Packard who employed Orville Wright as a consultant. Their idea was to bring auto industry

mass production techniques into aviation—a plan that was more difficult than they anticipated.

The first "sample" DH-4 arrived in the United States in July 1917, but it was not until February 1918 that the first nine Dayton-Wright–built DH-4s rolled off the assembly line. By October 1918, production reached 1,000 aircraft a month. The war ended a month later, with less than 200 Dayton-Wright DH-4s arriving in France. This entire inventory was destroyed rather than shipped home in a disastrous display of waste that was dubbed the "Billion-Dollar Bonfire." A total of 4,846 were built by Dayton-Wright through the middle of 1919, and they remained on duty with the U.S. Army, U.S. Marine Corps, U.S. Post Office Department, and the Border Patrol until as late as 1932.

The DH-4 had a wingspan of 42 feet 5.5 inches and a length of 30 feet 8 inches for the British

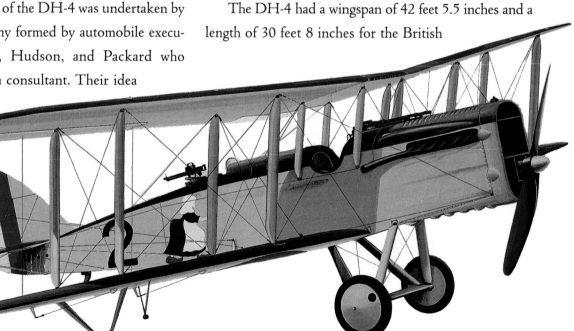

The remarkable de Havilland DH-4 was the brainchild of British aviation pioneer Geoffrey de Havilland and was widely used by the Allies during World War I.

(Left) *British-designed, the DH-4 was built in the United States by the Dayton-Wright Company.* (Bottom left) *A restored example of one of the several thousand DH-4s that were built for the U.S. Army Air Service in the United States. The U.S. Post Office obtained surplus army planes, such as the DH-4s, to serve as airmail planes.* (Bottom right) *A close-up of a DH-4 used by Dayton-Wright as a camera plane. The system was set up to shoot the film over the pilot's head, although the camera could be elevated to shoot another airplane flying above.*

version and 29 feet 11 inches for the Dayton-Wright variant. The British DH-4 weighed 3,472 pounds, and the Dayton-Wright machine had a gross weight of 3,582 pounds. While the British DH-4 was powered by the Rolls Royce Eagle engine, Dayton-Wright used the ubiquitous American-made 400-horsepower Liberty 12. The two engines provided top speeds of 143 miles per hour and 124 miles per hour, respectively. The service ceilings were listed at 23,500 feet and 19,500 feet.

In July 1917, the British introduced an improved variation on the DH-4 designated as the DH-9. The improvement was not all that was hoped for, and it was withdrawn from service a year later. The DH-9 had a wingspan of 45 feet 11 inches and a length of 30 feet 3 inches. It weighed 4,322 pounds and was powered by the American 400-horsepower Liberty 12. Like the DH-4, the DH-9 was produced in the United States—designated as USD-9A—but not in large numbers.

ONE OF THE FIRST French pursuit planes to address the "Fokker Scourge" of 1915, the maneuverable Nieuport 11 evolved from the Nieuport 10 racer. The Nieuport 10 was designed by Gustave Delage for the 1914 Gordon Bennett Cup Trophy Race.

The French Nieuport 11 fighter was known affectionately as Bébé because of its small size. The Bébé, along with other Nieuport models and British planes, bolstered the Allies' air power.

An extremely agile plane because of its small size, the Nieuport 11 was affectionately nicknamed "Bébé" (Baby). It had a wingspan of only 24 feet 6 inches and a length of just 19 feet. It weighed 1,210 pounds and was powered by an 80-horsepower, nine-cylinder, air-cooled Gnome A or Le Rhône 9C engine that gave it a top speed in excess of 97 miles per hour. It had a ceiling of 15,090 feet and an endurance of 2 hours on a tank of fuel.

The Bébé was more than a match for the early Fokker Eindeckers, and it was flown by great French aces such as Charles Nungesser and Georges Guynemer. Over the battlefield of Verdun in February 1916, these men—flying Nieuport 11s—scored impressive victories over the Germans. The Nieuport 11 was also used by the air forces of Russia, Britain, and Belgium as well as Italy, where it was produced under license as the Nieuport-Macchi Ni11.

A major shortcoming in the Nieuport 11 was the lack of synchronization for machine guns so the Bébé carried its Lewis machine gun on top of the upper wing. Some aircraft were also equipped with Le Prieur rockets for use in attacking German long-range observation balloons and dirigibles.

Most of Bébé's failings—such as lack of synchronization—were successfully addressed when Gustave Delage designed his masterpiece, the Nieuport 17, a larger and sturdier aircraft. The Nieuport 17 fighter had a wingspan of only 26 feet 10 inches and a length of 18 feet 11 inches. It weighed 1,246 pounds and was powered by a 110-horsepower, nine-cylinder air-cooled Le Rhône 9J engine that provided a top speed of 110 miles per hour—the same as the Bébé. It had a ceiling of 17,390 feet and an endurance of 2 hours.

The greatest Nieuport aircraft ever to see action, the 17 appeared in March 1916 and was readily accepted by Nungesser and Guynemer as well as by William Bishop, the great Canadian ace. As with the Nieuport 11, the air forces of Russia, Belgium, and Italy—as well as France and Britain—embraced the Nieuport 17, but Imperial Russia received relatively few before it collapsed in the 1917 Revolution. In late 1917, the American Expeditionary Force Air Service also took delivery of Nieuport 17s, but they were soon superseded by superior Nieuport 28s.

Gustave Delage continued to design new aircraft for Nieuport, and although the Nieuport 27 and 28 were substantial improvements, they were never produced in sufficient quantities to allow them to match the operational success of their predecessors the Nieuport 11 Bébé and the Nieuport 17.

(Above) *This Nieuport 17 pursuit craft is led onto the field by a team of U.S. Army Air Service crewmen, who are still new to the care and operation of combat aircraft. By the end of 1917, they would become veterans.* (Left) *Before the United States entered World War I, American pilots went to France to fly with the Lafayette Escadrille, a mostly American squadron in the French Air Force. The squadron scored 39 victories against the Germans, but nearly a third of the unit died in the effort.*

IN 1914, ON THE EVE of World War I, the great airman and engineer Louis Blériot took over as president of a failing French aircraft company called Société pour les Appareils Deperdussin. He renamed the company Société pour l'Aviation et ses Derives (SPAD) and went on to produce a series of aircraft that are recognized as having been the best Allied combat aircraft of the war.

For most of the first two years of the war, Allied aircraft—with the noted exception of the Nieuport 11—were con-

This photo shows a restored early-model SPAD. Built in France, the SPAD was one of a very few French types to see service with the British during World War I.

siderably outperformed by the German Fokkers. The first SPAD fighter, the A.2 designed by Louis Béchereau, was among the Allied disappointments. Béchereau went back to the drawing board. By 1916, he had designed the SPAD VII. It had a single fully synchronized machine gun and was designed around a powerful 150-horsepower V-8 engine created for France's Hispano-Suiza by its owner, Swiss designer Marc Birkigt. The SPAD VII had a wingspan of 25 feet 6 inches and a length of 20 feet 1 inch. It weighed a mere 1,550 pounds and had a top speed in excess of 119 miles per hour. It had a ceiling of 18,000 feet and an endurance of over 2 hours.

The SPAD VII was in service with the French Aviation Militaire by September 1916—only five months after its first flight—and with the Italian Air Force in March 1917. Eventually 5,600 were built in France alone.

Béchereau continued to refine his design to create the great SPAD XIII, which was considered by some to be the best

Allied aircraft of the war. Béchereau enlarged the basic format of the SPAD VII and incorporated not one but a pair of fully synchronized Vickers machine guns. The SPAD XIII had a wingspan of 26 feet 4 inches and a length of 20 feet 4 inches. It weighed 1,811 pounds and was powered by a 235-horsepower, liquid-cooled Hispano-Suiza 8BEc V-8 engine that gave it a top speed of 138 miles per hour. This engine provided more power than the engines of Germany's Albatros fighters, but it was not always reliable. The SPAD XIII had a ceiling of 22,000 feet and an endurance of 2.5 hours.

Béchereau's masterpiece helped provide ultimate air superiority to the Allied air forces, and over 8,400 SPAD XIIIs were delivered before the Armistice. After May 1917, few of the top Allied pilots used anything else. The French aces Rene Fonck, Charles Nungesser, and Georges Guynemer all flew the SPAD XIII, and it was embraced by the leading American Air Service pilots, including Frank Luke and Eddie Rickenbacker.

EDWARD "EDDIE" VERNON RICKENBACKER

A race-car driver turned pilot, Eddie Rickenbacker was the highest-scoring American ace of World War I and a national luminary. Born in Columbus, Ohio, Rickenbacker went on the racing circuit when he was barely 20 and earned a reputation for speed and coolness. When the United States entered World War I, he tried to organize an "aero" squadron composed of his racing pals, but after he enlisted, General John J. "Blackjack" Pershing requested Rickenbacker as his personal driver.

In August 1917, he was transferred to the U.S. Army Signal Corps aviation section and signed up for flight training. After training at Issoudon, France, in 1918, he joined the 94th Aero Pursuit Squadron. Rickenbacker scored his first half-credit aerial victory on April 18, and on June 18, he scored his first full victory flying a Nieuport 28. He shot five down that day and became the first American ace of World War I.

Grounded briefly with an ear infection, he returned to combat in August as his squadron upgraded to the SPAD XIII. During the last three months of the war, he distinguished himself by bringing his score to 26 and demonstrating the heroism that earned him the

Medal of Honor. He assumed command of the 94th Aero Squadron on September 24, 1918.

After the war, he organized the Rickenbacker Motor Company and served as its president until 1928, when he went to Fokker Aircraft Corporation as vice president. Between 1932 and 1935 he served in various posts for American Airways (American Airlines) and North American Aviation. In 1934, he joined Eastern Airlines as general manager, and in 1938, he bought the airline and became its president.

An excellent view of a SPAD XIII, the ultimate pursuit machine built by the Société Pour l'Aviation et ses Derives (SPAD). The fully synchronized Vickers machine guns are seen on the top of the nose above the exhaust lines streaming from the engine.

THE BIGGEST AND most unpleasant surprise faced by the airmen of Britain and France in World War I were the airplanes known collectively as the "Fokkers." The term became a synonym for effective—and dangerous— enemy fighter aircraft. Dutch-born aeronautical designer Anthony Fokker, who formed his first aircraft company in Germany in 1912, oversaw the creation of a series of fighters

A Fokker E.III Eindecker (monoplane) in flight. The E.III was the most important of the Fokker monoplanes that dominated the skies of Europe during the first two years of World War I.

that were virtually unmatched through the first half of the war and legendary for the entire war.

The first important Fokker warplanes were the Eindeckers (monoplanes). These planes, designated E.I through E.III, were in action during the first six months of the war. It was for the Eindeckers that Fokker, working with Heinrich Luebbe, developed a synchronization system that allowed a machine gun to be fired through the arc of a spinning propeller without any bullets hitting the propeller blade. When this apparatus made its debut over the Western Front in April 1915, Allied pilots were all but helpless; for a year they were at the mercy of the "Fokker Scourge."

The Fokker E.III, perhaps the most important monoplane in a war dominated by biplanes, had a wingspan of 32 feet 8 inches and a length of 23 feet 6.5 inches. It weighed 1,342 pounds and was powered by a 100-horsepower, Oberursel UI

nine-cylinder, air-cooled rotary engine that gave it a top speed of 87 miles per hour. This speed was adequate for 1914 and early 1915 but slower than comparable French machines. Before abandoning the Eindecker concept for other designs, Fokker developed the E.IV. This Fokker aircraft was heavier than the E.III and was powered by a 160-horsepower Oberursel nine-cylinder, air-cooled engine. A total of 400 E.IVs were built, but their service career was short. The E.IIIs were shunted off to the Eastern Front where they dueled with the Czar's dwindling air force until the Revolution of 1917 brought an end to both the Russian Empire and the combat career of the Fokker Eindecker.

Meanwhile, Fokker was experimenting with a new design concept. Whereas the Eindeckers had one wing, Fokker's most well-known aircraft of this era had three. The Fokker Dr.I Driedecker (triplane) was not the first triplane, but it was the most famous. The first operationally successful triplane to enter

In 1915, when Anthony Fokker developed a successful machine gun synchronization system for a Fokker monoplane, it revolutionized aerial combat.

combat in World War I was the British Sopwith Triplane, which made its debut in the spring of 1917. And what an illustrious debut it was: Canadian ace Major Raymond Collishaw reportedly shot down 16 Germans in a month. Though the Triplane was superseded by the Sopwith Camel, it got everyone's attention—including Anthony Fokker.

The Fokker Dr.I was unstable; but this instability in the hands of a skilled pilot translated to remarkable maneuverability. Fokker's Dr.I reached front-line units by mid-summer 1917, and in one three-week period in September, Werner Voss alone claimed ten aerial victories with his Dr.I. It was turning out to be a one-plane Fokker Scourge.

The Dr.I was a small airplane with a wingspan of 23 feet 7.5 inches and a length of 18 feet 11 inches. It was nearly 10 feet tall, giving it the visual impression of being almost as tall as it was long. The wings were fixed by means of struts, theoretically

eliminating the need for bracing wires, but structural failures caused by excessive vibration forced the Dr.I to be withdrawn from service briefly in the autumn of 1917 for retrofitting. Subsequent bracing modifications corrected the problem but somewhat hindered maneuverability.

The Dr.I weighed 1,298 pounds and was powered by a French-designed, German-built 110-horsepower, nine-cylinder, Le Rhône 9J air-cooled rotary engine that gave it a top speed of 103 miles per hour. It could climb to 14,000 feet in 17 minutes and had a ceiling of 19,685 feet, although it was criticized as not being effective at higher altitudes.

One of the first and most famous squadrons to use the Dr.I was Jagdgeschwader (Fighter Squadron) No. 1, commanded by Baron Manfred von Richthofen. Jagdgeschwader No. 1 was known to the Allies as the "Flying Circus" because all the aircraft were painted in loud, brilliant colors. Richthofen flew an

This splendid cutaway drawing shows the internal structure of the Fokker Dr.I and its French-designed, German-built air-cooled radial engine. Aft of the engine are the two fully synchronized Spandau machine guns and an armored tub for their ammunition. The pilot's lower back was protected by an armor plate behind the cockpit. Also note the tubular metal frame of the fuselage and the more complex wooden framing in the wings.

A flight of brightly painted Fokker Dr.I triplanes over a castle on the Moselle River in Germany. The German Jagdgeschwader (Fighter Squadron) No. 1 was called the "Flying Circus" because all the aircraft were decorated in especially lavish color schemes.

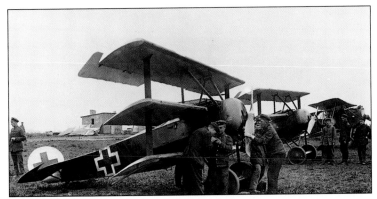

Shown here are several German mechanics with a pair of Fokker Dr.I Driedeckers. The Dr.I was not the first triplane used in front-line service in World War I, but it was the most famous.

all-red Dr.I, which earned him the well-remembered nickname of "Red Baron."

While the Dr.I was probably the signature Fokker airplane of the First World War, the best Fokker was the D.VII. The Fokker D.VII was the culmination of a line of conventional biplane fighters that began with the D.I through D.V, a series of variations on the same idea that was seen as influenced by the French Nieuport 11. The performance of these aircraft was deemed inferior to that of contemporary Allied airplanes and only 565 were built. After 1916 they were used almost entirely as trainers or sold to Austria-Hungary.

In terms of biplane designs, Fokker finally hit his stride in early 1918 with the D.VI, which was much better than its predecessors, and with the D.VII—introduced almost simultaneously—which was much better than the D.VI and every other aircraft produced in Germany at that time. While both planes made their debut at the same time, the D.VI is all but forgotten, and the D.VII had an illustrious—albeit brief—career.

In service in large numbers from the spring of 1918, the Fokker D.VII outperformed the Sopwith Camel and met its

BARON MANFRED VON RICHTHOFEN

The top-scoring ace of World War I and probably the best-remembered combat pilot in history, Manfred von Richthofen graduated from the Berlin War Academy in 1911. He enlisted in the cavalry of the Imperial German Army and served in both Poland and France during 1914.

As the ground war was reduced to static trench warfare, there was little use for cavalry so Richthofen transferred to the newly organized air service. He served briefly as an observer, gunner, and bombardier before applying for pilot training. In September 1916, Richthofen was handpicked by Oswald Boelke to join his Jagdstaffel 2 squadron on the western front; within a month, Boelke's young protege was an ace.

Richthofen soon earned a reputation as a skilled fighter pilot and a dangerous adversary. By June 1917, he was the highest-scoring German ace with 52 victories. At that time, he was given command of Jagdgeschwader No. I. He transformed the squadron into the most feared unit in the German air force. The pilots painted their airplanes in loud and garish colors, earning them the nickname "The Flying Circus." Richthofen painted his own Fokker Dr.I red, and thereafter he was known as the "Red Baron."

On April 21, 1918, Richthofen's victories came to an end. While the question of who shot the Red Baron down is still disputed, one account is that Canadian Captain Roy Brown, flying a Sopwith Camel, got on the Red Baron's tail over Allied lines in a sector controlled by Australian troops. The Dr.I crashed and the Baron was found dead, with a single bullet in his heart. Australian gunners claimed their fire from the ground was what brought Richthofen down. A controversy persists to this day over whether the bullet was Canadian or Australian.

FOKKER E.III, DR.I, AND D.VII

(Above) A restored Fokker D.VII in the gaudy colors of Baron von Richthofen's legendary "Flying Circus" squadron is pursued by a SPAD with French markings in a mock battle. (Right) A group of Fokker D.VII fighters belonging to Jagdstaffel 71 of the German air force. This aircraft was so potent that it was singled out in negotiations that concluded World War I. (Below) With its powerful 160-horsepower Mercedes D.III or 185-horsepower BMW IIIa engine, the Fokker D.VII was able to outfly and outfight every Allied aircraft in the sky—with the possible exception of the SPAD XIII.

only real competition with the S.E.5a, Sopwith Snipe, and SPAD XIII. The D.VII was larger than the Dr.I, weighing 1,870 pounds and having a wingspan of 29 feet 3.5 inches and a length of 22 feet 11.5 inches. Two different engines were used during the D.VII production run: the 160-horsepower, water-cooled, six-cylinder Mercedes D.III and the 185-horsepower BMW IIIa. The D.VII biplane had a top speed in level flight of 124 miles per hour and a ceiling of 19,685 feet, with a fast rate of climb.

By Armistice Day November 11, 1918, over 800 D.VIIs were delivered to 40 front-line squadrons and the aircraft was still in production. The final World War I Fokker, the D.VIII high-wing Eindecker, had appeared by this time, but only 100 had been placed into service.

After the war, the Fokker D.VII had the distinction of being singled out in a special provision in the Armistice negotiations. The aircraft was so potent that the agreement that concluded the war specifically required Germany to turn over all the D.VIIs to the Allies for disposal. Anthony Fokker, however, shipped a large number of them—along with parts and manufacturing equipment—into neutral Holland. When the dust had settled, Fokker was back in business. He continued to produce the D.VII for the Royal Netherlands Air Force, and he also sold a sizable number to neighboring Belgium—ironically, the nation most badly trampled by Germany during the war—as well as to Switzerland, which, like the Netherlands, had remained neutral throughout the war.

The Fokker D.VII was still in production during the 1920s, and it evolved into the Fokker C series of biplane fighters, some of which were still flying with the Royal Netherlands Air Force when World War II began.

ANTHONY HERMAN GERARD FOKKER

Known affectionately as "The Flying Dutchman" and revered at the apex of the pantheon of Netherlands aviation greats, Anthony Fokker was born to Dutch parents in Kediri on the island of Java in what was then the Netherlands East Indies. He went to Haarlem in the Netherlands to study engineering and earned his pilot's license in 1911. He combined his interests in 1912, starting an aircraft factory in Johannisthal, Germany. Fokker Flugzeugwerke, as his company was known, built both private aircraft and trainers for the German Army.

When World War I began, Fokker Flugzeugwerke produced the Eindecker combat aircraft that dominated the aerial battlefield and led the British to squeal "Fokker Scourge." Fokker, along with Heinrich Luebbe, developed the machine gun synchronization system that gave the German air service an overwhelming air superiority in the early part of the war. Fokker also developed the legendary Dr.I triplane and the D.VII, which he continued to produce in the Netherlands after Germany's defeat in 1918. After 1918, Fokker also built commercial transports for Royal Dutch Airlines (KLM).

In 1924, Fokker established the New Jersey–based Atlantic Aircraft Corporation, which was later named the Fokker Aircraft Corporation of America. In September 1925, Fokker introduced the F.VII, a trimotor transport that was widely used by airlines around the world as well as in a number of important record flights.

When General Motors acquired Fokker of America in 1929, Fokker stayed on briefly as technical manager (and as a 20 percent shareholder). In the late 1930s, Fokker moved to Switzerland.

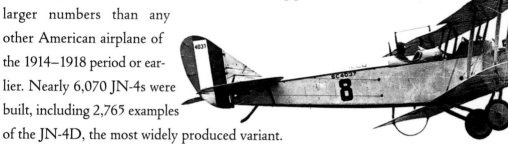

KNOWN FAMILIARLY as the "Jenny," the JN series, especially the JN-4, had the distinction of being produced in larger numbers than any other American airplane of the 1914–1918 period or earlier. Nearly 6,070 JN-4s were built, including 2,765 examples of the JN-4D, the most widely produced variant.

The development of the Jenny began in a London rainstorm in 1913. American aircraft builder Glenn Curtiss was in Britain to visit Thomas Sopwith's plant in Kingston, and two of Sopwith's men traveled back to London with Curtiss at the end of the day. Taking shelter from the storm, Curtiss and one of the men, B. Douglas Thomas, got to talking. This discussion led to

Curtiss hiring Thomas and then to Thomas designing the Curtiss Model J, which evolved into the Model N and ultimately the JN dynasty.

During the course of developing the J and N, Thomas and Curtiss varied the wing length considerably. The Model J originally had a 30 foot wingspan, but later examples were built with a 40 foot 2 inch upper wing. The Model N had a span of 38 feet 2.5 inches on both wings, although the shape of its upper wing was the same that was used in the JN series.

Fewer than 200 Model J and Model N two-seat biplane trainers were built for the U.S. Army and U.S. Navy before

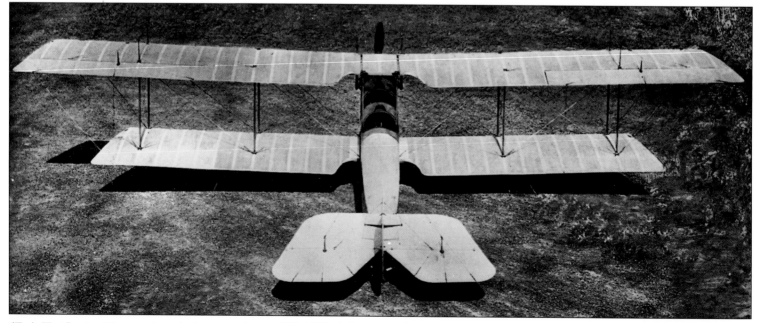

(Top) *The Curtiss JN-4 was the only American-designed World War I classic aircraft. Though it never saw action, it was used extensively as a trainer.* (Above) *After the war, the Curtiss JN-4 was employed for nonmilitary purposes as well. Barnstormers often purchased war-surplus, bargain-priced Jennies, and the first airmail flight in U.S. history was made by a Curtiss Jenny on May 15, 1918.*

Curtiss decided in 1915 to launch the Model JN series.

Only 11 JN-1 and JN-2 aircraft (with 36-foot equal span wings) and two JN-3s (with extended span uppers) were built, with two delivered to the Navy as floatplanes and the rest delivered to the U.S. Army to equip its 1st Aero Squadron. The JN-2s and JN-3s of the 1st Aero Squadron took part in the first use of aircraft in an American military operation.

Before going on to fight in Europe, many U.S. pilots were trained to fly with the Jenny. This American-designed plane was used as a trainer during and after the war.

In 1916, when the Mexican bandit Francisco "Pancho" Villa started raiding American towns on the Mexican border, Brigadier General John J. "Blackjack" Pershing was ordered to pursue him into Mexico with U.S. Army troops. The 1st Aero Squadron was assigned to support Pershing's operations as aerial observers. The Jennies did poorly in their baptism of fire. They were grossly underpowered with their Curtiss V-8 engines and had a great deal of trouble in the thin air of the high-plateau country of the Sonoran Desert, much less in the high peaks of the Sierra Madre. At the same time, Blackjack Pershing also had failed. His troops pushed deep into Mexico—to Chihuahua City and beyond—but they never caught Pancho Villa.

In two years, however, both the general and the Jenny were vindicated. Pershing led the American Expeditionary Force to France and tipped the tide of victory in World War I, while the JN-4 Jenny was the aircraft that helped train almost every pilot from the United States and Canada that served in the war.

The JN-4 appeared late in 1916 and incorporated the lessons painfully learned south of the border. It weighed 2,130 pounds and was powered by a 90-horsepower, Curtiss OX (typically OX-5) V-8 liquid-cooled engine that gave it a top speed of 75 miles per hour and an effective service ceiling of 11,000 feet. It had an upper wingspan of 43 feet 7 inches and a length of 27 feet 4 inches. The 1,200 JN-4Cs that were built under license by Canadian Aeroplanes, Ltd., (Canuck) had the same wing dimensions but were slightly shorter and had a gross weight listed at 1,920 pounds.

While the Jenny's performance was slack by the standard of the combat aircraft of the First World War, the durability and reliability of the Jenny made it an ideal trainer.

THE GOLDEN AGE OF FLIGHT

THE INTERWAR PERIOD, from 1919 to 1939, was a time of triumph and change for aeronautical engineering and for the aviation industry. It began with the airways dominated by wood and fabric biplanes that were held together by wires, and it ended with large all-metal, multiengine monoplanes with soundproofed passenger cabins and the ability to cruise comfortably at altitudes that would have intimidated 1919's pilots.

The war years saw a refinement in the reliability and performance of airframes as well as an improvement in "aeroengine" technology. The sputtering four-cylinder engines of the early days were replaced by thundering V-8s.

More power and better airplanes meant more speed and maneuverability for the classic dogfights, but engineers were also working on an improvement in range and altitude that would

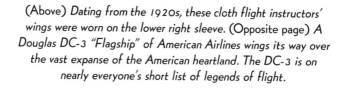

(Above) *Dating from the 1920s, these cloth flight instructors' wings were worn on the lower right sleeve.* (Opposite page) *A Douglas DC-3 "Flagship" of American Airlines wings its way over the vast expanse of the American heartland. The DC-3 is on nearly everyone's short list of legends of flight.*

make profitable commercial aviation a reality after the war. Before the war, there were no real airlines. In 1919 and the early 1920s, airlines started cropping up everywhere, especially in Europe and North America. Some were organized to connect to only two or three cities and they eventually faded away, but others began with a vision of a truly comprehensive air transport network. A good example of the latter is Royal Dutch Airlines (Koninklijke Luchtvaart Maatschappij, KLM), which began in the early 1920s with a few domestic routes plus a flight from Amsterdam to London and is a major worldwide carrier today.

By 1939, many of the airlines that are familiar to us today were flying routes that still form the heart of their service areas. In Europe there was KLM, Swissair, Finnair, and Deutsche Luft

In the 1920s, the French airline Fleche d'Orient offered to fly passengers, freight, and mail to Istanbul, with stops all across central Europe.

Hansa (Lufthansa). In the United States there was United Air Lines, Northwest Airlines, American Airlines, and TWA (Trans-World Airlines), which was then known as Transcontinental & Western Airlines. The gone but not forgotten giants such as Eastern Airlines and Pan American World Airways were also well established by 1939.

Military aviation also evolved in the interwar period. After World War I, declining budgets meant that aircraft then in service or on the drawing boards were the mainstay through the mid-1920s. Gradually new types of aircraft evolved, and the urge to improve paralleled that of the commercial aircraft industry.

Combat aircraft were continually improving not only in speed and range but also in terms of their armament. Most of the large bombers of

1939 carried their ordnance in internal bomb bays rather than on brackets under the fuselages. The planes still carried numerous machine guns for defensive armament as they had in 1919, but these were now in powered turrets enclosed in plexiglass.

Even as the technology changed, an even more important change was taking place among a new generation of pilots. After World War I, many pilots sought new opportunities in aviation. From 1919 through the 1930s, the newspaper headlines were filled with a myriad of "firsts." In 1919, John Alcock and Arthur Whitten-Brown became the first to fly the Atlantic nonstop. In 1923, Oakley Kelly and John MacReady were the first to fly across the United States nonstop. In 1927, Charles Lindbergh became the first to fly the Atlantic solo. In 1931, Wiley Post and

In 1919, Anglo-French aviation pioneer Henri Farman began a commercial air service between London and Paris. He later expanded his service across northern Europe.

Harold Gatty flew around the world in less than nine days.

Women were also matching the accomplishments of men. In 1930, Amy Johnson became the first woman to fly from England to Australia, and in 1932, Amelia Earhart became the first woman to fly solo across the Atlantic.

During this era, airplanes carried passengers from New York to Los Angeles and overflew both the North and South Poles as well as Mount Everest. Speed and distance records were broken almost as soon as they were set. New innovations provided greater safety and endurance.

It was truly a golden age. Airplanes were fulfilling dreams that could hardly have been imagined in 1903 when the Wright brothers started it all. The 1920s and 1930s were exciting times for the pilots and for the history of aviation.

LOCKHEED VEGA ★

ALLAN AND MALCOLM LOUGHEAD (pronounced Lockheed) first began building airplanes in San Francisco in 1916, but their company folded in 1921. In December 1926, the brothers resurfaced in Hollywood, California, with new investors, to form the Lockheed Aircraft Company. The first product was the Vega, a high-wing monoplane designed by an up-and-coming young airplane designer named John K. Northrop.

The four-passenger Vega was one of the first important and successful American commercial transports, and it marked the beginning of one of the world's most important aircraft makers. The aircraft was named for the fifth brightest star visible from the Earth, setting for Lockheed the tradition of naming aircraft after stars and other astronomical features.

Though the prototype Vega—the *Golden Eagle* flown by Jack Frost—was lost in the infamous Dole Derby race from California to Hawaii in August 1927, the Vega attracted a good deal of interest from pilots intent on endurance flights and later from commercial airlines.

One of the first great endurance flights to feature the Vega came in April 1928 when Captain George Hubert (later Sir Hubert) Wilkins and Alaskan bush pilot Carl Ben Eielsen flew across the Arctic from Point Barrow, Alaska, to Spitzbergen, Norway, in 20 hours. On December 20, 1928, Wilkins and a team of pilots took a pair of Vegas to Antarctica to conduct aerial mapping of 100,000 square miles of the frozen continent.

Meanwhile, the original four-passenger Vega 1 evolved into the much more capable Lockheed Model 5, or Vega 5. The Vega 1 had a wingspan of 41 feet and a length of 27 feet 6 inches. It weighed 2,900 pounds fully loaded and fueled and

This marvelous cutaway drawing of Wiley Post's Winnie Mae clearly shows the Vega's compact crew compartment and its powerful Pratt & Whitney R-1340 Wasp engine.

WILEY HARDEMAN POST

The son of a Texas oil driller, Wiley Hardeman Post became the personal pilot to millionaire oil man F. C. Hall in 1930. Post flew Hall's Lockheed Vega, which was named *Winnie Mae* in honor of his daughter. Through the early 1930s, Post and Hall's *Winnie Mae* became legendary for fast transcontinental flights. With Harold Gatty aboard, Wiley and

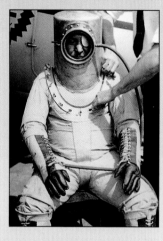

Winnie set a round-the-world speed record in 1931. At *Winnie's* controls two years later, Post became the first man to fly around the world solo, completing the feat in just over a week.

After establishing his reputation as a distance flyer, Wiley Post became interested in distance flying at extremely high altitudes. Post realized that long distance flying at high altitudes required a means of adapting human bodies to the environment. In 1934, he modified a deep-sea diver's suit and created the world's first high-altitude aircraft pressure suit.

By supercharging *Winnie Mae's* Pratt & Whitney Wasp engine and with his pressure suit, Post was able to reach altitudes approaching 55,000 feet. At this point he discovered the jet streams—fast-moving "rivers" of air flowing in a westerly direction in the high stratosphere. He believed that if an airplane flew in the jet stream it could fly faster using less fuel than it could at lower altitudes, and he was right.

In 1935, Hall and Post retired the *Winnie Mae* in favor of a hybrid aircraft made up of Orion Explorer parts. To break in the new plane, Post and author-humorist Will Rogers decided to make a highly publicized flight to Europe by way of Alaska. On August 15, 1935, the plane crashed after takeoff, and both men were killed instantly.

The Lockheed Vega was considered designer John Northrop's "dream ship." Ahead of its time, Northrop designed the Vega with no visible means of support on the wings. The Vega made its initial flight on July 4, 1927.

had a service ceiling of 15,000 feet. It was powered by a single 225-horsepower, air-cooled nine-cylinder Wright Whirlwind J-5 engine that gave it a cruising speed of 118 miles per hour and a range of 900 miles. The Vega 5 had the same dimensions as the Vega 1 and had a gross weight of 4,265 pounds. It was powered by a single 450-horsepower, air-cooled Pratt & Whitney R-1340 Wasp engine that gave it a cruising speed of 155 miles per hour.

One of the most important Vega 5 operators was Wiley Post. Between June 23 and July 1, 1931, he and navigator Harold Gatty succeeded in flying around the world with Post's Vega 5 in eight days 15 hours and 51 minutes. The first-ever round-the-world flight was achieved only seven years earlier, taking 175 days. Post's flight demonstrated how far aviation had come in just a few years.

Not willing to rest on his accomplishment, Post set out in 1933 to top his record. Between July 15 and 22, 1933, he flew his Vega 5 *Winnie Mae* around the world again but this time in seven days 18 hours and 43 minutes. He would have done it faster, but when he landed in Alaska on the last leg, he damaged

One of the great names in the history of airplane manufacturing, John Northrop was more of an aeronautical genius than a businessman. Indeed, his early work was in the service of other great names in the early history of the business: Lockheed and Douglas.

Northrop grew up in Santa Barbara, California, and after early work as a garage mechanic and carpenter, he landed a job in 1916 with Allan and Malcolm Loughead designing wings for their F-1 seaplane. He joined the Army when the United States entered World War I in 1917 but was furloughed back to the Lougheads where his talents better served the war effort.

In 1923, after the collapse of the Loughead brothers' first company, Northrop was hired by Donald Douglas to work at his Santa Monica, California, plant. After a few years with Douglas, Northrop moved back to the newly constituted Lockheed Company. It was here that Northrop designed his first masterpiece, the Lockheed Vega.

In 1928, Northrop moved again, this time to the Avion Corporation in Burbank, California, where he hoped to try out some of his own more innovative designs. Northrop developed a theory that the most efficient airplane would be one that was *all wing* since lift is produced only by wing surfaces. The fuselage was just dead weight, and in Northrop's ideal airplane, it would be eliminated. The dream of a "flying wing" was a theme that ran through Northrop's entire career.

Avion became Northrop Aircraft Corporation in 1928, and the first flying wing was in the air the same year. It had no fuselage; the tail was attached to the wing by narrow booms. Northrop also built a series of popular conventional low-wing, fixed gear monoplanes—the Alpha, Beta, Gamma, and Delta—which were acquired by various customers such as TWA.

During World War II, Northrop built a modest number of aircraft, notably the sophisticated and effective P-61 Black Widow night fighter. Meanwhile, John Northrop continued to build small flying wing aircraft. Finally, as the war was at its crescendo, Northrop received a contract to build the giant B-35, a pure flying wing bomber. The first B-35 flew in June 1946, after the war had ended, but the U.S. Army Air Force (USAAF) was satisfied and ordered it into production. Meanwhile, Northrop suggested, and the USAAF agreed, to convert two B-35s from piston engines to jet engines or turbo props.

The all-jet flying wing, designated as the B-49, first flew in October 1947 just as the USAAF was becoming the U.S. Air Force. After a promising start, however, fewer than 20 flying wing bombers of both types were built as the Air Force decided to focus its attention on the more conventional Convair B-36.

Through the 1950s, Northrop built a number of experimental aircraft, as well as the conventional F-89 Scorpion interceptor and the SM-62 Snark cruise missile. In the meantime, the company developed what evolved into one of the most successful supersonic jet fighters in history. The N-156 Freedom Fighter was designed primarily for the export market. It was an efficient and high-performance jet fighter that was also economical. The U.S. Air Force bought a large number as the T-38 trainer and the F-5 fighter, but the majority of the more than 4,000 that were built went to over two dozen other air forces.

Though John Northrop retired in 1952, he continued to serve as a consultant to the company that bore his name. As a final irony and a tribute to his vision, at the time of his death, the Air Force had commissioned the Northrop company to build the gigantic flying wing that first flew in 1989 as the B-2 stealth bomber.

The Lockheed Vegas that equipped Sir Hubert Wilkins' 1929 expedition to Antarctica were painted orange for high-visibility and carried the markings of his corporate sponsors: Penzoil, Atlantic Richfield, and, of course, the Detroit News.

his propeller and lost seven hours waiting for repairs. Post had not only bested his own record, but in the process, he also became the first person to fly around the world *solo*.

Even as Wiley Post was chalking up accomplishments in the *Winnie Mae*, others were setting new records in their Vegas. These daredevil aviators included Amelia Earhart, Jimmie Mattern, Ruth Nichols, and Roscoe Turner. Known as "The Flying Debutante," Ruth Nichols set both transcontinental endurance and altitude (28,743 feet) records in her Vega, while Amelia Earhart became the first woman to fly the Atlantic solo.

Earhart's Atlantic flight is a testimony to the Vega's durability. She landed in Ireland on May 21, 1932, after a flight of 14 hours 54 minutes. During this flight, her Vega suffered severe icing while trying to climb over a weather front and went into a 3,000-foot plunge from which Earhart was able to recover.

Eventually, over 128 Vegas were built, including the Model 4 Air Express, which was built for Western Air Express (later known as Western Airlines) and for the Texaco Oil Company. Though the two aircraft were similar, the Model 4 Air Express differed from the Vega in that it had a parasol wing and the pilot was positioned in an open cockpit behind the passenger cabin. The Lockheed Sirius, Altair, and Orion were the successors to the Vega throughout the early 1930s. They were in the same size and weight class as the Vega, and like the Vega, they were powered by single radial engines. These were low-wing aircraft, and the Altair and Orion had retractable landing gear. Just as they had done with the Vega, many important pilots of the era flew her low-wing sisters. Charles Lindbergh operated a Sirius, and Jimmy Doolittle flew an Orion for the Shell Oil Company.

Achievements by women aviators in the early days of aviation are more often than not overshadowed by those of their male counterparts. But there is one woman who gets instant recognition. Amelia Earhart, born in Atchison, Kansas, learned to fly in 1921. She was not among the first women to earn a pilot's license, but she was a member of the post–World War I generation of pilots who wanted to push the limits and set records.

She had already amassed an impressive number of hours in the cockpit by 1928 when she flew as a passenger with Wilmer L. Stutz and Louis E. Gordon in their Fokker F.VII to make history. They flew 2,000 miles from Newfoundland to Wales, and Earhart became the first woman to cross the Atlantic by airplane.

On May 21, 1932, five years to the day after Lindbergh's solo Atlantic crossing, Amelia Earhart's Lockheed Vega touched down in Ireland in the second such solo flight and the first ever by a woman. She landed near Derry in Ireland after a flight from Newfoundland lasting 14 hours 54 minutes. The flight also gave her the record for the longest nonstop flight—2,026 miles—by a woman. Congress awarded her the Distinguished Flying Cross, making her the only woman so honored until well after World War II.

Only three months after her Atlantic flight, Amelia became the first woman to fly nonstop across the United States. In doing so, she set a new women's distance record of 2,447.8 miles. In January 1935, she became the first woman pilot to make a solo, long-distance flight over the Pacific, flying from Honolulu, Hawaii, to Oakland, California.

Often compared to Lindbergh, Earhart received celebrity treatment from the media, which relished her every achievement. By 1937, there was one obvious challenge left to be met: to become the first woman to pilot an aircraft around the world. All previous flights "around the world" were made by shortcuts within the Northern Hemisphere. Amelia Earhart planned to be the first pilot of either gender to circle the globe at its widest, close to the equator.

On May 21, 1937, she flew east out of Oakland in a specially modified twin-engine Lockheed Model 10E Electra. Accompanying her were her husband of six years, publisher and explorer George Palmer Putnam, and her crew. This crew included mechanic Bo McNeely and navigator Fred Noonan. Leaving Putnam and McNeely in Florida on June 1, 1937, she and Noonan flew from Miami to South America. They crossed the Atlantic at its narrowest in one hop and flew across Africa and the Asian subcontinent by way of Khartoum, Karachi, and Calcutta. With stops in Singapore and Australia, they reached Lae, New Guinea, poised for the long flight across the Pacific by way of Howland Island and Hawaii.

On July 1, she and Noonan took off from Lae, flying over open water toward Howland, which was 2,556 miles away. Their last radio transmission was heard aboard the U.S. Coast Guard cutter *Itasca* 20 hours 16 minutes after they took off. The Electra never arrived at Howland, and Amelia Earhart was never seen or heard from again. The disappearance without a trace of the Electra has become one of aviation's most enduring unsolved mysteries.

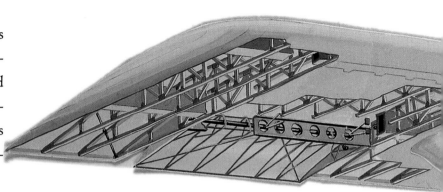

FOR MUCH OF THE 20TH CENTURY, it was the most famous one-of-a-kind aircraft in the United States. Its accomplishment was significant, its renown was enormous, and it touched the hearts and minds of the public more deeply than can be imagined today. It was at the right time, at the right place, and it was piloted by the man who was the central casting image of the perfect American hero for the times.

It began with an idea. Flying an airplane nonstop—alone—across the Atlantic Ocean was a concept that a vast portion of the American and European public found appealing. Even more than the Pacific, the Atlantic seemed to be the perfect barrier over which aviation should triumph. In June 1919, British pilots John Alcock and Arthur Whitten-Brown succeeded in flying from Newfoundland to Ireland nonstop, but it wasn't from the North American continent to continental Europe, and there were two of them. Six men had died trying to fly it solo, and the hero's laurel still awaited the pilot who succeeded.

Charles Lindbergh was a quiet young man flying the airmail out of St. Louis who dreamed the dream and decided to do something about it. With the financial backing of a syndicate of St. Louis businessmen, he approached Claude Ryan in San Diego, California, to build a special aircraft based on the Ryan M-1 mailplane but with the range to fly from New York to Paris.

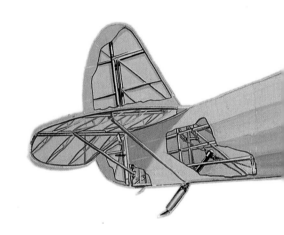

Ryan agreed, and the result was designated as the Ryan NYP ("New York to Paris"). The airplane bore the name *The Spirit of St. Louis* in deference to the people who put up the $6,000 to build the plane. The Ryan NYP had a wingspan of 46 feet and a length of 27 feet 5 inches. It weighed 5,245 pounds—over half of the weight in fuel—and had a service ceiling of 16,400 feet. It was powered by a single 220-horse-power, air-cooled, nine-cylinder Wright J-5C Whirlwind engine that gave it a cruising speed of 112 miles per hour.

To achieve the specified range of 4,100 miles, *The Spirit of St. Louis* had to carry 2,700 pounds of fuel in a huge fuel tank in the forward part of the fuselage ahead of the cockpit. The pilot's only forward vision was through a small periscope. To cut down on weight, the flight instruments were held to a minimum.

Because it was based on the existing M-1 mailplane, the NYP took only two months to build. It was then delivered to

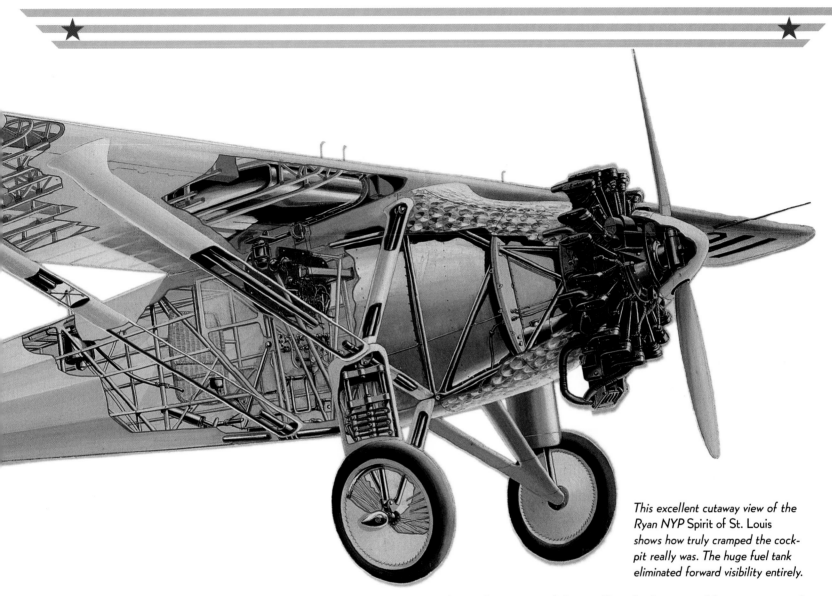

This excellent cutaway view of the Ryan NYP Spirit of St. Louis shows how truly cramped the cockpit really was. The huge fuel tank eliminated forward visibility entirely.

Lindbergh, who took off and flew nonstop from San Diego to St. Louis in just 14 hours 30 minutes. From there, he flew to Roosevelt Field on New York's Long Island, the point at which the do-or-die flight to Paris would begin.

Even though he had been awake for 36 hours, Lindbergh decided to take advantage of the high pressure that pushed fair weather over the Atlantic, and he took off at dawn on May 20, 1927. Straining under the weight of its own fuel—which pushed its tires into the muddy field—*The Spirit of St. Louis* struggled

down the runway, lifting off at the last possible moment and barely missing telephone lines at the end of the field.

Though the weather was predicted to be good, storms near Nova Scotia battered the NYP as the pilot fought to keep himself awake. At the 28-hour mark, Lindbergh sighted land—the Irish coast. He headed on to France, navigated toward the French capital, spotted the lights of the City of Lights, and landed at Le Bourget Field 33 hours 30 minutes 30 seconds after he'd taken off from Roosevelt Field.

The Ryan NYP Spirit of St. Louis *in flight with Charles Lindbergh at the controls. While he was not the first to fly the Atlantic nonstop,"Lucky Lindy" was the first pilot to do it with just the hum of the engine to keep him company.*

Like its pilot, *The Spirit of St. Louis* was treated heroically. Carried back to the United States courtesy of the U.S. Navy, the small Ryan monoplane subsequently carried Lindbergh on an extensive series of publicity flights throughout the Western Hemisphere. Finally, Lindbergh donated *The Spirit of St. Louis* to the Smithsonian Institution where it became the star attraction. Though its importance has faded, the airplane that carried Lindbergh to Paris still occupies a place of immense prominence not only in the Smithsonian's National Air & Space Museum in Washington, D.C., but also in the history of aviation.

(Above) Lindbergh took the Spirit of St. Louis *on numerous demonstration flights. He was not always able to land at the most perfect of airfields.*
(Left) This close-up view of a Ryan NYP replica shows the Wright J-5C Whirlwind engine with the Hamilton Standard logo on the propeller blade.

In the late 1920s and early 1930s, Charles Augustus Lindbergh and Anne Morrow Lindbergh were the first couple of American adventure and favorites of the American media. They epitomized strength and wholesomeness and characterized everything that Americans admired in their national character.

Charles Lindbergh was born in Detroit, Michigan, and grew up in Little Falls, Minnesota. He was the son of Charles Lindbergh, Sr., a Republican congressman. The young Lindbergh attended the University of Wisconsin to study mechanical engineering but later dropped out to take flying lessons. He became a barnstormer, flying at fairs throughout the Midwest.

Anne Spencer Morrow was born in Englewood, New Jersey, and was the daughter of banker Dwight Whitney Morrow. She graduated in 1928 from Smith College, where she received honors for her distinguished literary work.

In 1924, as Anne entered Smith, Charles enrolled as a cadet in the U.S. Air Service Reserve at Brooks Field, Texas. He was commissioned as a second lieutenant in November 1925, and in April 1926, he made his first long-distance airmail flight.

During this glorious era, young men such as Lindbergh were dreaming of the limitless possibilities of aviation. Well known to this generation of pilots was the $25,000 that French hotel magnate Raymond Orteig had previously offered in 1919 to the first aviator to fly nonstop from New York to Paris.

Bankrolled by a consortium of St. Louis financiers, Lindbergh had an aircraft built by Claude Ryan in San Diego, California, and set out to conquer the Atlantic. On May 20, 1927, Lindbergh took off from Roosevelt Field, New York, in his sturdy Ryan monoplane *The Spirit of St. Louis* and headed for Paris.

Cursed by having had a sleepless night before taking off, Lindbergh had a miserable flight, battling both the weather and his own exhaustion. He persevered and landed safely at Le Bourget Field near Paris after dark on May 21. The welcome was tumultuous. Crowds of well-wishers mobbed him, and he needed a police escort to get off the field. For the media, "Lucky Lindy" was its dream of an American hero. President Calvin Coolidge sent the U.S. Navy to bring him home, and he returned to New York to a ticker tape parade.

He became an overnight celebrity, and the Guggenheim Foundation sponsored his air visits to 75 cities in the United States. Dwight Morrow, now the American ambassador to Mexico, sponsored a Lindbergh goodwill tour to that country, and it was there that Charles met Anne. Lindbergh married Anne in 1929, and for the next several years, he rarely flew alone.

Anne learned to fly and accompanied her husband on many flights throughout the world. Together, they set a transcontinental speed record and surveyed commercial air routes through Central America for Pan American Airways. In 1931, they surveyed air routes to the Far East, flying to China by way of Alaska, Siberia, and Japan. Two years later, they conducted a 29,000-mile flight that took them to Europe via Greenland and back to the United States by way of West Africa and Brazil.

Meanwhile, disaster struck the Lindberghs in 1932 when their two-year-old son Charles was kidnapped for ransom and murdered. Bruno Hauptman was arrested, tried in what was then known as "the trial of the century," and executed. The Lindberghs never fully recovered from their tragedy.

When World War II began, Charles Lindbergh urged American isolation and neutrality, which was an unpopular opinion that caused the once-adoring public to turn on him. During World War II, as a civilian, he helped train Allied pilots and developed techniques for conserving fuel over long ocean flights and for taking heavily loaded planes aloft from difficult war strips. The Lindberghs later retired at a secluded home near Hana on the Hawaiian island of Maui.

DOUGLAS WORLD CRUISERS

THE 1920s WERE AN expansive era in the history of aviation technology. The generation of pilots that came of age flying in the First World War were anxious to outdo one another with amazing endurance flights. The phrase "First to fly..." was commonly found on the front pages of the newspapers of the 1920s. The feat that captured the imagination most was to be the first to fly around the

The Douglas World Cruisers Boston, Chicago, New Orleans, and Seattle began their epic globe-circling flight officially on April 6, 1924, taking off from Seattle, Washington.

world. By 1923, flights across the United States, across the Atlantic, and between Europe and the Far East had been accomplished. The dangers and complexities were known and had been pushed to the limits. A flight around the world would be no easy task.

The U.S. Army Air Service decided to undertake the project, using several aircraft and a network of support sites prearranged around the globe. Five aircraft were ordered from the Douglas Aircraft Company of Santa Monica, California. Based on the U.S. Navy's DT-2 torpedo bomber, they would be known as the Douglas World Cruisers (DWC). The Douglas World Cruisers were two-place, open-cockpit aircraft, with a wingspan of 50 feet and a length of 35 feet 6 inches. They weighed 6,995 pounds fully loaded and fueled and had a service ceiling of 7,000 to 10,000 feet. They were powered by a single 420-horsepower, liquid-cooled Liberty 12A V-12 in-line engine

that gave them a top speed of about 103 miles per hour, depending on altitude.

A 600-gallon fuel capacity provided an unrefueled cruising range up to 2,200 miles, although the longest planned flight segment on the route was only 875 miles. To permit the Cruisers to use a variety of landing sites, they were designed to be converted back and forth from landplanes to seaplanes as they made their epic voyage. Four of the five DWCs were earmarked to make the flight, with a fifth held as a spare. The four planes were individually named for four cities of the United States: *Boston, Chicago, New Orleans,* and *Seattle.*

The flight crews were Army Air Service officers and enlisted men, all of them chosen and trained for the mission as carefully as the first American astronauts would be four long decades later. They included Major Frederick L. Martin, the commander of the contingent; First Lieutenant Leslie Arnold, an Army Air Service exhibition flyer who was a former summer stock actor and who became the group spokesman; Second Lieutenant John Harding, an engine maintenance specialist who had taken part in an earlier series of flights circumnavigating the borders of the United States; Staff Sergeant Alva Harvey, another ace flight mechanic who rose through the ranks to become an Army general in World War II; First Lieutenant Erik Nelson, a pilot-engi-

(Above) *The Douglas World Cruiser* New Orleans *was piloted by Second Lieutenant John Harding, an engine maintenance specialist. The* New Orleans *was one of two World Cruisers to make it all the way around the world.* (Left) *Crowds wait patiently at Douglas's Clover Field in Santa Monica, California, for the World Cruisers to take off on their long journey. Ultimately, they would return to this spot six months later.*

The Douglas World Cruiser fleet is readied for takeoff. The aircraft began their flight from Santa Monica as landplanes but were converted to a seaplane configuration for the island-to-island hops across the Pacific and Atlantic.

neer whose expertise was in long-duration endurance flying; Second Lieutenant Henry Ogden, a sergeant when the flight began and also the team's top mechanical trouble-shooter; Lieutenant Lowell Smith, holder of 16 flying records and pioneer of techniques for air-to-air refueling; and First Lieutenant Leigh Wade, a test pilot who had once suffered frostbite to set an altitude record for multiengine aircraft.

As history reveals, the success of the world flight is attributed as much to a carefully planned global support network as to the World Cruiser airplanes and crews. The State Department obtained clearances for the flight from 15 different governments. Interservice rivalries were suspended as the U.S. Navy prepositioned supplies, spare parts, and support teams at key points in various remote areas and stationed support ships at intervals along major overwater stretches of the route. The worldwide effort made it one of the most prodigious military logistics operations ever attempted up to that time.

On March 17, 1924, the fully fueled DWCs took off from Santa Monica and headed for Alaska by way of Seattle, which was the official starting point for the historic flight. The DWC *Seattle* was lost in April in stormy weather, hitting a mountain in Alaska. The crew survived, however, and walked out of the wilderness ten days later.

The other three planes plowed on through the spring of 1924, becoming the first aircraft to cross the Pacific, albeit at the northern edge. They reached Tokyo on May 22, Shanghai on June 4, and Saigon on June 6. They crossed the Asian subcontinent during the hot and muggy summer, hitting Calcutta on June 26 and Karachi on the fourth of July.

Four days later, Baghdad shimmered in the heat, but Istanbul was somewhat cooler on July 10. Two days later, they landed in Bucharest, having become the first—and the last for many years—to fly from the United States to Europe traveling west to east. A fast, three-day European tour took them to Vienna, Paris, and London, where they rested for two weeks before resuming the flight.

For the flight across Asia and Europe, the three DWCs had been configured as landplanes, but they left from Brough, Eng-

The Douglas World Cruiser 2, Chicago, is seen here in its seaplane configuration flying over Puget Sound, en route west to circle the globe in its historic 1924 round-the-world flight.

land, on July 30 with their seaplane pontoons reattached. On August 21, *Boston* was lost off Iceland on the 875-mile flight to Frederksdal, Greenland—the longest leg of the flight. Now only the *Chicago* and the *New Orleans* were left to continue the flight.

In Pictou, Nova Scotia, on August 6, the fifth DWC, which was christened *Boston II*, was flown in to join her sisters for the flight to Boston, Massachusetts, and then across the United States. The triumphal American tour took the three DWCs to Washington, D.C.; Chicago, Illinois; Muscogee, Oklahoma; and El Paso, Texas. Among the four namesake cities, New Orleans was, for some reason, not included in the flight plan.

On September 23, at 2:25 pm, *Chicago* and *New Orleans*, along with *Boston II*, touched down in Santa Monica. Only Smith and Arnold in *Chicago* and Nelson and Harding in *New Orleans* had made the entire circumnavigation. As though it were a victory lap or as a tribute to the first DWC lost, the three aircraft continued on to Seattle, touching down on September 28 after a flight of 27,553 miles.

Boeing P-26 Peashooter

A DECADE AFTER WORLD WAR I, the U.S. Army's Air Corps still looked like its wartime Air Service. The open-cockpit biplanes were newer, but they still consisted of wood and fabric construction. Even though more metal was used in construction and the engines were better, the overall performance and durability of the planes had improved only slightly from 1918.

By the early 1930s, it was time for a wake-up call. The purpose of the Army's pursuit squadrons was to defend against enemy bombers. In order to do that, a pursuit plane had to be faster than the bombers it was pursuing. A glance at the rapidly improving capabilities of bombers produced in Europe, and even in the United States, showed Air Corps planners that a new generation of fighters was needed.

Several fighter prototypes were considered before the Air Corps finally settled on a Boeing design. This fighter was ordered under the designation P-26. It was promptly given the nickname "Peashooter" because the gunsight protruding from the cockpit looked exactly like a peashooter.

The Peashooter was the U.S. Army Air Corps' last open-cockpit, fixed-landing-gear fighter, but at the same time, it was also the first all-metal monoplane fighter to reach squadron service with the Air Corps. The prototype was first flown on March 20, 1932, and a production contract for 111 P-26As was issued the following January.

The P-26A had a wingspan of 27 feet 11 inches and a length of 23 feet 7 inches. It weighed 3,012 pounds and had a service ceiling of 28,300 feet. It was powered by a single 600-horse-

Shown here is a side view of the XP-26 at Boeing Field in 1933. The prototype was not yet equipped with the gunsight that protruded from the cockpit to give the aircraft its nickname "Peashooter."

A formation of Boeing P-26A Peashooters fly on a routine training flight out of March Army Air Field, circa 1935. The P-26A was the first U.S. monoplane fighter.

power, air-cooled, nine-cylinder Pratt & Whitney R-1340 Wasp engine that gave it a cruising speed of 199 miles per hour. The P-26A had a range of 620 miles.

The first of the P-26As was flown in January 1934, and all of the production aircraft were delivered by June. However, the airplanes had to be retrofitted with flaps to reduce the landing speed of the fast little machines, and a headrest/roll bar was added to protect the pilot in case his Peashooter overturned. A small number of P-26Bs were delivered to the U.S. Army Air Corps in June 1934. These were equipped with landing flaps, and they also had new fuel-injected R-1340 Wasp engines.

To carry out its combat mission, the P-26 was armed with a pair of machine guns, and it had the capacity for two 116-pound bombs. The guns were located in the fuselage adjacent to the pilot's knees. They were originally to be .30 caliber weapons, but provisions were made for replacing the right machine gun with a .50 caliber unit.

The Peashooter ultimately had a combat career, but it was not with the U.S. Army. Nine P-26s were reported in combat with the Philippine Army Air Force in December 1941. A few days after the attack on Pearl Harbor, as the Japanese pressed their offensive on the Philippines, the Peashooters made their combat appearance. The Philippines were overrun and subjugated in a matter of weeks, and the P-26, which had been revolutionary in 1933, was now outmoded. Thus, the P-26 faded away, never again to see action.

BOEING 247

IN THE EARLY YEARS after World War I, commercial air travel was an interesting novelty enjoyed by a few daring travelers willing to put up with the noise and vibration of the early transports in order to travel between New York and Chicago or between Frankfurt and Berlin in half the time that it took to go by train.

By the early 1930s, however, there were many who saw commercial air travel as no longer a novelty but as an emerging form of transportation. One of those who saw this view of the future was William Edward Boeing. His airplane factory in Seattle, Washington, was one of the fastest growing in the country. Boeing also owned the Hamilton Standard Propeller Corporation. The Boeing Air Transport System, a combination of small regional lines, was founded, and Boeing instructed the engineers at his Boeing Airplane Company to build an all-metal monoplane transport that was more advanced than anything then in service.

The result was the Boeing 247, a ten-passenger airliner that was 70 miles per hour faster than any other airliner

Wien Alaska Airlines was one of the pioneer airlines in the vast territory that would one day become America's 49th state. The airline began operating in the 1940s, with two Boeing 247Ds.

This Boeing Model 247D wears the livery of United Air Lines, circa 1940. The Model 247 was originally introduced in 1933 when United Air Lines and Boeing were both part of the same conglomerate.

in service and equipped with more soundproofing measures than used previously.

Meanwhile, Boeing was imagining an empire that would not only create an airline but build the aircraft to fly on that airline. His holdings were combined into an entity known as United Aircraft & Transport Corporation. The first 247 flew in February 1933, and within the year, 60 were delivered to the United Aircraft & Transport Corporation.

In 1934, the improved 247D made its debut as an entry in the MacRobertson air race from London to Melbourne, Australia. Equipped with the new Hamilton Standard variable-pitch propeller and piloted by Clyde Pangborne and Roscoe Turner, the 247D came in second in the transport category and third overall, making a notable debut. Most of the remaining 247s built became 247Ds, although a single "militarized" 247Y was built for a Chinese warlord.

Except for the windshield, which did not slant back as on the earlier 247s, the 247D was generally similar in appearance

When it was first introduced in 1933, the Boeing 247 was marked with a United Air Lines logo that carried the Boeing logo at its center. Within a year, the two components would be separate companies.

to its predecessors. It had a wingspan of 74 feet and a length of 51 feet 7 inches. It weighed 13,650 pounds and had a service ceiling of 25,400 feet. It was powered by a pair of 550-horse-power, air-cooled, nine-cylinder Pratt & Whitney R-1340-S1H1G Wasp engines that gave it a cruising speed of 189 miles per hour. It had a range of 745 miles.

The 247D won the 1934 Guggenheim medal for "successful pioneering and advancement in aircraft manufacturing and transport." However, this award was overshadowed by United Aircraft & Transport's insurmountable turbulence of its own. In 1932, the Roosevelt Administration was keen to break up corporate monopolies that it perceived as contrary to the good

of the American economy, and United Aircraft & Transport was seen as such a monopoly.

The Black-McKellar Act was passed in 1934, prohibiting a single company to own both airplane manufacturing and airline operations. In September, Bill Boeing resigned as his empire broke up. The airline portion went on to become United Air Lines; the Boeing Airplane Company evolved into the largest producer of commercial aircraft in the world.

The 247s and 247Ds continued to fly for United and for other customers as well. Although these planes were soon outclassed by the immortal Douglas DC-3, the Boeing monoplanes would have a long life, lasting several decades.

ONE OF THE MOST interesting series of recurring air races held in the years before World War II were the Schneider Trophy seaplane races, a brainchild of French armsmaker and aviation patron Jacques Schneider. The Schneider Trophy Race actually dated to before the First World War, with the first two held in 1913 and 1914 at Monaco. The races resumed in 1919 amid a row between Britain and Italy over who would host the race. Britain won that contest, but the race turned into a farce when the only plane to finish, an Italian Savoia S.13, was compelled to make an extra lap in order to win the trophy but ran out of fuel in the process.

In 1920 and 1921, the race was held in Venice and won by the Italian entrant each year. In 1922, Briton Henri Beard took the trophy to England with a 146 miles per hour win at Naples. Beard's aircraft was a Supermarine Sea Lion II, a remarkable plane that became a precursor to the Supermarine seaplanes that dominated the final years of the Schneider Trophy Race in the 1930s.

In 1923—amid growing interest in air races and demonstration flying in the United States—the U.S. Navy decided to enter the Schneider Trophy Race. The aircraft of choice was the Curtiss CR-3. In retrospect, it may have seemed strange or even extravagant that the U.S. Navy had an interest in air racing;

Powered by a 600-horsepower Curtiss engine, the U.S. Army's R-6 race plane was a sister ship to the Curtiss P-6 Hawk pursuit aircraft. The heavy-duty struts shown here were not standard on the pursuit version.

however, it was seen as a good exercise in developing both fast and maneuverable high-performance aircraft.

The Navy became so involved in racing that, from 1922 to 1928, they actually assigned an official "racer" designation in their nomenclature. When Congress looked with disapproval at this practice a few years later, race planes started receiving new "fighter" designations. The three aircraft types to receive the "racer" designation were all from Curtiss: the CR, the R2C, and the R3C. (The latter two later became F2C and F3C, respectively.) The first CR, the CR-1 was built expressly for the 1921 Pulitzer Race. Powered by a 405-horsepower Curtiss CD12 engine, it came in first. In 1922, the Navy raced another CR-1 plus a CR-2, which was actually a modified CR-1. After they came in a disappointing third and fourth in the race, the Navy changed engines and developed the CR-3.

The CR-3, two of which competed in the 1923 Schneider Trophy Race, had a wingspan of 22 feet 8 inches and a length of 25 feet 10 inches. It weighed 2,746 pounds fully loaded and fueled. It was powered by a 450-horsepower Curtiss D-12 liquid-cooled V-12 engine that gave it a top speed of 188 miles per hour. It had a range of 520 miles.

In September 1923, Navy Lieutenant David Rittenhouse took the Schneider Trophy in one of the CR-3s, turning in a

(Above) *When the U.S. Navy decided to enter air races, they turned to Glenn Curtiss. The first racer was the CR-1 and was built expressly for the 1921 Pulitzer Race. This plane later evolved into the CR-3, which first competed in the 1923 Schneider Trophy Race.* (Left) *Based on the F6C pursuit plane, the Curtiss R2C-1 race plane won the 1923 Pulitzer Race in St. Louis. Its successor, the Curtiss R3C-2, won the 1925 Schneider Trophy Race held at Bay Shore Park, Maryland.*

A U.S. Navy Curtiss Model R-3 is shown here in a twin-float seaplane configuration. Powered by a 160-horsepower Curtiss VX engine, the Model R-3 was similar to the R-2 landplane that flew an aerial review for General John "Blackjack" Pershing on August 22, 1916.

time of 177.38 miles per hour and edging out Lieutenant Rutledge Irvine in the other CR-3. This stunning performance, held near Cowes on Britain's Isle of Wight, buoyed the spirits of those at the Navy's Bureau of Aeronautics. However, it was soon eclipsed by another triumph.

Less than a month later, a pair of R2Cs took the top spots at the Pulitzer Race in St. Louis. On October 6, 1923, Lieutenant Alford Williams set a new world speed record of 243.673 miles per hour in his R2C, followed by Lieutenant Harold Brow in another R2C—who also beat the previous world record—with a time of 241.779 miles per hour.

The 1924 Schneider Trophy Race was canceled because the British and Italian aircraft were "not ready;" the Americans agreed to a postponement. This set the stage for an interesting race that would pit Italy's Macchi M.33 and Britain's Gloster IIIA and new Supermarine S.4 monoplane against the latest of the Curtiss Navy racers.

The Curtiss R3C-2, designed for the 1925 Schneider Trophy event, was a trim biplane with a wingspan of 22 feet and a length of 22 feet. It weighed 2,738 pounds fully loaded and fueled. It was powered by a 565-horsepower Curtiss V-1400 liquid-cooled V-12 engine that gave it a top speed of 245 miles per hour. It had a range of 290 miles. This time, an Army pilot would be at the controls for the race. Army test pilot Lieutenant Jimmy Doolittle established an aviation career that flourished 15 years later during World War II.

The 1925 Schneider event was held at Bay Shore Park in Baltimore, Maryland, and was the first of only two Schneider

Trophy Races hosted by the United States. During pre-race trials, the Supermarine entry, whose cantilever wing was subject to flutter, stalled out and side-slipped into the water. The Macchi came in third, and the Gloster was second. Doolittle piloted the R3C to victory with a speed of 232.57 miles per hour. He was the only pilot to break the 200 miles per hour mark. Ironically, it had been an Army pilot who piloted a Navy Curtiss racer to its final international triumph.

The 1926 Schneider contest—held off Hampton Roads, Virginia—had a political dimension not previously seen. Italian dictator Benito Mussolini took a personal interest in Schneider Trophy racing, and he insisted that Italy should win. Appropriating a great deal of research and development money, he oversaw the development of the new Macchi M.39 monoplane as well as the powerful 800-horsepower, 12-cylinder Fiat AS.2 in-line engine. The U.S. Navy fielded an R3C-2 and an R3C-4, which was an R3C-3 plane with a 700-horsepower Curtiss V-1550 engine.

Held on November 13, 1926, it was the fastest Schneider Trophy Race to date. U.S. Navy Lieutenant George Cuddihy in the R3C-2—powered by the V-1400 engine—managed to reach a speed of 232.42 miles per hour, but the fuel pump failed and he ran out of fuel before he crossed the finish line. The Italian investment paid off as Major Mario de Bernardi's Macchi won the race with a speed of 246.496 miles per hour.

This was the last Schneider Trophy Race for the Curtiss racers and for the United States. The official explanation was that costs were prohibitive. Ironically, the Italians, who had gone all out to win in 1926, never won the cup again. All the Schneider races after 1926 were dominated by the British Supermarine monoplanes, and the event was held for the last time in 1931.

JAMES "JIMMY" DOOLITTLE

One of America's greatest military airmen and a leading figure in the pantheon of aviation, Jimmy Doolittle joined the U.S. Army Air Service during World War I. Although he served as a flight and gunnery instructor, he never got into action.

In 1929, he led the effort to develop blind-flying instruments. In the early days of flying, pilots were at considerable risk from bad weather and fogged-in runways. Doolitle became the first pilot to take off, maneuver for 15 miles, and land safely, relying only on the aircraft's instruments rather than looking outside his aircraft.

In 1931, Jimmy Doolittle won the Bendix transcontinental air race with a time of 11 hours 16 minutes and an average speed of 223 miles per hour. The following year, he flew the Granville Gee Bee raceplane with a world record speed of 294 miles per hour and won the Thompson Trophy. Doolittle and Roscoe Turner were the only pilots to win both the Bendix and Thompson trophies.

He returned to active duty during World War II, and in 1942, he organized what would be his most famous achievement. Lieutenant Colonel Doolittle established a seemingly impossible air raid on Tokyo, using USAAF B-25 medium bombers launched from a U.S. Navy aircraft carrier. On April 18, 1942, all 16 planes of Doolittle's strike force successfully took off from the USS *Hornet*. While the physical damage to Japan was negligible, the mission boosted the American morale.

All of Doolittle's crews, except one, safely reached China. Doolittle was awarded the Medal of Honor. Promoted to brigadier general, he went on to command the 12th and 15th U.S. Army Air Forces. As a lieutenant general, he commanded the USAAF 8th Air Force for the last 18 months of the war.

THE PIPER CUB'S STORY began in 1929 when William T. Piper, Sr., became an investor in C. Gilbert Taylor's Taylor Brothers Aircraft Company in Bradford, Pennsylvania. A year later when the aircraft company went bankrupt, Piper took control, and in 1937, when Taylor left the firm, it was reorganized as the Piper Aircraft Corporation.

In 1931, as Piper became

The four-passenger Piper PA-6 Skysedan, seen here during May 1946 flight tests near Lock Haven, Pennsylvania, was one of many aircraft that crowded onto the postwar general aviation market.

actively involved in the company, he insisted that Taylor—a self-taught aeronautical engineer—build a light, two-place airplane that was both reasonably powerful and affordable to the average person. Essentially, Piper's idea was to airplanes what Henry Ford's was to automobiles when he introduced the mass-produced Model T a generation earlier.

The result of Piper's idea was the E-2 Cub. It was a plane of modest performance but at a modest price: Piper sold over 200 E-2s at a price of $1,300. In 1936, the company produced the J-2 Cub, which was later followed by the immensely successful J-3 Cub. Well over 14,000 J-3s were built. Tens of thousands of private pilots who learned to fly in the 1930s and 1940s learned in Cubs.

The J-3 Cub had a wingspan of 35 feet 2.5 inches and a length of 22 feet 4.5 inches. It weighed just 1,220 pounds fully loaded and fueled, and it had a service ceiling of 11,500 feet. It was designed to have a range of just over 200 miles. The Cub

was powered by various air-cooled four-cylinder engines manufactured by such firms as Franklin, Continental, or Lycoming. The standard engine was the 40-horsepower Continental A-40-4, although many were built with the 50-horse-power Continental A-50-5, the Lycoming O-145, and the Franklin AC-150. The Cub's cruising speed was typically about 80 miles per hour.

The J-3 Cubs were complemented by the J-4, which was introduced in 1938, and the three-seat J-5, which was introduced in 1940. Just under 3,000 of these two models were produced, and all of them were powered by the 75-horsepower Continental A-75-8 engine.

During World War II, Piper delivered over 5,700 Cubs to the American armed forces. The USAAF took thousands under the designations L-4, C-83, O-59, and L-14 (the three-seat version). The Navy bought them under a variety of designations, notably the HE-1 air ambulance version, which had a hinged fuselage top to accommodate a stretcher.

After World War II, Piper continued to produce improved versions of the Cub. The PA-11 Cub Special came on-line in 1947. Over 1,400 were built, and most Cub Specials had a 65-horsepower Continental A-65-8 engine. The longest running production Cub was the PA-18 Super Cub. Over 6,000 were built between 1949 and 1978.

(Top left) *Photographed in a field somewhere in Normandy two weeks after the June 1944 invasion of Europe, this USAAF Piper L-4 Cub liaison plane is marked with the same kind of "invasion stripes" as larger combat aircraft.* (Top right) *When it was displayed at the Flushing, New York, airport on April 12, 1950, this Piper Super Cub was billed in a press release as "the world's slowest airplane currently in production." The idea behind the press release was to underscore that the Super Cub could cruise at 30 miles per hour in still air.* (Above left) *The Piper PA-28 Turbo Arrow, seen here in 1980, was powered by a Continental TSIO-360-F turbocharged engine rated at 200-horsepower. It had a high tail but a fuselage similar to that of the Piper Cherokee.* (Above right) *The Piper Comanche 400—as seen here in 1964, which was the first year of a four-year production run—was a limited edition, 400-horse-power version of the Comanche 260. Both were powered by Lycoming IO-540-series engines.*

The Piper PA-18 Super Cub had a wingspan of 35 feet 3.5 inches and a length of 22 feet 6 inches. It weighed 1,750 pounds fully loaded and fueled. Various engines were used through the years, but the last Super Cubs from the 1970s were usually powered by the 175-horsepower Lycoming O-320. The Super Cub's cruising speed was typically about 115 miles per hour, and it had a range of just over 450 miles.

Though never known for its speed, its power, or for breaking any records, the Piper Cub was legendary for its numbers. It has been estimated that over a third of the nonmilitary aircraft sold in the United States during the middle decades of the 20th century were Cubs. Indeed, Cubs were in production for almost two generations and were the most widely produced nonmilitary aircraft in U.S. history.

PEOPLE ARE FOND of top ten lists, and if aviation historians were asked to write such a list for great airplanes, there is one airplane that would almost certainly be on every list. The Douglas DC-3 is one of the undisputed greats of aviation, and no mention of it is complete without a nod to its immediate predecessors, the DC-1 and the DC-2.

As airlines and potential passengers started to get serious about air transport as a viable service, aircraft builders started getting serious about building aircraft to meet their needs. Boeing was developing its modern 247 airliner for Boeing Air Transport, its sister company under the umbrella of United Aircraft & Transport Corporation. Meanwhile, the competition, Transcontinental & Western Air (TWA) looked at what was happening at United. In order to successfully compete with United, TWA needed to compete with the Boeing 247.

In August 1932, Jack Frye, the vice president for operations at TWA, wrote to the major planemakers, requesting a bid on ten new airliners. These planes needed to be fast, reliable, and capable of crossing the Rocky Mountains safely. Douglas Aircraft Company put its best designers to work on the project.

Though Boeing's 247 was delivered sooner, Douglas finished the prototype DC-1 in less than a year. The big silver bird

The DC-2 first entered service with Transcontinental & Western Air, but American Airlines soon became a customer. The latter company, in turn, became the airline that helped to launch the DC-3.

was larger than the 247, and after the initial engine problems were overcome, it flew beautifully. The DC-1 first flew on July 1, 1933, and it was delivered to TWA on September 13, 1933.

The Douglas DC-1 had a wingspan of 85 feet and a length of 60 feet. It weighed 17,500 pounds fully loaded and fueled and had a service ceiling of 23,000 feet. It was powered by two 710-horsepower, air-cooled Wright Cyclone SGR-1820-F3 radial engines that gave it a cruising speed of 190 miles per hour. It carried 12 passengers and had a range of 998 miles.

TWA was so delighted with the DC-1's performance, they placed an order for 25 more production planes. These new planes differed slightly from the DC-1 and were delivered under the designation DC-2. The Douglas DC-2 first flew on May 11, 1934, and the first airline delivery went to TWA two days later.

The DC-2 had a wingspan of 85 feet and a length of 61 feet 11 inches. It weighed 18,560 pounds fully loaded and fueled and had a service ceiling of 23,600 feet. It was powered by two 835-horsepower, air-cooled Wright SGR-1820-F3 radial engines that gave it a cruising speed of 185 miles per hour. It carried 14 passengers and had a range of 1,225 miles. The DC-2 was almost

(Above) *Customers for the great Douglas transports included both airlines and other types of companies. This DC-2, for instance, was operated by the Standard Oil Company of California, now known familiarly as "Chevron." Note the company monogram adjacent to the door and the red, white, and blue chevron on the tail.* (Left) *The Douglas DC-2 differed externally from the DC-3 by its narrower fuselage and its prominent headlights. It was powered by two 835-horsepower, air-cooled Wright SGR-1820-F3 radial engines.*

An American Airlines Douglas DC-3 flies over the Woolworth Building and other skyscrapers of lower Manhattan, with the East River and the borough of Queens in the distance.

identical to the DC-1, but it was faster, carried more passengers, and had a longer range.

Placed into service between Chicago and Newark an unprecedented two days after its delivery flight, the first DC-2 actually broke the speed record for that route four times in just over a week. The DC-2 was also promptly exported to Europe when Royal Dutch Airlines (KLM) became the second customer after TWA to buy the aircraft. After a KLM DC-2 plane

came in second place at the October 1934 MacRobertson London-to-Melbourne Air Race, commercial orders poured in from around the world.

Pan American World Airways purchased them for its Chinese and Latin American subsidiaries, and the DC-2 became the first of a long line of DC liners acquired by American, Braniff, Eastern, Northwest, and Western in the United States. The United States military also bought 26 DC-2s under the U.S.

Army Air Corps designations C-32, C-33, C-34 (with special VIP interiors), and C-38 as well as the U.S. Navy/U.S. Marine Corps designation R2D.

The plane's reputation was so renowned that the DC-2 won Donald Douglas the 1936 Collier Trophy for aviation achievement—presented personally by President Roosevelt—and solidly launched his company into the world of commercial avi-

ation. After producing 185 DC-2s, Douglas turned to a similar but larger and improved version.

C. R. Smith of American Airlines helped to make the next generation of DC liners possible. In 1934, he went to Douglas with the idea for a transcontinental airliner with sleeping berths like the railroads offered. The resulting aircraft, with a wider fuselage than the DC-2, was the Douglas Skysleeper Transport

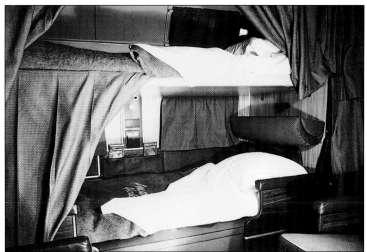

(Above left) *This close-up of the forward section of a mirror-brilliant Piedmont Airlines DC-3 provides a good view of the two 1,200-horsepower, air-cooled Wright R-1820 Cyclone engines.* (Above) *The original version of the Douglas DC-3 was the Douglas Skysleeper Transport (DST), which offered the type of sleeping accommodations available on Pullman railroad cars.* (Left) *A gleaming silver Douglas DC-3 in the livery of Eastern Air Lines. In the late 1930s, the DC-3 was the standard of excellence on all of the world's premier airlines.*

(DST). The DST first flew on December 17, 1935. That day was now not only known for the 32nd anniversary of the Wright Brothers' first flight but was significant for another aviation milestone of almost equal importance.

The DST, which was redesignated as the DC-3 when configured as a day-use, nonsleeper, offered luxury and reliability that could not have been imagined only a few years before. It carried varying numbers of passengers depending on its internal arrangement but typically the number was 21 in regular seating or 14 in the DST sleeper configuration. Its "Sky Room" was literally a suite with washroom facilities.

The DC-3 had a wingspan of 95 feet and a length of 64 feet 6 inches. It weighed 30,900 pounds fully loaded and fueled and had a service ceiling of 20,800 feet. It was typically powered by two 1,200-horsepower, air-cooled Wright R-1820 engines that gave it a cruising speed of 192 miles per hour. Its range was 1,200 miles.

The first DST/DC-3 airline delivery was to American Airlines on August 8, 1936, and soon TWA, Eastern, and United placed orders. Hundreds of DC-3s were sold over the next few years. So many of them were in service that it was estimated that

at the beginning of 1939, nine out of every ten airliners operated by United States airlines were either a DC-2 or a DC-3, and a total of 455 DC-3s were delivered to airlines around the world.

Even before World War II began, the U.S. Army Air Corps (U.S. Army Air Forces after June 1941) and the U.S. Navy started to acquire DC-2s and DC-3s to satisfy their needs for transport aircraft. The first military DC-3 had been a single C-41 delivered in October 1938 as an executive aircraft for the use of General Henry "Hap" Arnold, the head of the U.S. Army Air Corps. In addition, there were the hybrid C-39 and C-42, which were DC-2s with the empennage and outer wings of the DC-3.

During World War II, they were purchased primarily under the USAAF designation C-47 and the Navy designation R4D. The C-47/R4D aircraft were similar to the commercial DC-3, but they lacked the airline interiors, and they had heavier floors, stronger landing gear, and a large cargo door. After the United States entered the war, they also incorporated various subtle design changes that would facilitate a rapid and high rate of production.

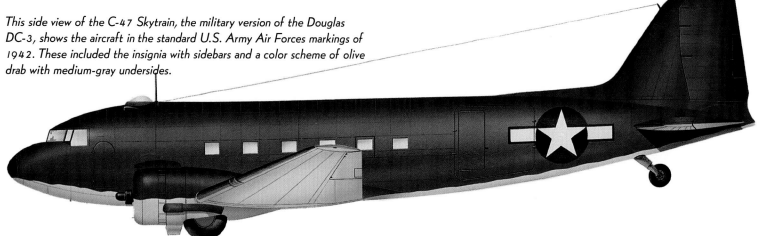

This side view of the C-47 Skytrain, the military version of the Douglas DC-3, shows the aircraft in the standard U.S. Army Air Forces markings of 1942. These included the insignia with sidebars and a color scheme of olive drab with medium-gray undersides.

A variation on the C-47 that was designed specifically for paratroopers had a smaller door and was delivered under the designation C-53. The official name for the C-47 was Skytrain, and for the C-53, it was Skytrooper. Those of both types that were transferred to Britain for use by the Royal Air Force or other Commonwealth air forces were known simply as "Dakotas." The most common unofficial nickname for the C-47 was "Gooney Bird." This nickname was borrowed from the Albatross, which, like the C-47, had a not-so-graceful appearance while landing that was in marked contrast to its quite graceful appearance in flight.

Having built 455 commercial DC-3s, Douglas produced another 10,174 military versions, including C-47s, Dakotas, C-53s, and R4Ds. On top of this, nearly 2,000 were produced in the Soviet Union and in Japan under license.

The Skytrains, Skytroopers, and Dakotas served the Allies in every theater of World War II, from the South Pacific to Europe. These planes spearheaded the Normandy invasion by towing troop gliders and dropping paratroopers behind enemy lines. They survived and even thrived in every imaginable environment, from the ice of Alaska to the constant bone-chilling rain in Britain and the unbearable heat of North Africa. They dodged the worst flying weather in the world, and they carried loads that far exceeded that for which they were designed.

In an appropriate tribute, Allied Supreme Commander General Dwight Eisenhower credited them with being the single most important airplane contributing to the Allied victory.

After World War II, DC-3s and surplus C-47s flooded into the surplus market and continued to be a mainstay with many regional airlines well into the 1950s. Indeed, there were still an estimated 1,000 of them in use during the 1990s.

DONALD WILLS DOUGLAS

One of the greatest entrepreneurs in aviation history, Donald Douglas was born in Brooklyn, New York. In his youth, Douglas developed a love of sailing that would endure throughout his life, and in 1909, he earned an appointment to the U.S. Naval Academy.

In the fall of 1912, he entered the Massachusetts Institute of Technology and earned his bachelor's degree in engineering by the spring of 1914, graduating two years ahead of schedule. MIT was so impressed they hired him as an assistant professor of engineering. In August 1915, after a year at MIT, he was hired by Glenn Martin, one of America's premier airplane builders.

In 1917, the United States entered World War I, and the U.S. Army suddenly realized the need for a staff that understood airplanes. For their first chief aeronautical engineer, the aviation section of the Army Signal Corps summoned Douglas. After World War I, he went back to work for Martin and designed the MB-1 bomber, which was the largest aircraft yet developed for the U.S. Army.

During World War II, Douglas produced tens of thousands of transports and combat aircraft, becoming one of the world's biggest planemakers. For two decades after the war, Douglas continued to produce large numbers of innovative and successful military and civilian aircraft and moved into building rockets used in the American space program.

In the mid-1960s, however, the good fortune that had smiled upon Douglas began to fade. The high cost of gearing up to build jetliners combined with the inflation brought about by the Vietnam War pushed the company to the edge of bankruptcy. This was averted only by a 1967 merger with McDonnell Aircraft of St. Louis.

WORLD WAR II

THE PERIOD OF THE SECOND WORLD WAR, from 1939 to 1945, was a major turning point in aviation history. First of all, there has been no other six-year period in history when so many airplanes were manufactured or so many pilots trained to fly. On a typical day in 1943 or 1944, there were probably more airplanes in the air around the world than there are today.

British industry, which was producing 9,000 aircraft annually in 1940, went on to produce a wartime total of over 125,000. The United States was in World War II for just four years, but American industry produced almost 300,000 aircraft in that time. In the peak year of production, 1944, American factories manufactured nearly 100,000 planes, including over 16,000 four-engine bombers. In the Soviet Union, more than 8,000 aircraft were produced in 1942—a year when most of its industrial centers were in the hands of the German Army—but the following year

(Above) The Air Medal was awarded for valor to American pilots during World War II. (Opposite page) The great Supermarine Spitfire evolved from the Supermarine S.6B. The remarkable S.6B, with its Rolls-Royce engine, not only won the 1931 Schneider Trophy Race but it led to the development of the Spitfire fighter.

production totaled 30,000. In the first half of 1945, Soviet industry turned out 25,000 aircraft.

On the Axis side, Germany reached a wartime peak of 40,000 aircraft in 1944—despite Allied bombing—by dispersing their manufacturing into small, easier to conceal, and often underground, factories. Even in the final four months of the war, 8,000 aircraft rolled

The U.S. Army's 9th Armored Division was operational on the Western Front during World War II. The division depended on air support from the USAAF 9th Air Force.

off the hidden assembly lines. In Japan, the 1944 peak was over 28,000, and in 1945, a battered industry turned out over 11,000.

In terms of aircraft production, the world will never see another remarkable year like 1944, when over 225,000 airplanes were built in just five countries. In that same year, an even greater number of pilots

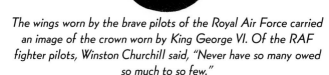

The wings worn by the brave pilots of the Royal Air Force carried an image of the crown worn by King George VI. Of the RAF fighter pilots, Winston Churchill said, "Never have so many owed so much to so few."

earned their wings. The year that the United States entered World War II, the U.S. Army Air Force (USAAF) had 150,000 personnel, but at the beginning of 1944, there were 2.4 million people in USAAF uniforms, many of them pilots and aircrew members.

The story of the 1939–1945 period is more than a story of numbers. In terms of aircraft technology, it was a story of monumental advances. In 1939, many of the aircraft in the world's air forces were still open-cockpit biplanes or open-cockpit monoplanes with ranges under 200 miles. It was almost as if time had stood still at the end of the previous world war. At the end of World War II, however, aircraft with a range of 5,000 miles were flying routine missions in the stratosphere with pressurized flight decks.

Also during 1939, one experimental jet aircraft was tested for the first time, and the technology was considered a novelty. By the autumn of 1944, the jet fighter squadrons had become fairly operational in Germany. In Britain, a jet airplane, the Gloster Meteor, was in full production and used by the RAF near the end of the war. Several types of jet aircraft that were on drawing boards in 1945 were in the air within three years.

In 1939, radar existed, but it was massive, ground-based equipment that was experimental, temperamental, and top secret. By 1945, ground-based radar was common, and night fighters equipped with airborne radar were shooting

In early 1941, when he said "You buy 'em, we'll fly 'em," this Army Air Corps pilot meant that money spent to buy Defense Bonds and Stamps went to the purchase of government aircraft. After December 7, they were War Bonds and Stamps.

down enemies they couldn't see. Bombers were also using radar to "see" through clouds.

With the notion of "the sky's the limit," a new generation stepped into and perpetuated an amazing quarter-century boom of unprecedented promise and prosperity. This was a clear combination of both technology and the will and vision to use that technology successfully.

The jet, rocket, and radar technology developed during World War II was combined to create new craft that could not have been imagined in 1939. Rockets were prepared to probe the edge of space, to open humankind's imagination to travel beyond our earth, and to see a human landing on the moon less than 24 years after the guns fell silent.

CURTISS P-40 WARHAWK

WHEN WORLD WAR II BEGAN, the P-40 Warhawk was the standard front-line fighter in the U.S. Army Air Corps (USAAF after June 1941). In fact, from 1940 to 1942, more P-40s were produced in the United States than all other fighter types combined. Warhawks saw action at Pearl Harbor, and they went on to serve in combat in every theater of the war where the United States was involved. They were also exported to Allied services, especially to China and to Britain's Royal Air Force (RAF).

Perhaps the most famous group to use Warhawks against the Axis was the American Volunteer Group (AVG) commanded by Claire Chennault. The AVG was a group of American military pilots who, before the United States entered the war, gave up their commissions to fly in China as civilians and help fight the Japanese. The AVG men painted fearsome, brilliantly colored jaws on their P-40s' prominent cowling, earning themselves and their airplanes the nickname "Flying Tigers." After the United States entered the war, the Flying Tigers became part of the USAAF 14th Air Force.

During the 1920s and early 1930s, Curtiss was one of the leading builders of fighters for both the U.S. Army and U.S. Navy. These aircraft were primarily radial-engine biplanes for which Curtiss established a solid reputation. By 1934, the Air Corps was making the transition to monoplanes, and the Curtiss entry, while not the first monoplane fighter, was among the first generation of Air Corps monoplane fighters. The Curtiss Model 75 Hawk first flew in May 1935 and was soon delivered to the U.S. Army Air Corps under the designation P-36. Eventually the Hawk would be the first American airplane of which over 1,000 were produced.

USAAF 14th Air Force pilots scramble for their P-40N Warhawks, circa 1943. After the United States entered World War II, the Flying Tigers became the nucleus of the 14th Air Force.

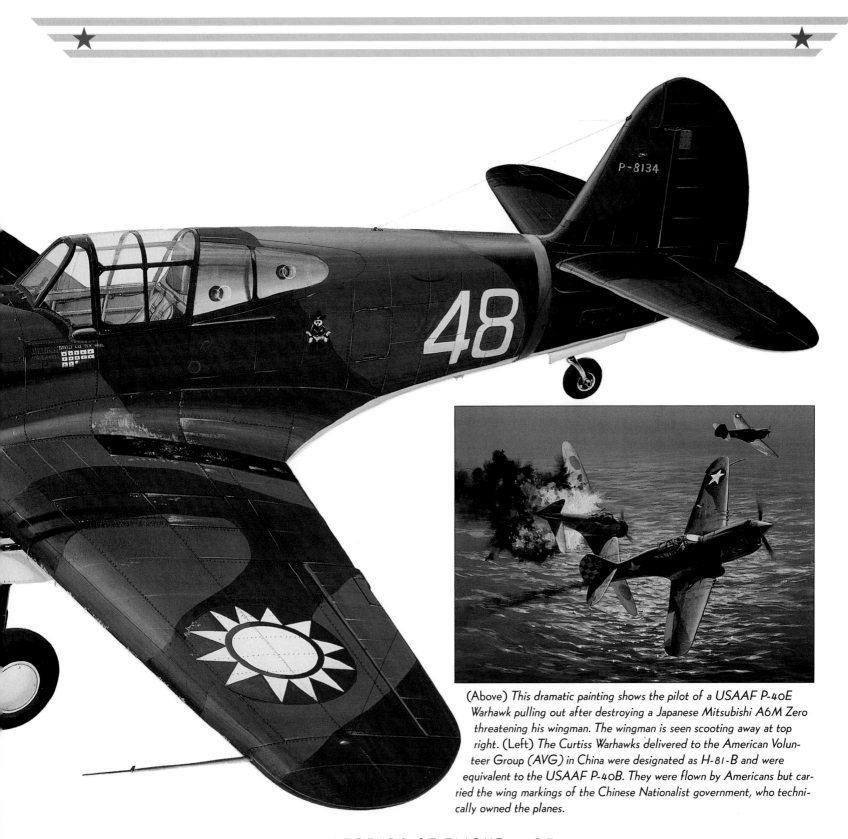

(Above) *This dramatic painting shows the pilot of a USAAF P-40E Warhawk pulling out after destroying a Japanese Mitsubishi A6M Zero threatening his wingman. The wingman is seen scooting away at top right.* (Left) *The Curtiss Warhawks delivered to the American Volunteer Group (AVG) in China were designated as H-81-B and were equivalent to the USAAF P-40B. They were flown by Americans but carried the wing markings of the Chinese Nationalist government, who technically owned the planes.*

The Warhawk was equipped with a supercharged in-line engine for better high-altitude performance. First flown in October 1938, the Warhawk was delivered to the Army for evaluation in January 1939. Orders for 524 P-40s were forthcoming, and an export version was also sold to France.

Deliveries began in the spring of 1940, with the Air Corps assigning theirs to Langley Field, Virginia; Hamilton Field, California; and Selfridge Field, Michigan. France was invaded by Germany in May and defeated in June before any of their deliveries were made. Britain took over the French contracts, and between September and December 1940, 558 aircraft were delivered to the RAF under the British-assigned name "Tomahawk."

Meanwhile, the U.S. Army Air Corps was beginning to take delivery of its own version of the newer Tomahawk-type aircraft under the appellation P-40B Warhawk. These were followed by the Tomahawk II/P-40C series in the spring of 1941. The British immediately sent 300 Tomahawk IIs into combat in the Middle East, and they achieved their first aerial victory near Alexandria on June 8, 1941. Against the legendary German Messerschmitt Bf109, the Tomahawks did reasonably well. Though they were slower in the climb, they could outmaneuver the Messerschmitts.

In May 1941, Curtiss introduced the P-40E type, of which over 2,000 were built, including 1,500 to be delivered to the RAF as the Kittyhawk I. The Curtiss P-40E Warhawk had a

A pair of Curtiss P-40 Warhawks display the 1941-vintage USAAF markings. These P-40s were painted with red and white stripes on the rudder, but in early 1942, the red was deleted to avoid confusion with Japanese insignia.

wingspan of 37 feet 4 inches and a length of 31 feet 2 inches. It weighed 8,280 pounds fully loaded and fueled. It was powered by an Allison 1,150-horsepower, liquid-cooled V-1710-39 engine that gave it a top speed of 354 miles per hour. It had a service ceiling of 29,000 feet and a range of over 700 miles. Armament consisted of six wing-mounted .50 caliber machine guns.

When the Japanese attacked the Hawaiian Islands on December 7, 1941, the USAAF Warhawks performed well, with Lieutenant George S. Welch shooting down four of the attackers in a P-40B. In the coming weeks, five outnumbered Warhawk squadrons (mostly equipped with P-40Es) faced the Japanese, and Lieutenant Boyd D. Wagner shot down eight of the enemy in his P-40E to become the first American ace of World War II.

The need for better high-altitude performance led Curtiss to replace the Allison engine with the Rolls-Royce-designed, Packard-manufactured, 1,300-horsepower V-1650 Merlin engine in the P-40F through P-40L. These aircraft were then sent to the North Africa and Mediterranean Theaters with the USAAF in the latter half of 1942. They also were supplied to the RAF in the same theaters as the Kittyhawk II. Merlin-powered Warhawks were also widely active in the Pacific during 1942 and 1943, serving in combat from Guadalcanal to New Guinea.

The most widely produced Warhawk was the P-40N, of which over 5,000 were produced. They entered USAAF service in March 1943, and although the superior P-47 and P-51 were on-line at the same time, P-40Ns were produced so rapidly, they gave the USAAF a chance to concentrate large numbers of aircraft in the field while waiting for production momentum on the P-47 and P-51 assembly lines to build up.

The P-40N Warhawk had a wingspan of 37 feet 4 inches and a length of 33 feet 4 inches. It weighed 7,400 pounds fully loaded and fueled. It was powered by an Allison 1,360-horsepower, liquid-cooled V-1710-81 engine that gave it a top speed of 378 miles per hour. It had a service ceiling of 38,000 feet and a range of 240 miles with 500-pound bombs carried and 1,400 miles when ferried. Armament consisted of six wing-mounted .50 caliber machine guns, and there were wing racks for bombs.

By 1944, the P-40 was gradually phased out of service with the USAAF and the RAF. The last of over 13,700 P-40s was delivered in November 1944, and except for northern Europe, where their role had been entirely usurped by the P-51D, they continued in service on most fronts until the end of the war.

CLAIRE L. CHENNAULT

Born in Commerce, Texas, and educated at Louisiana State, Claire Chennault was the principal of a Texas high school when the United States entered World War I. He quit his job to become an Army pilot, but the war ended before he earned his wings. He decided to remain in the Army after the war, and by 1925, he was commanding a pursuit squadron in Hawaii. Chennault became one of the Air Corps' rising stars in the field of combat tactics for pursuit planes (fighters), and he was named to head the Pursuit Section.

Chennault retired from the Army in 1937 and was hired by China's first lady Madame Chiang Kai-shek to set up a school in China to train military pilots. China was then involved in a losing war with the Japanese, and Chennault watched the situation deteriorate from bad to worse. The Chinese Air Force was losing badly at the hands of the Japanese. In 1940, Chennault put together the American Volunteer Group (AVG), a fighter squadron composed of former American military pilots.

Better known as the "Flying Tigers," the AVG achieved amazing results against the Japanese because of the tactics they practiced. In 1942, after the United States entered World War II, Chennault became a USAAF major general and was placed in command of USAAF units in China. Originally known as the China Air Task Force, Chennault's command became the 14th Air Force in 1943.

Commander of the Flying Tigers, Brigadier General Claire L. Chennault (far right) seen here with pilots of the 23rd Fighter Group.

Under Chennault, the 14th Air Force won and maintained air superiority over China despite difficult supply problems.

After World War II, Chennault retired from the USAAF to start an air-freight system to serve the interior of China. In 1946, he founded the airline Chinese Civil Air Transport. When the Chinese Nationalist government was overthrown by the communists in 1949 at the end of the Chinese Civil War, the aircraft owned by Chinese Civil Air Transport were seized, and Chennault returned to the United States.

REMEMBERED TODAY as perhaps the greatest American fighter of World War II, the Mustang ironically began its career as a plane the British Royal Air Force ordered. In 1940, British aircraft manufacturing capacity was pushed to the limit, and they needed more aircraft. They were buying large numbers of Kittyhawks (P-40Ds) from Curtiss, but they needed more planes than even Curtiss could produce. For this reason, North American Aviation was asked if they could build Kittyhawks. The answer was affirmative, but North American countered with what they believed was a better idea.

North American proposed to the British that they could design a better airplane—using the same Allison V-1710 engine—and build a prototype in four months. This was done and the prototype first flew in October 1940. The U.S. Army Air Corps took a passing interest in the sleek, new plane and ordered a couple for tests under the designation XP-51.

Production aircraft, known as Mustang I, reached England in October 1941. Tests showed them to be superior to the Kittyhawk, and they even bested the great Spitfire in low-altitude operations. Armed with four 20mm cannons, the first Mustang Is were used in the ground attack role. When the United States entered the war, the first USAAF orders for the Mustang saw it in the photo-reconnaissance aircraft role rather than as a fighter. In another twist in the Mustang story, the first large order was

The North American P-51D Mustang, with its powerful Rolls-Royce-designed, Packard-manufactured Merlin engine and the extended range provided by underwing drop tanks, was the top USAAF fighter of World War II.

(Above) *A formation of USAAF 8th Air Force/361st Fighter Group P-51D Mustangs in flight over England during the summer of 1944. By this time, the Mustang literally ruled the skies over all of Western Europe. (Below left) This beautifully restored P-51D Mustang is one of several hundred that still survive in flying—and even racing—condition a half century after their glory days during World War II. (Below right) This excellent close-up shows a restored P-51D Mustang in flight. One of the key design features of the D model Mustang was the bubble canopy, which gave the pilot a 360-degree field of view.*

for it to be configured as a dive bomber under the designation of A-36 Apache. The A-36 began combat operations against targets in Italy from Tunisia and continued these activities from bases in Italy until the middle of 1944.

Meanwhile, in parallel development with the A-36, the USAAF was almost reluctantly putting the P-51 fighter into production. The Achilles' heel of the early Mustangs—as discovered by the British and confirmed by the Americans—was the relative weakness of the Allison

This sunset photograph shows a P-51D Mustang marked with the wide black and white "invasion stripes" painted on all Allied aircraft taking part in the June 1944 Normandy invasion. The stripes allowed antiaircraft gunners on the ground—as well as other aircraft—to quickly distinguish friend from foe.

engine. Britain began using the Rolls-Royce Merlin, and the results were so good that the Packard Motor Company built the Merlin in the United States under the designation V-1650.

Powered by the 1,595-horsepower Packard V-1650 Merlin, the first production P-51B was finally delivered to the USAAF in May 1943. It was a moment of profound revelation for those who had doubted the Mustang's promise. Not only was it fast and maneuverable, it had long range. The P-51B had a wingspan of 37 feet and a length of 32 feet 3 inches. It weighed 8,350 pounds fully loaded and fueled. The Merlin gave it a top speed of 441 miles per hour at 29,800 feet, and it had a service ceiling of 42,000 feet and a range of 2,200 miles. Armament consisted of four .50 caliber machine guns.

Over 3,700 P-51Bs and P-51Cs were built before the P-51D came on-line in the spring of 1944. The P-51D represented a major design change. The high-topped rear fuselage was cut down, and the greenhouse canopy was replaced by a bubble canopy, giving the pilot a 360-degree field of view. The P-51D became the definitive Mustang, and nearly 8,000 were manufactured at the two North American Aviation plants at Inglewood, California, and Dallas, Texas. Most went to the USAAF, but a few went to the Royal Air Force—who had been first to realize the Mustang's potential—as the Mustang IV.

The P-51D/Mustang IV had a wingspan and length matching those of the P-51B, but it had a gross weight of 10,000 pounds. It was powered by a 1,720-horsepower, liquid-cooled

Packard V-1650-7 engine that gave it a top speed of 440 miles per hour at 25,000 feet and the ability to climb 3,450 feet in one minute. It had a service ceiling like that of its older sibling and a range of 2,300 miles with wing fuel tanks. Armament consisted of six, rather than four, .50 caliber machine guns.

By the time the war ended, the largest P-51 user was the USAAF 8th Air Force, with 14 fighter groups, among them, the 357th, which had scored 609 aerial victories with P-51s. The Mustang scored more such kills than any other Allied aircraft of the war, with 4,950 confirmed kills in the European Theater alone. Mustangs also saw service with the 5th Air Force in the Pacific, the 10th Air Force in India, and the 14th Air Force in China. During the final offensive against Japan, three groups of P-51Ds were based on Iwo Jima to escort the B-29 bombing missions against Japanese targets.

The P-51 continued to evolve, with the most significant "post-D" Mustang being the P-51H, which appeared in February 1945, and of which only 555 were built. It was one of the fastest piston-engined aircraft in production during the war, with its V-1650-9 Merlin giving it a speed of 487 miles per hour. Ultimately, over 15,400 Mustangs—more than half P-51Ds—were produced, most of them during the last two years of the war.

After the war, the Mustang was retained in a front-line role until finally replaced by jets. Redesignated as F-51s in 1947, they were delegated to the Air National Guard but recalled to active duty when the Korean War started in 1950. Used primarily in a ground support role, the F-51s flew over 62,000 sorties and remained in service with the air forces of South Korea, South Africa, and Australia, as well as the United States, until the last year of the war. In the 1990s, Mustangs continued to fly in the air show circuit and at major competitive events.

BENJAMIN O. DAVIS, JR.

Benjamin Davis was born in Washington, D.C., the son of a U.S. Army officer. He graduated from high school at the top of his class and entered the U.S. Military Academy at West Point. As part of the Class of 1936, he was the first African American to graduate from West Point in the 20th century.

Davis was eager to become a pilot, but at the time, African Americans were not accepted for flight training, and he was assigned to the infantry. However, four years later, the U.S. Army Air Corps established Tuskegee Army Air Field. The purpose of the field was specifically to train African Americans as pilots. Because the Army was still officially segregated, the "Tuskegee Airmen" were formed into all-black fighter squadrons.

Ultimately, four such units were sent overseas to the Mediterranean Theater: the 99th, 100th, 301st, and 302nd. Led by Ben Davis, the first to go was the 99th. After distinguished service in North Africa and Italy, Davis, now a colonel, was assigned to organize the 322nd Fighter Group, which became the umbrella organization for all four Tuskegee Airmen squadrons.

In 1948, after segregation was officially phased out in all branches of the armed services, Davis was assigned to the Pentagon, where he served until sent to Korea in 1953 to command a fighter wing. In 1954, Davis pinned on his first general's star and was made vice commander of the 13th Air Force.

Through the 1950s and early 1960s, Davis served tours in Taiwan, Germany, Korea, and at the Pentagon before receiving the rank of lieutenant general and taking command of the 13th Air Force at the height of the Vietnam War. In 1970, he retired from the U.S. Air Force.

IN 1921, WHEN GENERAL Billy Mitchell used his Martin bombers to sink the German battleship *Ostfreisland*, he saw it as a triumphant demonstration of the potential of air power—specifically bombers—as an important weapon of war. However, the U.S. Navy, whose battleship fleet was touted as "America's first line of defense," was outraged. They did not want to believe that air power had the potential to defeat warships.

Mitchell died 15 years later. His ideas were officially discredited, but they were alive among a growing group of Air Corps officers who had an eye on the future. It was in the mid-1930s when the U.S. Army Air Corps began to seriously plan for long-range heavy bombers. The first milestone in this genre was the one-of-a-kind Boeing XB-15, which first flew in 1937. While it never actually served as a bomber, the gigantic, four-engine bomber was important in terms of what the design and construction process taught the Boeing engineers who would build the more practical XB-17.

The XB-17 program started later than that of the XB-15, but the prototype actually flew two years earlier. Meanwhile, the Air Corps had requested proposals from aircraft manufacturers for a "multiengine" long-range heavy bomber, and Boeing submitted its four-engine B-17 for their approval. The term "multiengine" meant different things to different people. When the contracts were announced in early 1937, the Air Corps had bought 133 twin-engine Douglas B-18s and only 13 four-motored B-17s. Within a few years, it was evident that a mistake had been made. Ultimately, the B-18 became a footnote in aviation history, and the B-17 became the best-remembered heavy bomber of World War II.

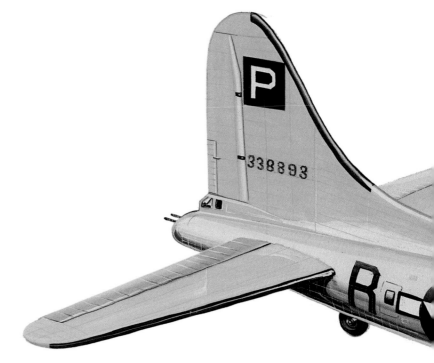

The Boeing B-17G Flying Fortress was the ultimate B-17. It was armed with powered turrets in the chin, as well at the top and bottom (not visible) of the fuselage. Additional guns were located in the tail and at various other points in the fuselage. This aircraft served with the 8th Air Force's 447th Bombardment Group.

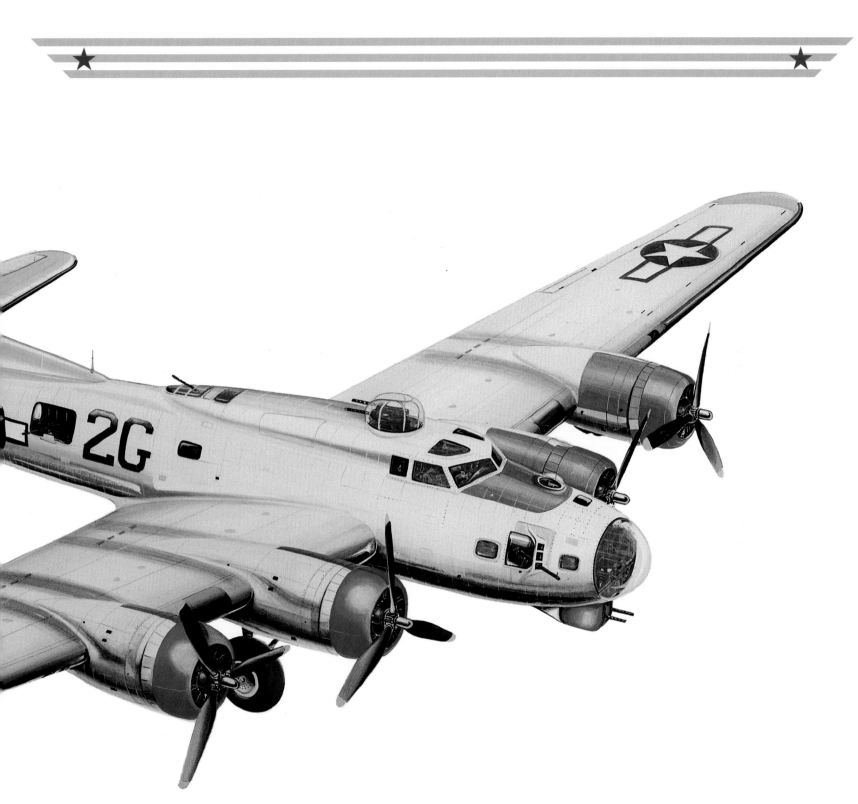

When World War II began in Europe in 1939, the U.S. Army began planning for the long-range defense of the Western Hemisphere against both Germany and Japan. The key heavy bomber at that time was the B-17, which had earned the official name Flying Fortress from having a defensive armament that included .50 caliber machine guns firing from its nose, its waist, and later its tail and belly. The first of the series to go into combat were those delivered to the Royal Air Force in the spring of 1941 under the designation Fortress I. The Air Corps equivalent, designated B-17C, was soon superseded by the similar B-17D.

A flight of U.S. Army Air Corps Y1 B-17s over New York City. First delivered to the 2nd Bombardment Group in 1936, the Y1 B-17 was the first production model Flying Fortress.

In late 1941, only 150 B-17Cs and B-17Ds were in the United States' inventory, and ironically, they were deployed to the areas where the war would first strike American Forces: Hawaii and the Philippines. Many of these planes were damaged or destroyed in the December 7 attack. A few in the Philippines flew on but were ineffectual in stemming the Japanese onslaught and those Flying Fortresses that survived retreated to Australia.

As early as 1940, it had become evident that a major flaw in the Flying Fortress was its lack of defensive armament in the tail. It was a six-sided fortress with guns omitted from its most vulnerable side. With this in mind, Boeing developed the B-17E, which had the tail turret that would be standard in the rest of the production series. The B-17E was also the first Flying Fortress produced in large numbers and the first to see combat on a regular basis. The first B-17Es were deployed to Australia in early 1942, and in July 1942, they arrived in England to become the nucleus of the USAAF 8th Air Force. This squadron would later undertake the great strategic offensive against Germany.

After 512 B-17Es, Boeing brought out the B-17F, which had the Sperry "ball" turret beneath the fuselage as standard equipment. The B-17F was in widespread service by early 1943 and was augmented by the B-17G from the autumn of 1943. The B-17G had the ball turret as well as the familiar forward-firing "chin" turret that made it a true Flying Fortress. The B-17G had a wingspan of 103 feet 9 inches, like all previous B-17s, and a length of 74 feet 4 inches, which was slightly longer than the two previous models and 6 feet longer than the Flying Fortresses that had no tail turrets. It weighed 55,000 pounds fully loaded and fueled, which was 40 percent more than the B-17C.

(Above) *Dawn breaks over a USAAF 8th Air Force bomber base in England, catching the tail of a B-17G in its fiery glow. The tail markings identify this bomber as belonging to the 401st Bombardment Group of the 94th Wing/1st Bombardment Division.* (Left) *When the Japanese struck American bases in the Philippines in December 1941, the USAAF launched counterstrikes with underarmed B-17Cs. The absence of the tail guns and powered turrets that would characterize later Flying Fortresses made the B-17C much more vulnerable to enemy aircraft.*

(Top) The Boeing B-17Fs (and early B-17Gs) had all of the defensive armament found on the ultimate "G" model, except the chin turret. (Above) One of the most famous Flying Fortresses in the 8th Air Force, the Memphis Belle made its 25th bombing mission in 1944. During its notable service career, the Belle downed eight enemy planes, damaged 12, and scored five "probables." (Right) The Memphis Belle was the first 8th Air Force bomber to fly back to the States from the European Theater with its original crew. Plane and crew are seen here on June 16, 1944, with USAAF chief General Henry "Hap" Arnold (in khaki uniform, second from right).

The B-17G was powered by four 1,200-horsepower, air-cooled Wright R-1820-97 engines that gave it a cruising speed of about 182 miles per hour and a top speed of nearly 300 miles per hour. It had a service ceiling of 35,600 feet and a range of 3,400 miles (or 2,000 miles with three tons of bombs). Armament consisted of up to 13 .50 caliber machine guns. It typically carried a bomb load of 6,000 to 9,600 pounds.

In addition to Boeing, both Douglas and Vega were called upon to build B-17Fs and B-17Gs, and they built almost half of the 3,405 B-17Fs and 8,680 B-17Gs that were delivered through April 1945.

Though a few B-17s were used in the Pacific, the vast majority formed the backbone of the 8th Air Force and 15th Air Force air offensive against German-occupied Europe. They dropped over 640,000 tons of bombs on Germany and German positions—or roughly half of the overall total. These raids systematically destroyed the German railroad network and their ball-bearing production, thereby severely crippling the German ability to build warplanes and motor vehicles.

When the war ended in Europe, B-17s were earmarked for the final offensive against Japan, but the war ended before they were redeployed. After the war, most B-17s were cut up for scrap, but a few survived to be used in guided missile testing and as search and rescue aircraft. Civilian B-17s continued to be used for four decades to attack forest fires with borate. By the 1990s, a handful of B-17s survived on the air show circuit.

This interesting composite view shows a Boeing B-17F over a flight of Stearman PT-17 Kaydets. Boeing, which bought the Stearman company before World War II, built both types at its Wichita, Kansas, factory.

THE HELLCAT WAS THE U.S. Navy's top fleet air superiority fighter for most of World War II, and it performed gloriously in what was the biggest dogfight of the Pacific Theater. In June 1944, in the Philippine Sea off the Mariana Islands, the aircraft carriers of U.S. Navy Task Force 58 met a Japanese task force under Vice Admiral Ozawa. In the skies over the ensuing sea battle, another battle raged—one that the Hellcat pilots would remember as "the Great Marianas Turkey Shoot." The Japanese lost 400 aircraft that day, and Task Force 58 lost only 27, with half the pilots rescued.

The F6F was part of a line of radial-engine fighters built for the U.S. Navy by the Grumman Corporation since the early 1930s. The first monoplane among them was the F4F Wildcat, which entered service early in 1940 with the U.S. Navy, as well as with the British Royal Navy and Royal Air Force, who designated it as Martlet I. When the United States entered World War II, the F4F Wildcat was the Navy's standard carrier-based fighter, and it was also in service in the Southwest Pacific Theater with U.S. Marine Corps units.

The process of designing the F6F Hellcat as the successor to the Wildcat was underway at the time the United States entered the war, and the first flight of the prototype occurred in June 1942. Production aircraft were first delivered at the end of 1942, and by the end of 1943, over 2,500 Hellcats had been delivered,

The F6F Hellcat was the star performer in the biggest dogfight of the Pacific Theater of World War II. This action took place in June 1944, in the Philippine Sea off the Mariana Islands.

(Left) *The red-rimmed United States insignia seen on this F6F Hellcat was used briefly by both the USAAF and U.S. Navy in the summer of 1943. The red outline was replaced by a blue one that remains to this day, although a red bar was added to the white sidebar in 1947.* (Below left) *The production model F6F-3 was in combat only 14 months after the first flight of the first Hellcat prototype. The first ships to receive Hellcats were the new carriers USS Yorktown and USS Independence. These carriers saw the F6Fs through their "baptism by fire" in August 1943.* (Below) *The Grumman F6F Hellcat sported a 2,000-horsepower, air-cooled Pratt & Whitney R-2800-10W engine that gave it a top speed of 375 miles per hour. It was armed with six wing-mounted .50 caliber machine guns.*

The pilot of a Grumman F6F Hellcat lowers his gear in preparation for landing. Based on the record accumulated during the 1943–1945 period, the Hellcat was the most effective carrier-based fighter in history.

allowing the U.S. Navy to equip every fighter squadron on its entire "fast carrier" force with F6Fs. Meanwhile, the Wildcats were relegated to service on the growing number of convoy escort carriers.

During this period of the war, the standard Hellcat was the F6F-3, which had a wingspan of 42 feet 10 inches and a length of 33 feet 7 inches. It weighed 12,441 pounds fully loaded and fueled. It was powered by a 2,000-horsepower, air-cooled Pratt & Whitney R-2800-10W engine that gave it a top speed of 375 miles per hour. It had a service ceiling of 37,300 feet and a maximum range of 1,590 miles. Armament consisted of six wing-mounted .50 caliber machine guns.

The F6F-3 was in combat only 14 months after the first flight of the first Hellcat prototype. The first ships to receive Hellcats were the new carriers USS *Essex*, USS *Yorktown*, and USS *Independence*, which were involved in the August 1943 attack on Marcus Island. Eventually, over 4,100 F6F-3s were manufactured, including over 300 that were sold to the British under the designation Hellcat I.

The definitive Hellcat was probably the F6F-5, which first flew in April 1944 and of which over 7,800 would be built. It featured a modified cowling, more armor and provisions for beefed up armament that included having two of the .50 caliber machine guns replaced by 20mm cannons, and the addition of attachment equipment for six rockets or two 1,000-pound bombs. The F6F-5 had the same dimensions as the F6F-3 but weighed 12,740 pounds fully loaded and fueled. It was powered by the same Pratt & Whitney R-2800-10W engines that gave it the same performance as the F6F-3.

Of note are the facts that over 1,400 of the F6F-5s were fitted out as night fighters and that nearly 1,000 were delivered to the British as the Hellcat II. Though they were inferior to the

Vought F4U Corsair in terms of performance, the Hellcats remained the standard carrier-based U.S. Navy fighter through the end of the war.

The Hellcat had a remarkable combat record. Of the 9,282 enemy aircraft shot down by U.S. Navy and Marine Corps aircraft during World War II, 5,156—over half—were dispatched by Hellcats. This was against the loss of only 270 Hellcats in aerial combat. Indeed, the Hellcat had a better record overall than the great P-51 Mustang had in the European Theater. The top-scoring U.S. Navy aces of World War II achieved all their victories in Hellcats: Captain David McCampbell with 34, Commander Cecil E. Harris with 24, and Commander Eugene Valencia with 23.

Over 12,000 Hellcats were manufactured, but after the war, they were quickly retired in favor of Corsairs. Some retirees were delivered to the French, who used them during their vain effort to reassert control over their lost colonies in Indochina. Others were resurrected during the Korean War to be used as radio-controlled cruise missiles for attacking bridges.

The Hellcat's lasting legacy was in its successor, the Grumman F8F Bearcat, which was first delivered in February 1945, and was en route to the Pacific Theater when the war ended in August. It was similar to the Hellcat in most respects, but it had a bubble canopy for 360-degree vision, and its Pratt & Whitney R-2800-34W gave it a top speed nearly 450 miles per hour. Remembered by some as the "best piston-engined fighter of World War II," the Bearcat never fired a shot and was retired before the Korean War. Many survived into the 1990s as race planes, and their continued performance at events such as the Reno National Air Races have earned them the distinction of being perhaps the fastest piston-engined aircraft ever built.

DAVID S. McCAMPBELL

The top-scoring U.S. Navy ace of World War II and the third highest scoring American ace of World War II, David McCampbell was born in Bessemer, Alabama. He graduated from Georgia Tech before attending the U.S. Naval Academy at Annapolis where he earned a degree in Marine Engineering.

In 1938, he became a carrier pilot as part of an air wing attached to the USS *Ranger*, and in 1940, he was transferred to the USS *Wasp*. In October 1942, he was promoted to lieutenant commander and placed in command of VF-15 (fighter squadron 15), then making the transition to the Grumman F6F Hellcat.

In 1943, McCampbell was chosen to command Carrier Air Group 15, which included VF-15, aboard the USS *Essex*. He scored his first aerial victory in June 1944 during the Battle of the Philippine Sea, which was known to Hellcat pilots as "the Great Marianas Turkey Shoot."

From June through November 1944, when the *Essex* concluded its cruise, Air Group 15 also took part in the Battle of Leyte Gulf and supported the recapture of the Philippines. During this time, McCampbell scored a total of 34 victories. On October 24, 1944, he shot down nine Mitsubishi A6M Zeros. The next day, he coordinated an air strike by three carrier air groups against Japanese targets in which they sank an enemy aircraft carrier, a light cruiser, and two destroyers. McCampbell was awarded the Navy Cross for this action, and in January 1945, President Roosevelt awarded him the Medal of Honor. David McCampbell saw no more combat action after November 1944, but his career in the Navy and in naval aviation continued until his retirement in 1964.

MITSUBISHI A6M REISEN ZERO

THE MOST IMPORTANT aircraft to be produced in the first half century of the Japanese aviation industry, the A6M was also arguably the best combat aircraft in widespread service in Asia and the Pacific from 1940 through 1942.

Mitsubishi had been producing aircraft for the Imperial Japanese Navy since the early 1920s, and its first monoplane fighter, the open-cockpit A5M, had gone into

The sight of an A6M in flight today will invariably involve a replica, such as we see here, rather than an original. All but a handful of the 10,499 Zeros produced between 1939 and 1945 were destroyed by 1945.

service in 1937. Sent into combat in China, the A5M was a successful aircraft, but it lacked the range needed to escort bombers deep into the interior. Noting this, as well as their expansionist plans for the near future, the Imperial Japanese Navy issued its 12-Shi requirement for a long-range air superiority fighter that could match the performance not only of the Chinese fighters but of the then-current British and American fighters they expected to face.

Mitsubishi A5M designer Jiro Horkoshi accepted the challenge and went to work developing an aircraft that pushed the limits of aeronautical technology. First flown in April 1939, the A6M would be his masterpiece.

The name "Zero" came from the developmental designation A6M Type 0, with the "0" being the last digit of the year it was expected to enter service, the Japanese year 2600 (A.D. 1940).

In Japanese, it was known as Rei Shiki Sento Ki (Type Zero Fighter), or Reisen for short. The Allies (following the code name practice of giving fighters male names and bombers female names) officially called the A6M "Zeke," but in practice, everybody called it "Zero."

From the moment that the first A6M2s went into action in China in July 1940, it was evident that it was the best air superiority fighter in Asian skies. The A6M2 had a wingspan of 39 feet 4.25 inches and a length of 29 feet 9 inches. It weighed 6,164 pounds fully loaded and fueled. It was powered by a 950-horsepower, air-cooled, 14-cylinder Nakajima NK1C Sakae 12 engine that gave it a top speed of 332 miles per hour, better than anything then in service on either side of the Pacific. It had a service ceiling of 32,810 feet and a maximum range of 1,930 miles. Armament consisted of two machine guns and two 20mm cannons, and the A6M2 was configured to carry 250 pounds of bombs.

In the surprise Japanese attack on Pearl Harbor on December 7, 1941, the Zero itself was one of the biggest surprises. American intelligence knew of its existence but drastically underestimated its performance. The Zero was a lethal weapon in the early part of the war, greatly outperforming the P-40 Warhawks it met in the Philippines and the F4F Wildcats it battled with in

The A6M5 was probably the best member of the A6M family to be put into widespread service during World War II. Crews are seen here preparing for a long-range mission, with external fuel tanks attached to their Zeros.

In 1938, Mitsubishi designer Jiro Horkoshi was given the task of creating an air superiority fighter combining the most advanced elements of aircraft technology. The result was the A6M Reisen.

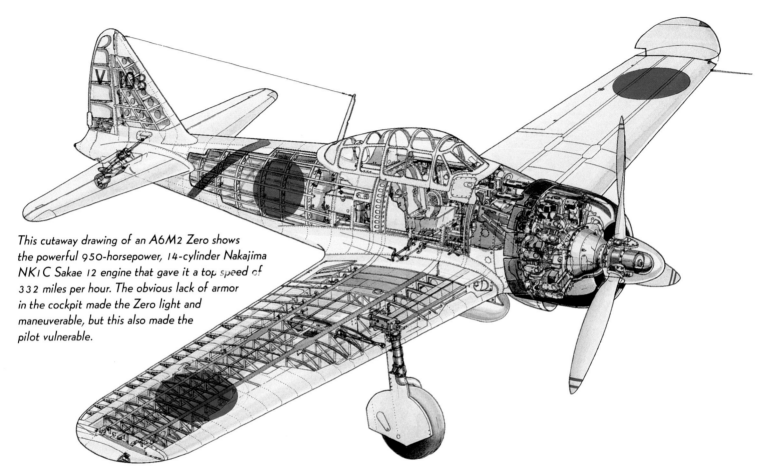

This cutaway drawing of an A6M2 Zero shows the powerful 950-horsepower, 14-cylinder Nakajima NK1C Sakae 12 engine that gave it a top speed of 332 miles per hour. The obvious lack of armor in the cockpit made the Zero light and maneuverable, but this also made the pilot vulnerable.

the skies over Guadalcanal and the Southwest Pacific. In 1940, American military planners had discounted it as probably an inferior copy of an older American aircraft. In 1942, the Zero was regarded as an almost mythical secret weapon.

In the Battle of Midway in June 1942, Americans faced the A6M3. The Zero was still superior, but the losses in aircraft carriers and pilots that began here would mark the beginning of the end, although that would not become fully evident for another year. The Zero's primacy extended into 1943 with the introduction of the A6M5. It had a wingspan of 36 feet 1 inch and a length of 29 feet 11 inches. It weighed 6,025 pounds fully loaded and fueled.

The A6M5 was powered by an 1,130-horsepower, air-cooled, 14-cylinder Nakajima NK1F Sakae 21 engine that gave it a top speed of 351 miles per hour. While this was better than the A6M2, it was not an even match against the F6F Hellcat, P-38 Lightning, and the F4U Corsair, which it faced in ever-growing numbers in 1943. The A6M5 had a service ceiling of 38,520 feet and a range of 1,194 miles, which was less than the A6M2 since range was sacrificed for performance. The armament was the same as the A6M2. What the A6M5 lacked were features then standard on American fighters, such as self-sealing fuel tanks and adequate rear cockpit armor. These were omitted to reduce weight and achieve maximum performance.

In one-on-one combat, an A6M5 in the hands of a good pilot outmaneuvered its American opponents. The A6M5 was probably the best of the widely used zero types. But by late 1943, a large number of good pilots had been lost, and the training system wasn't replacing them adequately. Conversely, the quality of American pilots' performance was steadily improving.

By the end of 1944, the Imperial Japanese Navy began to resort to its kamikaze tactics, recklessly throwing away both pilots and Zeros in a desperate attempt to sink aircraft carriers. By early 1945, the Zero's era of air superiority was a distant memory. With the losses in carriers, pilots, and Zeros, the Japanese no longer met their foe in air battles reminiscent of 1942 and 1943.

Meanwhile, Mitsubishi had developed the A6M8, powered by a 1,560-horsepower Mitsubishi Kinsei engine, as well as the Zero's successor, the A7M Reppu, powered by a 2,070-horse-power 18-cylinder Mitsubishi Ha43-11 engine. The former would have been the ideal fighter for 1943, but it was not available until April 1945. The latter would have been a formidable fighter in 1945, but the B-29 attacks had so seriously disrupted industrial production and transportation that there was no place to build them and no way to get needed parts. When the war ended, eight prototypes had been manufactured, and there were a few half-finished production models.

The A6M remained in production to the last, with a few Zeros coming off the assembly line even as the emperor pondered surrender. There were 10,499 Zeros produced between 1939 and 1945, making it the most-produced airplane in Japanese aviation history. Despite its dismal last chapter, the story of the Zero is one of a brilliantly designed airplane that was ideal for its time and proved that fact well.

RICHARD IRA BONG

The highest-scoring American ace of World War II, Richard Bong was born in Superior, Wisconsin. He decided to join the USAAF in 1941. Bong earned his wings and was assigned as an instructor, but he was anxious to get into combat.

The USAAF was reluctant to transfer him because he was a good instructor, so Bong engineered an infraction of rules. He flew under the center span of the Golden Gate Bridge in San Francisco, and as a penalty, he was sent to join the 5th Air Force in Australia in September 1942.

Flying a Lockheed P-38 Lightning, Bong scored his first two aerial victories in December 1942 over New Guinea. By March 1943, he had scored nine, including an A6M Zero and six Ki43 Oscars. In late July, Bong had equaled the best score in the 5th Air Force with 16 and went on to top 20. In April 1944, Bong pushed his score to 27, becoming the first American ace of World War II to surpass Eddie Rickenbacker's World War I score.

Bong went back to the United States in the summer of 1944 but then returned to the Pacific in September. Officially, he was a gunnery instructor, although he did fly combat missions. On the third anniversary of Pearl Harbor, he scored two victories, and on December 15 and 17, he shot down two more to bring his total to 40. With this, 5th Air Force commander General George Kenney decided to ground Bong. He was America's top-scoring ace, and he had just been awarded the Medal of Honor in a personal ceremony with General Douglas MacArthur.

Having scored all his victories in a Lockheed fighter, Bong was invited by Lockheed to test their new P-80 Shooting Star jet fighter. On August 6, 1945, while taking off from Burbank, California, Bong's P-80 suffered an engine flameout. It crashed, killing America's top ace.

THE MOST REVERED airplane in British history, and one of the greatest aircraft of World War II, the Spitfire had its roots in the marvelous racing seaplanes designed by Reginald J. Mitchell and built by Supermarine for the Schneider Trophy Races in the 1920s and 1930s. In the course of his work, Mitchell met and collaborated with Henry Royce of Rolls-Royce, and this association led to the Spitfire.

In a photograph taken during the Battle of Britain, a group of Spitfire Mk.Is are preparing for takeoff, while others seen in the background are returning from a mission.

The project got underway in 1934 as the Royal Air Force was beginning to evaluate aircraft to modernize its fighter fleet. Mitchell designed the Spitfire like a racing plane, aerodynamically trim and optimized for speed. Meanwhile, Royce was developing the 12-cylinder Merlin in-line engine, which itself was destined to be one of the true classics of World War II machinery. The Spitfire was a brilliant combination of power and grace.

The Spitfire and Merlin came together in a prototype that first flew in March 1936. Performance was far beyond expectations, and the Royal Air Force was ecstatic. The first Spitfire Mk.Is joined RAF Fighter Command in June 1938. By the time World War II began in September 1939, only 306 Spitfires had been delivered, but there were over 3,000 Spitfires in the order books.

The Royal Air Force saw relatively little action until the spring of 1940 and the massive German offensive against Western Europe. British forces, including Royal Air Force units, were sent in to action. Despite efforts at prewar planning, the British military establishment was utterly unprepared for the collapse of France in a matter of weeks. This left Britain facing the powerful German Army alone. The Germans were only 30 miles from Dover across the English Channel and preparations were made for the invasion of Britain itself.

Because a cross-channel invasion required air superiority, the first step was for the Luftwaffe to destroy the Royal Air Force.

The Royal Air Force was outnumbered four to one, with Fighter Command possessing fewer than 700 aircraft, including 19 squadrons of Spitfires. Between August and October, the Luftwaffe attacked relentlessly and the Royal Air Force—flying Hawker Hurricanes as well as Spitfires—fought back. For many dark days, the cause looked lost, but the Spitfires and their pilots inflicted damage far out of proportion to their own losses. With the loss of over 2,000 aircraft, the Luftwaffe finally gave up.

The Spitfire of the "finest hour" was the Mk.I. It had a wingspan of 36 feet 10 inches and a length of 29 feet 11 inches. It weighed 5,332 pounds fully loaded and fueled. The Mk.I was powered by the 1,030-horsepower, liquid-cooled Rolls-Royce Merlin II engine that gave it a top speed of 355 miles per hour. It had a service ceiling of 34,000 feet and a range of 500 miles. Armament consisted of four wing-mounted machine guns.

In 1941, Supermarine began deliveries of the Spitfire Mk.V, which was powered by the 1,470-horsepower, liquid-cooled Rolls-Royce Merlin 45 engine. For the Royal Navy's aircraft carriers, the Merlin 45-powered equivalent to the Mk.V was the Seafire Mk.IIC. In July 1942, the Spitfire Mk.IX was devel-

The Supermarine Spitfire Mk.IA, powered by the 1,030-horsepower Rolls-Royce Merlin II engine, proved to be a remarkable fighter for the Royal Air Force. The Spitfire, along with the Hawker Hurricane, successfully fended off the German Luftwaffe in the 1940 Battle of Britain.

oped, specifically to match the performance of the German Focke Wulf Fw.190. However, in 1942, the scope of the action had changed somewhat, and battles were more likely to take place over German-occupied territory than over Britain.

By 1944, with the Allies on the offensive, Supermarine delivered what was probably the most potent Spitfire to go into service during World War II. The Spitfire Mk.XIV was nearly three feet longer than the first Spitfires and weighed 10,280 pounds fully loaded and fueled. It was powered by a 2,035-horsepower, liquid-cooled Rolls-Royce Griffon 65 engine that drove a massive five-blade propeller and gave it a top speed of 448 miles per hour. It had a service ceiling of 43,000 feet and a range of 460 miles. Armament consisted of two 20mm cannons and four machine guns.

The Spitfire was one of the few fighter aircraft that was in production before World War II that stayed in production after the war. Notable among these were the Mk.XIX photo-reconnaissance aircraft and the F.24, which was the last Spitfire. A total of over 20,000 Spitfires and Seafires of over 40 different "marks" were manufactured, making it the most-produced British aircraft in history. Though the Spitfire was officially retired by the Royal Air Force in 1954, the RAF's "Historic Flight" still maintains a flying example for demonstration purposes and as a tribute to the finest few of the finest hour.

BUILT IN LARGER NUMBERS than any other warplane in history, the Bf109 was Germany's standard fighter through all of World War II. It was also one of the best piston-engined air superiority fighters in the world longer than any other, although this period probably ended midway through the war.

The development of this remarkable aircraft began in the middle 1930s as Germany was rearming and the Luftwaffe was looking for a high-performance fighter. The Bf109 was designed by Willy Messerschmitt and Walter Rethel at Bayerische Flugzeugwerke (BFW) in competition with designers from other important German planemakers, such as Heinkel and Focke Wulf. Powered by a 695-horsepower Rolls-Royce Kestrel V engine, the Bf109 prototype was first flown in September 1935,

with its remarkable speed and agility beating out the Heinkel He112 and the Focke Wulf Fw159.

Bayerische Flugzeugwerke was given a contract for production model Bf109Bs powered by German-made 610-horsepower Junkers Jumo 210A engines. These rolled of the assembly line in early 1937 and were flown with German Condor Legion "volunteers" in the Spanish Civil War. Its unqualified success in Spain gave the Bf109 an international reputation.

By July 1938, when Bayerische Flugzeugwerke was reorganized as Messerschmitt AG, the Luftwaffe's jagdstaffel (fighter squadrons) had taken delivery of about 300 Bf109s, with the Daimler-Benz–powered Bf109D now becoming available, and Switzerland in line as the first export customer.

This photograph, in which the national insignia have been retouched for reasons unknown, shows a Bf109E sporting the overall dark upper surface camouflage that was common to Luftwaffe aircraft early in World War II.

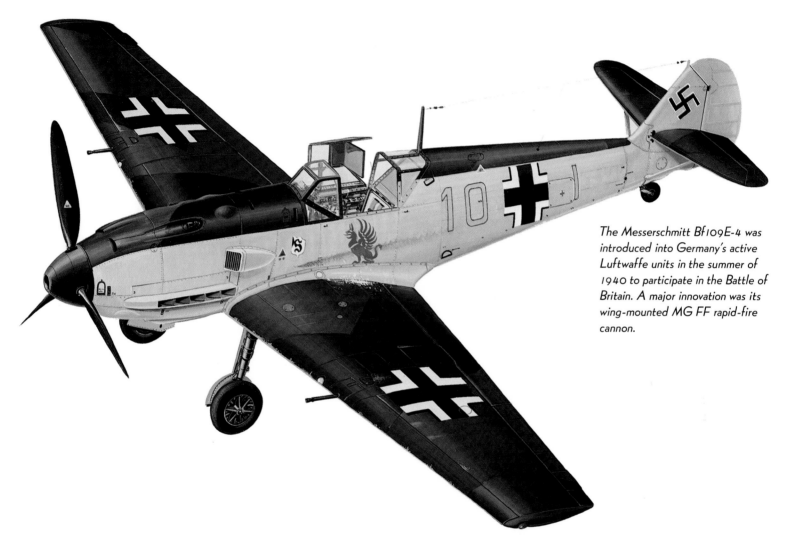

The Messerschmitt Bf109E-4 was introduced into Germany's active Luftwaffe units in the summer of 1940 to participate in the Battle of Britain. A major innovation was its wing-mounted MG FF rapid-fire cannon.

The first truly mass-produced model was the Bf109E, which entered Luftwaffe service early in 1939. It had a wingspan of 32 feet 4.5 inches and a length of 28 feet 10.5 inches. It weighed 4,431 pounds fully loaded and fueled. It was powered by a 1,050-horsepower, air-cooled V-12 Daimler-Benz DB 601 engine that was adopted in favor of the less-reliable DB 600 used in the Bf109D. This gave the Bf109E a top speed of 342 miles per hour. It had a service ceiling of 34,450 feet and a range of

410 miles. Armament consisted of two 20mm wing-mounted cannons, one 20mm cannon firing through the propeller spinner, and a pair of 7.9mm MG17 machine guns firing through the propeller arc.

When Germany launched the September 1, 1939, invasion of Poland that began World War II, there were 1,000 Bf109s in Luftwaffe service. The Luftwaffe's Bf109s easily overwhelmed the Polish Air Force and saw little other action in the war's first winter other than intercepting a few British bombing raids. In May 1940, with the invasion of France, the Luftwaffe had fewer than 1,500 Bf109s, but these were more than a match for the French defenders. Turning to the Battle of Britain in August 1940, the Bf109s faced their most potent adversaries, particularly in terms of the Royal Air Force pilots. In a dogfight between a Bf109 and a Spitfire Mk.1 or Hawker Hurricane, the outcome often depended on the skill—or luck—of the pilot. However, of the more than 1,100 aircraft lost by the Royal Air Force in the Battle of Britain, the vast majority were shot down by Bf109s.

The Bf109F type was introduced late in 1940, and these were a part of over 400 Bf109s available for the invasion of the Soviet Union in June 1941. While the Messerschmitts were clearly superior to the Soviet fighters, attrition alone took its toll on the Bf109 and production was stepped up.

In 1942, the Luftwaffe took delivery of the widely produced Bf109G, known as "Gustav." It had a wingspan of 32 feet 6.5 inches and a length of 29 feet 8 inches and weighed 6,834 pounds fully loaded and fueled. It was powered by a 1,475-horsepower, air-cooled V-12 Daimler-Benz DB 605 engine that gave the Bf109G a top speed of 386 miles per hour at 22,460

A Messerschmitt Bf109E-4 belonging to Luftwaffe Fighter Group II. Operational on the Western Front early in the war, Group II was active in Russia from 1942, where it was equipped with Bf109Gs.

(Above left) *Introduced in early 1939, the Emil was the first Bf109 equipped with the Daimler-Benz DB 601 engine.* (Right) *A group of Luftwaffe ground crewmen prepare a Messerschmitt Bf109G-6 assigned to Jagdstaffel 26 in northern France, circa late 1943. The G-6 did not have the pressurized cockpit incorporated into the G-5, but it was the first Bf109 that was factory-built to accept upgrade modifications in the field.*

feet, which was respectable but inferior to the P-51Ds and later "mark" Spitfires with which it would tangle. It had a service ceiling of 37,890 feet and a range of 530 miles. Armament consisted of one 20mm cannon firing through the propeller spinner and a pair of 7.9mm MG17 machine guns firing through the propeller arc. Some later Gustavs were equipped with provisions for wing-mounted Wfr.Gr.21 cm mortars and rocket launchers.

Production of the Bf109G reached a peak of 725 aircraft a month in July 1943, and Gustavs continued in production until well into 1944 when they were replaced on assembly lines by the Bf109K.

The Bf109Gs were used as interceptors for Reich air defense, and they served on every front that the Luftwaffe was active: from the Channel Coast to North Africa and from Italy to the Eastern Front. Other Bf109Gs were exported to neutral Switzerland as well as to Axis air forces such as those of Italy, Croatia, Slovakia, Spain, Romania, and the Royal Bulgarian Air

Force. Hungary not only used Bf109G, but a large number were manufactured there.

The last widely produced type was the Bf109K, which entered service in September 1944. It was similar to the Bf109G and was powered by a 2,030-horsepower DB 605ASCM engine. Both the Bf109G and Bf109K took part in the last major Luftwaffe offensive action, Operation Bodenplatte, which inflicted severe damage on the Anglo-American Allies in January 1945. The Allies were able to recover, but German production was no longer able to recoup from any losses; by February, the Luftwaffe was down to fewer than 1,000 Bf109s.

Amazingly, a handful of Bf109s were still produced in 1945, and they were still in combat during the war's final weeks. An incredible 33,000 Bf109s were manufactured between 1934 and 1945, and they continued to be produced by Hispano in Spain for a number of years. Bf109s continued in service in Switzerland until December 1949 and in Spain until the 1960s.

THE ULTIMATE BOMBER of World War II, the Super-fortress embodied all the principals of long-range strategic air power as expounded by General Billy Mitchell and others since the end of World War I. It was the largest bomber to go into production during World War II, and it had the longest range. To air-power purists and to many historians, the B-29—not the two atomic bombs dropped by a B-29—was the weapon that defeated Japan and ended World War II.

In January 1940, with the cloud of war already darkening Europe, the USAAF solicited top secret design proposals from aircraft builders for a bomber with a range of 5,333 miles—a bomber that could carry a full bomb load 2,000 miles from its base. Of the four companies approached, only Boeing and Consolidated took the challenge. Boeing's proposal took first honors, and a development contract was issued for an aircraft designated XB-29. Consolidated proceeded with their design—as a lower-priority backup—under the XB-32 designation.

Three prototype XB-29s were built in Seattle, and the first one was flown on September 21, 1942, with the great test pilot Edmund "Eddie" T. Allen at the controls. The plane was loosely based on Boeing's experience with the B-17, but there were so many entirely new features—all of them rushed to completion to meet tight deadlines—that there were many problems, especially with the new 2,200-horsepower Wright R-3350-13 engines. A major blow came on February 18, 1943, when an engine fire brought the second XB-29 down in flames over Seattle, killing Eddie Allen and everyone onboard.

Despite the crash and the nagging problems, the program pushed ahead briskly. The first production B-29 left the factory in September 1943. Meanwhile, both Martin and Bell were brought on-line to build Superfortresses as B-29A and B-29B, while Boeing continued to build B-29s and B-29As. Together, they built over 3,600 airplanes.

These three Superfortress types had a wingspan of 141 feet 3 inches and a length of 99 feet. They had various gross weights ranging from 110,000 pounds for the Bell-manufactured B-29B to 140,000 pounds for the Renton-built B-29A. They were all powered by variations of the 2,200-horsepower, air-cooled

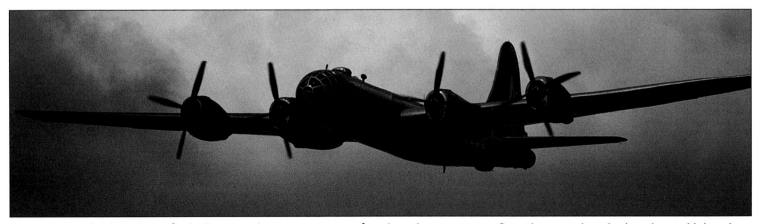

Unique among World War II aircraft, the B-29 was also an important aircraft in the early postwar years. Since they were the only plane that could drop the atomic bomb, Superfortresses became the keystone of the Strategic Air Command (SAC).

(Above left) *By the 1990s, the Superfortress nicknamed "Fifi" was the only B-29 left in flyable condition out of over 3,600 that were built between 1942 and 1945.* (Right) *The B-29 was heavily armed with four fuselage turrets having a total of 12 .50 caliber machine guns and a tail turret, which had machine guns as well as a 20mm cannon. Eventually, some or all of the turrets were pulled out to save weight.*

Wright R-3350 engine. Top speeds for the various B-29s ranged from 360 to 380 miles per hour depending on altitude. They had service ceilings above 30,000 feet, and the cabin was fully pressurized for long-range, high-altitude flying. They all had ranges in excess of the design spec of 5,333 miles, with the B-29B having a specified ferry range of 5,725.

Initially, the Superfortress armament included four fuselage turrets directed by a General Electric fire control system and a single manned tail turret. Each had a pair of .50 caliber machine guns except the top front turret, which had four, and the tail turret, which also carried a 20mm cannon. Later in the war, as the threat from enemy interceptors diminished to practically nil, some or all of the turrets were deleted in the field in order to save weight and carry a bigger bomb load at higher altitude.

By the time that the Superfortresses were ready for combat, the USAAF had decided to concentrate the entire force against Japan rather than to use some against Germany. USAAF com-mander General Henry H. Arnold even set up an all-new Air Force, the 20th, to manage the B-29 armada.

In 1944, the only bases available to the 20th Air Force that were within range of Japan were at Chengdu, deep in China. It was at the end of a long and difficult aerial supply line that crossed the Himalayas. The first B-29 mission was flown on June 5, 1944, against Japanese-occupied Bangkok from the 20th Air Force staging base in India. Similar operations continued through the summer and early autumn, but in October, the Mariana Islands—Guam, Saipan, and Tinian—were recaptured from the Japanese.

The 20th Air Force was promptly relocated to bases in the Marianas. They were closer to Japan, and they could be easily resupplied. Through the winter, the number of B-29s available grew rapidly and so did the intensity of the attacks on Japan.

In March 1945, General Curtis E. LeMay, commander of the 20th Air Force, decided to switch from high-altitude raids using high explosives to low-altitude raids using incendiary bombs. Because of the type of construction being used in Japanese cities, this tactic proved most effective. LeMay planned a series of raids against all the major Japanese industrial centers, and timed the missions so that at least 300 Superfortresses would be available for each. The raid on Tokyo on March 9, 1945, did more damage to the target than any other single air raid of the entire war.

The 20th Air Force continued this pattern through the spring and into the summer with the number of B-29s available for a single mission growing to 500 and to 600. On August 1, a total of 784 B-29s reached their targets. LeMay's plan was to defeat the Japanese so that a costly invasion would not be necessary.

On August 6, 1945, the Boeing B-29 bomber Enola Gay made history as it dropped the deadly uranium bomb called Little Boy on Hiroshima, Japan.

Meanwhile, however, the United States had developed the atomic bomb, and President Harry Truman had decided to use it to force the Japanese into an unconditional surrender. Because the B-29 was the largest bomber in the USAAF, the two available atomic bombs were designed to be dropped by B-29s.

The first nuclear weapon used in wartime was a 9,700-pound uranium bomb nicknamed *Little Boy* and was dropped on Hiroshima by the B-29 *Enola Gay* on August 6, 1945. The second was a 10,000-pound plutonium bomb nicknamed *Fat Man* and was dropped on Nagasaki three days later by the B-29 *Bock's Car*. Implicit in the two attacks three days apart was that the United States had the capability to drop many more in rapid succession, but this was not actually the case, and the B-29 force resumed conventional missions. The Japanese, however, saw that their misadventure that began at Pearl Harbor was now hopeless and agreed to an unconditional surrender on August 15.

After the war ended, B-29s were about the only wartime aircraft retained by the USAAF in undiminished status. They were, for the next several years, the only aircraft that could deliver a nuclear weapon, and they constituted the nucleus of the Strategic Air Command, formed in 1946.

By the time of the Korean War however, the mighty Superfortress was staring obsolescence in the eye. Three bomb groups were sent to Korea, but, while they were able to fly 21,000 effective missions—many of these reconnaissance flights—their vulnerability to Chinese and Soviet jet fighters made them less powerful a weapon than they were during World War II.

Hap Arnold was the man who created the largest air force in history. In 1938, when he became chief of the U.S. Army Air Corps, that service had fewer than 2,000 airplanes and 21,000 people. The Air Corps became the U.S. Army Air Forces in 1941, six months before the United States entered World War II. Arnold built the USAAF up to a peak wartime strength of 78,757 aircraft and 2,372,292 personnel.

Arnold was born in Gladwyn, Pennsylvania, and graduated from the U.S. Military Academy at West Point in 1907. His first post was in the Philippines, then an American colony, which was typical first duty for a young Army infantry second

lieutenant in those days. He returned to the states in 1909 and spent two years assigned to Governor's Island in New York Harbor.

In 1911, Arnold got the break that changed his life. He was ordered to report for pilot training with the Wright brothers. Having proven himself as a pilot, Arnold was assigned as a flight instructor at the Army's school at College Park, Maryland, a year later. While flying out of this field, he set a world altitude record of 6,540 feet.

Arnold was commander of the big Air Corps base at March Field, California, from 1931 to 1936, and in 1934, he commanded an important early exercise in air power force projection by leading a ten-bomber flight from Washington, D.C., to Fairbanks, Alaska. In 1936, he went to Washington as assistant chief of the Air Corps, and two years later, he was promoted to chief with the brevet rank of major general.

Now Arnold was in a position to effect important changes. Through the 1920s and 1930s, he had been one of a number of

young officers who believed in the idea that air power was an effective means of waging war and defending the United States. They believed that the Air Corps should not be a corps of the Army but rather an independent "Air Force" that was equal in official status to the Army and Navy. On June 20, 1941, the U.S. Army Air Force was created. By now, most of the world was at war, and Arnold faced the even bigger challenge of preparing for the inevitable United States entry into the war.

Arnold organized the USAAF into numbered air forces, each one assigned a specific task in a specific theater. He started with five, then added eight in 1942, and ended the war with 16 air forces. It was a herculean effort. Three years after World War II began, there were one hundred times as many personnel in Arnold's air force than there had been when he first became chief. Not only were there 35 airplanes in USAAF markings for every one in Air Corps insignia, they represented a vast qualitative and technological change. Reflecting Arnold's own intense interest in technology, the USAAF went from biplanes to jets in just a few short years.

A hard-working commander, Arnold—a five-star general—made long inspection tours of USAAF overseas operations during World War II, visiting both Europe and the Pacific and making one flight around the world. The long hours and long miles took their toll. Though his health was failing, Arnold remained at his post until the job was done and the war was won. He retired in 1946 and lived to see the USAAF become the fully independent U.S. Air Force a year later.

THE COLD WAR

THE COLD WAR, a period of long-term, broad-based conflict between the United States and the Soviet Union, began shortly after the end of World War II and soon evolved into an implicit threat of World War III—a threat that lasted until the collapse of the Soviet Union nearly half a century later. The evolution of military aviation during this postwar period was fueled by two key factors: the Cold War's regional tensions, which provided the need and the funding for development, and technology itself. In the 1950s and 1960s, progress in aircraft technology, aircraft engine technology, and aircraft electronics technology, or avionics, rapidly created further advances.

Each specialized type of aircraft evolved well beyond the technology represented by the early postwar jets. And so did items like military aircraft armament. Aerial rockets fired from planes became practical in World War II, and after the war, the 5-inch High

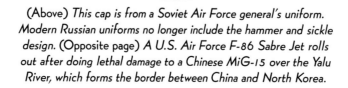

(Above) *This cap is from a Soviet Air Force general's uniform. Modern Russian uniforms no longer include the hammer and sickle design.* (Opposite page) *A U.S. Air Force F-86 Sabre Jet rolls out after doing lethal damage to a Chinese MiG-15 over the Yalu River, which forms the border between China and North Korea.*

Velocity Aerial Rocket (HVAR) was perfected. By 1950, the potent 2.75-inch Folding Fin Aerial Rocket (FFAR), or "Mighty Mouse," was introduced in the United States.

In the early 1950s, guidance system technology made guided missiles possible. The first family of air-intercept missiles were the AIM-4 Falcon, AIM-7 Sparrow, and AIM-9 Sidewinder, which were developed in the United States. The newer AIM-120 Advanced Medium-Range Air-to-Air Missile (AMRAAM) is similar to the Sparrow in appearance but is twice as fast and twice as effective in reaching and killing its target.

Just as guided air-to-air missiles evolved from the unguided aerial rockets of the 1940s, so too have guided air-to-surface missiles evolved from unguided rockets. These range from the AGM-65 Maverick, a short-range weapon, to that sophisticated family of weapons known as cruise missiles. Like airplanes, cruise missiles are very maneuverable. Their robot memory is preprogrammed with the route to the pre-

determined target. They know where to turn to avoid a hill, and they are hard to catch since they fly fast and low. With cruise missiles, bombers can hit a number of targets on one mission without exposing themselves to danger.

As military aircraft have evolved, the old distinctions and definitions have also evolved. In World War II there were fighters and there were bombers. After the war the U.S. Air Force had the Strategic Air Command (SAC) composed primarily of bombers and the Tactical Air Command (TAC) composed primarily of fighters. After the Gulf War, the U.S. Air Force merged the SAC and the TAC into a single Air Combat Command (ACC).

The large-scale development of military air transport fleets began with the U.S. Army Air Force (USAAF) C-47s and C-54s of World War II and evolved quickly after the war. During the Korean War, American four-engine transports ran continuously to the war zone, as they would in Vietnam. By Vietnam, however, the four-engine aircraft were jets, with twice the speed and twice the range, as well as up to three times the cargo capacity per flight. During the Gulf War, the tonnage that was hauled to the Middle East was staggering.

Another idea that took hold at this time was the concept of refueling one airplane from another. It was tried on a demonstration basis in the 1920s, but it wasn't until the late 1940s when the SAC began to perfect aerial refueling as a routine operation. KB-29 tankers were first used to support both fighter and bomber aircraft during the Korean War. By the mid-1950s, Boeing produced the KC-135 Stratotanker, which had the 600 miles per hour speed to stay ahead of the jet bombers. Despite its virtuosity, no one would have guessed in 1957 the KC-135 would still be in service after the turn of the century.

During the Cold War, reconnaissance aircraft evolved from bombers with cameras to sophisticated aircraft, such as the U-2, the SR-71, and the MiG-25, that could fly too high and/or too fast to be intercepted by other aircraft. Electronic warfare aircraft were children of the Cold War. As the technical complexity of radar defenses expanded so too must the means of defending attacking aircraft against it. In preparation for tackling well-defended potential targets in Eastern Europe, the U.S. Air Force converted about 20 B-66 tactical bombers to electronic warfare aircraft. Armed with radar, electronic countermeasures hardware, and a ton of aluminum foil "chaff" (to fool enemy radar), the EB-66s accompanied American fighter-bombers on their raids.

Of course, the military aircraft produced during the Cold War were not built to fight the Cold War. They were produced to fight a war that never happened. The air wars fought during the 1945–1992 period were small wars compared to World War I and World War II, but the aircraft used in those wars were remarkable for the technology that developed, and they were priceless for helping keep the Cold War cold.

★ LOCKHEED P-80/F-80 SHOOTING STAR ★

JET AIRCRAFT FIRST FLEW on the eve of World War II; projects to turn this new innovation into practical warplanes began in Germany, Britain, and the United States almost immediately. The first successful American jet fighter was the Lockheed P-80 (F-80 after 1948) Shooting Star. Ordered in June 1943, the first Shooting Star was designed and built in only 143 days. Britain, where engine development was moving faster than in the United States, provided a de Havilland Goblin turbojet engine for the new aircraft, and it made its historic first flight in January 1944.

By the summer of 1944, the intended American-made power plant, the General Electric J33 turbojet, was ready and the first of the flight-test YP-80As were flown. As Lockheed geared up for production of P-80As, the German Messerschmitt Me262 went into full-fledged squadron service and the need for Allied jet fighters was suddenly and painfully clear. The P-80As were ready for squadron service by April 1945, but the war ended on May 7 before the American jets could face their German counterparts in combat.

The P-80 remained in production after World War II, and the P-80A was superseded by the ejection-seat-

One of the first U.S. Air Force units to become operational with the Lockheed P-80 Shooting Star was the 94th "Hat in the Ring" Fighter Squadron. The 94th is perhaps best remembered as the outfit commanded by Eddie Rickenbacker during World War I.

equipped P-80B in 1947. The standard production Shooting Star was the F-80C, which entered service in 1948. The F-80C was heavier but the same size as the P-80A, with a wingspan of 39 feet 11 inches, a length of 34 feet 6 inches, and a gross weight of 15,336 pounds. It had a service ceiling of 42,750 feet and a range of 1,380 miles. It was powered by an Allison J33-A-23 turbojet engine, delivering 5,400 pounds of thrust and giving it

The Shooting Star prototype was fabricated at Lockheed's secret "Skunk Works" in Burbank, California. Designated XP-80 and nicknamed Lulu Belle, it made its first flight in January 1944.

a top speed of 580 miles per hour at 7,000 feet. Its armament consisted of four nose-mounted .50 caliber machine guns as well as wing racks with provisions for two 1,000 pound bombs or ten High Velocity Aerial Rockets (HVAR).

When the Korean War started in June 1950, the Shooting Stars were the first U.S. Air Force jet fighters to see action. On November 8, 1950, a P-80C shot down a Chinese MiG-15 in history's first jet-to-jet aerial battle. As the Korean War dragged on, however, the American jet fighter that might have bested the best the German Luftwaffe had to offer showed itself to be inferior to the feared MiG-15. The swept-wing MiG was more than a match for the straight-winged Shooting Star.

To counter the MiG-15 threat, the U.S. Air Force introduced the North American F-86 Sabre as its first-line air superiority fighter, and the Shooting Star was moved to the ground

support role. In total, the Shooting Star flew over 62,000 missions in Korea, with fewer than 150 of them lost to enemy action.

After the Korean War, the F-80 was withdrawn from service with the U.S. Air Force, but a variant of the Shooting Star remained in service for another three decades. The need for a two-seat jet trainer had become apparent in the late 1940s as the Air Force was abandoning piston-engined fighters for jets. Lockheed made a suggestion to develop a two-seat F-80; the first of these made its debut in 1948 as the TF-80C.

The production version of the TF-80C appeared in 1949 under the designation T-33A. Although the T-33A was also officially known as the Shooting Star, it was unofficially—and universally—known as the "T-Bird." While the U.S. Navy had shied away from the F-80 as a fighter, they ordered over 700 T-Birds under the designation TV (later T-33B).

THROUGHOUT THE early 1940s, it was widely theorized in aviation circles that jet propulsion was the way of the future for combat aircraft. However, the full extent of the jets' superiority over piston-engined types was not fully understood until jets actually entered combat. In the final months of World War II, the German Me262 jet fighter, with its 500-plus miles per hour speed and the ability to maintain its speed in a turn, made it the most potent aircraft in any aerial battle it entered. The exciting era of the jets had arrived.

An early photo shows a North American Aviation F-86A Sabre Jet in flight over the desert test range at Edwards Air Force Base in California. Edwards AFB has been the center of U.S. Air Force flight testing since World War II.

The United States and Britain were also working on jet fighter projects during World War II, unaware of exactly how far behind Germany they were. Not only were the Germans able to field several combat jets, they were technologically superior to those that were being developed by the Allies. For example, the American Lockheed P-80 and British Gloster Meteor had straight wings. After the war, the Allies had a chance to examine German aviation technology and aircraft, including the Me262 technology, up close. The data on swept wings prompted the redesign of a number of straight-winged jet fighters on the drawing boards in 1945. One such fighter was the North American Aviation Sabre.

The XP-86 (XF-86 after June 1948) Sabre made its first flight at Muroc Army Air Field on October 1, 1947, and flight tests showed it to be a very potent aircraft, capable of breaking the sound barrier in a dive. In February 1949, production F-86As equipped the 1st Fighter Group at March Air Force Base, California, and the 4th Fighter Group at Langley Air Force Base, Virginia. The latter was the first unit to actually fly Sabres in combat in Korea.

The F-86A Sabre had a wingspan of 37 feet 1 inch, a length of 37 feet 6 inches, and a gross weight of 15,876 pounds. It had a service ceiling of 48,000 feet, a range of 1,052 miles, and a combat radius of 330 miles. It was powered by a General Electric J47-GE-13 turbojet, delivering 5,200 pounds of thrust and giving it a top speed of 601 miles per hour at 35,000 feet. Its armament consisted of six nose-mounted .50 caliber machine guns.

When the United States led United Nations forces to counter the June 1950 North Korean invasion of South Korea, the U.S. Air Force sent straight-winged F-80 jet fighters and piston-engined F-51 Mustangs to fight the North Korean air force. For the first six months of the Korean War, these aircraft were up to the task. In November 1950, as United Nations troops

(Above) *This artist's conception shows a U.S. Air Force F-86 Sabre Jet moments after defeating a Mikoyan Gurevich MiG-15 in the skies over Korea, circa 1951. Note the gunpowder streaks behind the three gun ports in the Sabre's nose.*
(Left) *A restored Sabre Jet prepares for a demonstration flight four decades after its halcyon days as an air superiority fighter. In terms of its success in aerial combat, the North American Aviation F-86 Sabre Jet was the best jet fighter of its era.*

neared the Chinese border, communist China sent vast numbers of troops into the war. Just as these ground forces tipped the scales on the ground, the entry of the Chinese air force into combat changed things in the air.

Chinese squadrons were equipped with the extraordinary new Soviet jet, the swept-wing fighter known as the Mikoyan-Gurevich MiG-15. Flown by Chinese and Soviet pilots, these aircraft achieved air superiority of the Korean peninsula and the U.S. Air Force made the decision to send the F-86A to Korea. The Sabres made an impressive debut: They scored their first MiG-15 victory on their first day of combat, December 17, 1950.

During the early months of 1951, the Sabres wrested air superiority from the MiG-15 and went on to achieve a better than ten-to-one rate of combat success. F-86 pilots shot down 792 MiG-15s and 13 other aircraft while losing only 78 of their own. There were three dozen U.S. Air Force Sabre aces, topped by Captain Joe McConnell with 16 victories.

Late in the war, the F-86A was superseded by the improved F-86E and F-86F. The latter—which had become the standard Sabre by the time the war ended—had the same dimensions as the F-86A, but its gross weight was 17,921 pounds. It had a ser-

A Mikoyan-Gurevich MiG-15 dives onto the tail of North American Aviation F-86 Sabre Jet over Korea. The fast, swept wing MiG-15, which first flew in 1947, was perhaps the best combat jet designed in Europe between 1945 and the early 1950s.

vice ceiling of 48,000 feet, a ferry range of 1,615 miles, and a combat radius of 458 miles. It was powered by a General Electric J47-GE-27 turbojet, delivering 5,910 pounds of thrust. Its armament consisted of six nose-mounted .50 caliber machine guns like the F-86A, but a few were armed with four 20mm cannons instead.

The U.S. Navy version of the Sabre was the FJ-series Fury. The first Fury, the straight-winged FJ-1 appeared in 1946, but it was not suited for duty on aircraft carriers as were other aircraft of the time. The FJ-2, based on the F-86F, appeared in 1951, but it was also too heavy for efficient carrier use and was diverted to the U.S. Marine Corps. The final Fury was the FJ-4, which was largely designed to serve as an attack bomber. It was equipped to carry conventional bombs as well as the Mk.7 nuclear weapon and the Bullpup air-to-ground missile.

Meanwhile, North American Aviation produced an interceptor version of the Sabre for the U.S. Air Force under the designation F-86D, which was known as the "Sabre Dog" since the word dog was phonetic code for the letter D and the F-86D's black, nose-mounted radome gave it a slightly canine appearance.

Ordered in large numbers because of the threat of a growing number of Soviet bombers, the Sabre Dog entry into squadron service was delayed until 1953 because of problems with the E-4 fire control system that targeted its air-to-air rockets. The F-86D-1 had a wingspan of 37 feet 1 inch, a length of 40 feet 3 inches, and a gross weight of 18,183 pounds. It had a service ceiling of 49,750 feet, a range of 769 miles, and a combat radius of 277 miles. It was powered by a General Electric J47-GE-17 turbojet, delivering 5,425 pounds of thrust and giving it a top speed of 612 miles per hour at 40,000 feet. Its armament consisted of 24 2.75-inch "Mighty Mouse" Folding Fin Aerial Rockets (FFAR) carried in a fuselage weapons bay.

The Sabre Dog was superseded by the F-86K and F-86L "dog-nosed" interceptors, which remained in service with the Air National Guard until the mid-1960s. Several hundred Sabre interceptors were also sold to Japan and to NATO countries, and Fiat in Italy assembled over 200 for its own air force, as well as those of France and Germany.

The Sabre remained in production until 1956, with 6,210 F-86s and 1,112 Furies having been manufactured by North American Aviation, and 520 assembled by Mitsubishi and Fiat from parts made by North American. There were 1,815 manufactured by Canadair and 112 made by Commonwealth. Over 2,500 each were built of the F-86D and F-86F variants.

HOYT S. VANDENBERG

The first full-term U.S. Air Force chief of staff, General Hoyt Vandenberg graduated from the U.S. Military Academy at West Point in 1923. He took pilot training in the U.S. Army Air Service, and he earned his wings after completing advanced flight training in Texas.

In the spring of 1944, he became deputy commander of the Allied Expeditionary Air Force (AEF). The AEF had the task of carrying out the Operation Overlord invasion of Normandy. As such, Vandenberg assumed command of the USAAF 9th Air Force, which would undertake the tactical air campaign against German forces until the end of World War II.

After the war, Vandenberg returned to Washington to help direct USAAF intelligence activities, and in 1946, he became director of the Central Intelligence Agency (CIA). When the U.S. Air Force was created in 1947, Vandenberg became its vice chief of staff, and about a year later he became chief of staff.

Vandenberg undertook the task of rebuilding the Air Force. He oversaw the U.S. Air Force commitment to the Korean War. In 1953, after the Korean War, Defense Secretary Charles Wilson decided to drastically downsize the Air Force, depending only on a nuclear retaliation and defense. Vandenberg argued successfully that to do so would leave the United States no option other than nuclear war, and hence, it would be a great danger to the world.

Hoyt Vandenberg died on April 2, 1954. He had won the battle to preserve a strong Air Force, but he had lost his personal battle with cancer. Today, his name lives on at Vandenberg Air Force Base in California, the site of all U.S. Air Force missile tests and a primary site for launching spacecraft into polar orbit.

BOEING B-52 STRATOFORTRESS

THE DEEPENING OF the Cold War led to the expanded production that was never seen again for a large jet bomber. The B-52 Stratofortress was conceived in this Cold War environment—just as its smaller sister the B-47 was created. Unlike the Stratojet, which served for less than a decade, the B-52 has been a front-line weapon for more than 40 years. The B-52 has survived long enough to have been used by three generations of pilots.

Development of the aircraft that became the B-52

A turbofan-engined Boeing B-52H in 1980s-vintage camouflage markings during a training exercise. The B-52H's Pratt & Whitney TF33-P-3 turbofans, each delivering 17,000 pounds of thrust, distinguished it from earlier Stratofortresses.

began in the late 1940s with the idea of building an all-jet swept-wing bomber with a conventional as well as nuclear bomb capacity was a truly intercontinental range. The Convair B-36, a straight-winged behemoth that was designed during World War II, was the largest bomber in history. It had the intercontinental range but it was slow and cumbersome. For Boeing, the idea was to develop something entirely new that would break new ground and would remain in the arsenal until at least the 1960s.

The XB-52 prototype made its first flight in 1952 and production model B-52Bs entered service with the U.S. Air Force's SAC in 1954, a year after the Soviet Union exploded its first hydrogen bomb. Like that of the SAC itself, the principle job

of the B-52 in 1955—as today—was to deter nuclear aggression against the United States by demonstrating the capacity and readiness to deliver an equal counter blow against the aggressor. The eight-engine giants were described at the time by Defense Secretary Donald Quarles as "the most formidable expression of air power in the history of military aviation."

The first major production series were the B-52C/ B-52D aircraft manufactured in Seattle and Wichita, respectively. The B-52C and B-52D had a wingspan of 185 feet, a length of 156 feet 7 inches, and a gross weight of 450,000 pounds. They had a combat ceiling of 46,350 feet, a ferry range of 7,850 miles, and an unrefueled combat radius of 3,800 miles with a bomb load of 10,000 pounds. However, all B-52s were fully air-refuelable and had effectively unlimited range. They were powered by eight Pratt & Whitney J57-P-19W or J57-P-29W turbojets, each delivering 12,100 pounds of thrust, giving the B-52s a top speed of 634 miles per hour at 20,200 feet.

The early production Stratofortresses were designed to carry 27 conventional bombs weighing 1,000 pounds each or

(Above) *A Boeing B-52G Stratofortress thunders in for a late afternoon landing. The B-52G was the penultimate Stratofortress subtype to be delivered to the U.S. Air Force. The B-52Gs were retired in 1994, leaving only the B-52H in service. (Left) This B-52H is being refueled by a KC-135E Stratotanker. The glossy white undersurfaces of the Stratofortress were standard equipment for most of the fleet from the 1950s to the 1990s. The purpose was to reflect light and heat generated by the explosion of the nuclear weapons that the B-52s were designed to deliver.*

(Right) *This black-bellied B-52D is on the tarmac at Andersen AFB in Guam. The black undersurfaces were common to the B-52Ds that were used to fly night missions over Southeast Asia during the Vietnam War.* (Far right) *In the 1980s, the U.S. Air Force retrofitted its B-52Gs and B-52Hs with Low-Light Television (LLTV) and Forward-Looking Infrared (FLIR) turrets that were mounted under the aircraft's chin.*

one 43,000-pound nuclear weapon. Subsequent modifications, including wing-mounted pylons added during the Vietnam War, added to the aircraft's overall capacity. Its defensive armament consisted of four .50 caliber machine guns in a manned tail turret.

As with the B-47, the arming of the B-52s with the Bell GAM-63 Rascal air-to-surface missile was considered, but the Rascal was abandoned by the Air Force in favor of the North American Aviation GAM-77 Hound Dog, a 42-foot jet cruise missile with a stand-off range of 600 miles. It was a precursor to the air-launched cruise missiles that the Stratofortress would carry into war in the 1990s.

The final two B-52 models were the B-52G and B-52H, instantly recognizable by tails that were eight feet shorter than other models. The B-52G had a wingspan of 185 feet, a length of 157 feet 7 inches, and a gross weight of 450,000 pounds. It had a combat ceiling of 47,100 feet, a ferry range of 8,900 miles, and an unrefueled combat radius of 3,980 miles with a bomb load of 10,000 pounds. It was powered by eight Pratt & Whitney J57-P-43WB turbojets, each delivering 13,750 pounds of thrust, giving it a top speed of 637 miles per hour at 20,200 feet.

The final Stratofortress, and the one retained by the U.S. Air Force the longest, was also the only turbofan-powered Stratofortress. The B-52H had a wingspan of 185 feet, a length of 156 feet, and a gross weight of 450,000 pounds. It had a combat ceiling of 47,200 feet, a ferry range of 7,715 miles, and an unrefueled combat radius of 4,477 miles with a bomb load of 10,000 pounds. It was powered by eight Pratt & Whitney TF33-P3 turbofans, each delivering 17,000 pounds of thrust and giving it a top speed of 639 miles per hour at 20,200 feet.

In 1957, as a demonstration of their intercontinental range capabilities, three B-52s were flown (with aerial refuelings en route) nonstop 24,325 miles around the world. Five years later, a B-52H flew 12,532 miles nonstop without refueling, setting a distance record that stood until the flight of the *Voyager* a quarter century later. This type of operational capability gave the B-52 a much-deserved reputation for durability and tenacity.

The last two Stratofortress types were designed with conventional and nuclear bomb capacity as were their predecessors, but they were also upgraded with the addition of rotary launchers in their bomb bays and underwing pylons to carry such stand-off weapons as the Short-Range Attack Missile (SRAM). In 1993, B-52Hs became active with the AGM-129 Advanced Cruise Missile (ACM) carried on wing-mounted pylons. The B-52G's defensive armament consisted of four .50 caliber machine guns in a remotely operated tail turret.

B-52s were assigned to the Air Force Systems Command for various testing purposes, but the majority of the 744 Stratofortresses Boeing manufactured between 1951 and 1963 spent their entire careers in service with the SAC, until the SAC was merged into ACC in 1992. Since then, they have been included in the traditional SAC-type bomb wings, as well as the ACC's specialized, multipurpose bomb wings.

In 1965, after a decade of service only in a nuclear deterrent capacity, SAC B-52s were detailed to Vietnam for the Operation Arc Light carpet-bombing raids, which were part of the overall "Rolling Thunder" campaign. In 1972, SAC B-52s based in Guam and Thailand conducted an 11-day series of strategic bombing missions, the Christmas Bombings, against Hanoi. While the B-52s suffered their highest losses (15 planes) during the Christmas Bombings, their valiant efforts paid off. The missions largely destroyed North Vietnam's war-making capacity and paved the way for a cease-fire after nearly a decade of intense U.S. involvement in the war in Southeast Asia.

In 1991, B-52s went into action again during Operation Desert Storm. Flying extremely long-range missions from Diego Garcia in the Indian Ocean and from the United States itself, they were used to launch ALCMs against highly critical targets in Iraq, as well as to drop conventional bombs on armored and mechanized concentrations in Kuwait and Iraq. Five years later, during Operation Desert Strike in 1996, B-52s again flew half way around the world for ALCM strikes on Iraqi targets.

CURTIS EMERSON LEMAY

The most influential leader to hold the post of U.S. Air Force Chief of Staff, Curtis LeMay is best remembered as the commander of the Strategic Air Command (SAC) who built it from a handful of piston-engined bombers into the most formidable aerial strike force the world will ever know.

LeMay joined the U.S. Army Air Corps in 1928 as a flying cadet. He was assigned to the 27th Pursuit Squadron at Selfridge Field, Michigan, in 1929, and he spent the next eight years as a fighter pilot. In 1937, he transferred to bombers on the eve of the introduction of the B-17 Flying Fortress. The following year, he participated in the first massed overseas deployment of B-17s.

In 1944, the B-29 Superfortress was introduced. It was earmarked solely for the new 20th Bomber Command, and its mission was to undertake a strategic air campaign against Japan. LeMay was given command of the 20th, and in June 1944, he began B-29 raids against Japanese industrial targets.

As the number of bombers increased, LeMay was able to run 300-, 400-, and even 600-plane raids. In March 1945, he switched from high-altitude bombing to low-altitude attacks with incendiaries that badly mauled the enemy's urban infrastructure. In August 1945, B-29s were used to drop the nuclear weapons that ended the war, but LeMay always felt that Japan could have been defeated by conventional raids alone.

After the war, LeMay served as commander of U.S. Air Forces in Europe and as deputy Chief of Staff for Research and Development. In 1948, he was placed in charge of the SAC. In the nearly ten years that LeMay ruled the SAC, it became the most powerful air strike force in history.

McDonnell Douglas F-4 Phantom II

THE F-4 PHANTOM II, which had a service career spanning three decades and two major wars, was probably the most important fighter of its era and it will probably see a fifth decade of service somewhere. For the United States, it was a workhorse of the Vietnam War, where most of the enemy aircraft shot down were claimed by Phantoms, and where the only five Americans to become aces since 1953 did so in Phantoms.

The Phantom II was a fourth generation descendent of the McDonnell FH-1 Phantom, the U.S. Navy's first carrier-based jet fighter, which first flew in 1946. By 1954, McDonnell had added two additional fighters—the F2H Banshee and F3H Demon—to the catalog of aircraft they were developing for the Navy. It was at this time the Navy requested a design for a carrier-based attack bomber, which would be designated AH-1.

By 1955, when the new AH-1 aircraft was ready, the Navy had changed its mind and requested that the St. Louis aircraft maker reconfigure the AH-1 as a fighter. Redesignated F4H, the new aircraft was named Phantom II even though its wing plan made it very dissimilar to the smaller, straight-winged FH-1Phantom.

The first of 696 F4Hs entered Navy service in 1955, and a few years later the Air Force took an interest. In January 1962, they borrowed some from the Navy, and soon they decided to order 635 Phantoms of their own under the F-110 designation. In September 1962, the Air Force and Navy numbering systems were merged, and the Navy's Phantoms were redesignated F-4A and F-4B, with the Air Force variant becoming F-4C. In 1964, the Air Force ordered 703 F-4Ds, which were like the F-4C except they had a larger radar system.

The F-4B and F-4C had a wingspan of 38 feet 5 inches, a length of 58 feet 3 inches, and gross weights of 43,907 and 51,441 pounds, respectively, and they had service ceilings of over 56,000 feet. The F-4B was powered by a pair of General Electric J79-GE-8 turbojets delivering 17,000 pounds of thrust and giving it a top speed of 1,490 miles per hour at 40,000 feet. Its unrefueled ferry range was 2,076 miles, and it had a combat range of 1,297 miles with 6,000 pounds of bombs or much longer with aerial refueling. The F-4C was powered by a pair of General Electric J79-GE-15 turbojets, delivering up to 17,000 pounds of thrust and giving it a top speed of 1,433 miles per hour at 40,000 feet. Its unrefueled ferry range was 1,926 miles, and it had a combat radius of 323 miles with 8,250 pounds of bombs.

The F-4B Phantom IIs flown by the U.S. Navy's VF-84 fighter squadron carried the distinctive "Jolly Roger" tail marks. The VF-84 sailed to the Gulf of Tonkin off the coast of Vietnam aboard the USS Independence (CV-62) during the latter half of 1965.

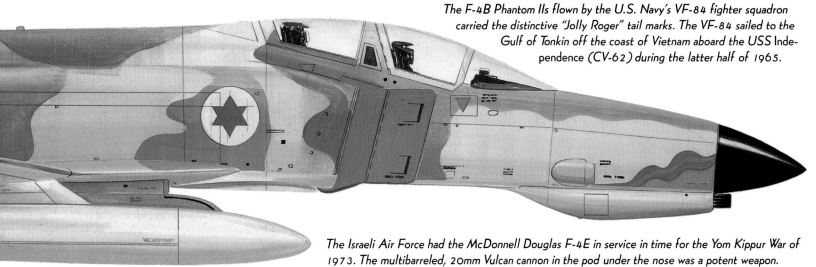

The Israeli Air Force had the McDonnell Douglas F-4E in service in time for the Yom Kippur War of 1973. The multibarreled, 20mm Vulcan cannon in the pod under the nose was a potent weapon.

(Above) *A flight of U.S. Navy F-4B Phantom IIs line up behind a McDonnell Douglas KA-3 aerial refueling aircraft. The effectiveness of the carrier-based Phantom II fighters was greatly enhanced by having a carrier-based refueling aircraft. (Right) This shot of U.S. Navy F-4J Phantom II was taken from the view of a U.S. Air Force KC-135 Stratotanker. The U.S. Navy Phantom IIs were designed with a refueling probe that folded out from the fuselage, while the U.S. Air Force Phantom IIs were refueled through a receptacle behind the cockpit.*

The F-4B and F-4C could carry up to two dozen 500-pound conventional bombs or a 2,040-pound Mk.28 nuclear weapon. Their defensive armament consisted of four AIM-7 Sparrow and four AIM-9 Sidewinder air-to-air missiles. The Phantom carried a crew of two, with the pilot in the forward cockpit and the weapons system operator (WSO) behind. The idea behind having a second crewman was traceable to the Phantom's origin as an attack aircraft; in these aircraft, with their wide variety of weapons types, it was essential to have a WSO—a "whizzo"—in addition to the pilot. Indeed, it was the presence of the backseater that helped to permit the adaptation of the Phantom to fighter-bomber and reconnaissance missions.

U.S. Air Force Phantoms were sent to Vietnam early the following year, scoring their first aerial victories in July 1965. It was during this baptism of fire in Southeast Asia that a major shortcoming in the Phantom's armament was discovered. The aircraft had evolved in the 1950s when the school of thought was

held that fighters could henceforth do their jobs entirely with air-to-air missiles—that guns were now obsolete in fighter aircraft. In the skies over Southeast Asia, when the Phantom actually began getting into dogfights, however, aircrews discovered that this assumption was incorrect—guns were essential. The Air Force F-4Ds were then hastily fitted with 20mm cannon pods bolted to their bellies as McDonnell (McDonnell Douglas after 1967) went to work designing an all-new Phantom II, the F-4E, which first appeared in 1967 and had an internally mounted 20mm cannon.

The F-4E had a wingspan of 38 feet 5 inches, a length of 63 feet, and a gross weight of 53,848 pounds. It had a service ceiling of 59,200 feet and a combat ceiling of 59,600 feet. It was powered by a pair of General Electric J79-GE-17 turbojets, delivering up to 17,900 pounds of thrust and giving it a top speed of 1,464 miles per hour at 40,000 feet. Its unrefueled ferry range was 1,885 miles, and it had a combat radius of 533 miles

Daniel "Chappie" James

Born in Pensacola, Florida, Chappie James studied at the Tuskegee Institute, an all-black college in Alabama established in 1881 by Booker T. Washington. After the United States entered World War II, he enrolled in the pilot training program at the Tuskegee Army Air Field. Here, he became part of the legendary group remembered as the Tuskegee Airmen.

In 1944, four African-American fighter squadrons were deployed to Italy, where they were consolidated into the 332nd Fighter Group. Flying P-51 Mustangs in support of USAAF bombers, they flew over 10,000 sorties, shot down over 100 Germans, and never lost a bomber to enemy fighters.

After the war, James decided to make the postwar USAAF (U.S. Air Force after 1947) his career. Having been cheated out of a chance at combat in World War II, he flew 101 missions in the Korean War and was awarded the Distinguished Flying Cross.

Transferred to the U.S. Air Forces in Europe, James commanded the 81st Fighter Wing at RAF Bentwaters. During the Vietnam War, he flew F-4C MiGCAP missions as vice commander of the 8th Tactical Fighter Wing, known as the legendary "Wolf Pack," commanded by World War II fighter ace Colonel Robin Olds. In January 1967, while with the Wolf Pack, James flew as a flight leader in Operation Bolo, which was the biggest air-to-air battle of the war.

After a tour at the Pentagon, James became the first African-American Air Force general to pin on a fourth star, and in 1975, he became Commander in Chief of the North American Air Defense Command (NORAD).

A U.S. Air Force F-4E touches down at Nellis AFB in Nevada after a day's action as part of the U.S. Air Force's annual Red Flag combat readiness exercise. The Phantom II was the backbone of U.S. Air Force power for almost two decades.

with 2,000 pounds of weapons or much longer with aerial refueling. The F-4E had a conventional bomb and nuclear weapon capability similar to that of earlier Phantoms. In addition to the four AIM-7 Sparrow and four AIM-9 Sidewinder air-to-air missiles included with earlier Phantoms, the F-4E's defensive armament also had an M61 20mm gatling gun.

The U.S. Navy's F-4J, introduced in 1966, had a wingspan of 38 feet 5 inches, a length of 58 feet 3.5 inches, and a gross weight of 46,833 pounds. It had a combat ceiling of 54,700 feet. It was powered by a pair of General Electric J79-GE-10 turbojets, delivering up to 17,859 pounds of thrust and giving it a top speed of 1,416 miles per hour at 36,089 feet. Its unrefueled ferry range was 1,956 miles, and it had a combat radius of 596 miles armed or much longer with aerial refueling. The F-4J had a conventional bomb and nuclear weapon capability similar to earlier Phantoms. Its defensive armament included the four AIM-7 Sparrow and four AIM-9 Sidewinder air-to-air missiles but not a gun as in the F-4E.

In May 1972, the U.S. Navy team of Lieutenant Randy "Duke" Cunningham and Lieutenant Bill Driscoll became the first American aces of the Vietnam War. Later in the year, U.S. Air Force Captains Jeffrey Feinstein and Richard "Steve" Ritchie became aces while flying the Phantom F-4E fighter.

The U.S. Air Force bought over a thousand F-4Es, and McDonnell Douglas sold several hundred others to various countries around the world. Other specialized Phantom IIs were developed for West Germany (F-4F) and the United Kingdom (F-4K and F-4M). The reconnaissance variant was the RF-4C, a variation of the F-4C, which entered service in 1964 with the job of devoting its supersonic speed and maneuverability of a fighter to the role of a reconnaissance aircraft. The RF-4C was used in Vietnam, taking reconnaissance photos of the effects of American bombing raids.

In use through the 1991 Gulf War, RF-4Cs were configured to carry state-of-the art reconnaissance equipment, although the state of the art has now changed to where the aircraft's camera bay included infrared target locating sensors, and conventional optical cameras were replaced by electro-optical sensors.

Over 5,000 Phantom IIs were produced by McDonnell Douglas through a period of a quarter century, and as a type, the aircraft will survive well into the 21st century in such diverse places as Israel, Greece, and Japan. In the U.S. Air Force, Phantom F-4s continued with reserve units and in the F-4G "Wild Weasel" antiradar configuration—that performed brilliantly in the 1991 Gulf War—until their controversial retirement in 1996.

(Above) *This close-up of a Phantom II front cockpit reminds us that the great fighter was designed during the era of analog dials, well before the commonplace use of digital electronics.* (Left) *The RF-4E was the U.S. Air Force photo-reconnaissance variant of the Phantom II. The camera was located behind the dark panel under the nose. This RF-4E was assigned to the U.S. Air Force Flight Test Center at Edwards AFB.*

ESIGNED AS THE WORLD'S ultimate air superiority fighter—with the Vietnam experience of the F-4 Phantom II in mind—the F-15 Eagle has never been beaten in aerial combat. It went to war with the U.S. Air Force in 1991 after a dozen years in service and chalked up a record 31 aerial victories against Iraqi fighter jets with no losses. This performance served to underscore the action over Lebanon's Baka'a Valley in June 1982 when Israeli F-15s tackled the best Soviet-built fighters in the Syrian air force and downed 80 of them with the loss of no Eagles.

The F-15 Eagle first flew in July 1972, and the first F-15As entered squadron service four years later, followed by the F-15C in 1979. The F-15B and F-15D are two-seat counterparts of the F-15A and F-15C, which are used in training but are also fully combat-capable. By the early 1980s, Eagles had already replaced F-4s as the Air Force's first-line fighters, and export deals were struck in which Eagles were exported to Israel, Japan, and Saudi Arabia.

The F-15C and F-15D have a wingspan of 42 feet 9.75 inches, a length of 63 feet 9 inches, and a gross weight of 81,000 pounds. The Eagle has a service ceiling of 60,000 feet, with a time-to-altitude record of 49,212 feet in 77 seconds. Since 1985, the F-15C and F-15D have been powered by two Pratt & Whitney F100-PW-220 turbofan engines, each delivering 23,450 pounds of thrust and giving them a top speed of Mach 2.5. Their maximum unrefueled ferry range is 2,762 miles. The weapons systems for the Eagles include an internally mounted M61A1 20mm cannon, as well as the four AIM-7 Sparrow and four AIM-9 Sidewinder air-to-air missiles, or the more sophisticated AIM-120 AMRAAM. In 1984, two squadrons of F-15s

A U.S. Air Force F-15C Eagle is refueled by a U.S. Air Force KC-135 Stratotanker. The powerful McDonnell Douglas Eagle became the U.S. Air Force's top air superiority fighter in the 1980s and served admirably in the Gulf War.

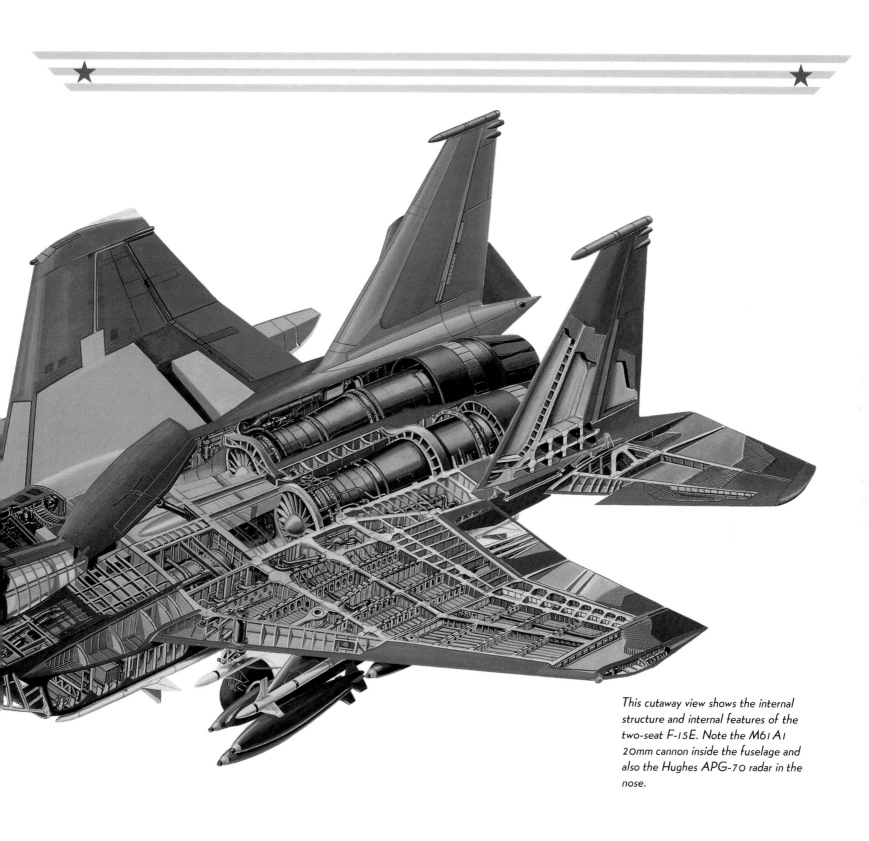

This cutaway view shows the internal structure and internal features of the two-seat F-15E. Note the M61A1 20mm cannon inside the fuselage and also the Hughes APG-70 radar in the nose.

were experimentally equipped with the ALMV/ASAT, a two-stage missile that could be fired into space to destroy satellites. After a successful test in 1985, Congress banned further testing of the system.

By 1986, with the completion of the 1,000th Eagle, McDonnell Douglas had delivered 931 F-15s to the air forces of the United States, Israel, Japan, and Saudi Arabia. Mitsubishi Heavy Industries, Ltd., of Japan had made 69 F-15s under license from McDonnell Douglas. The

This aft view of a McDonnell Douglas Eagle parked at Edwards AFB provides a good look at the distinctive twin tails, the twin tailpipes, and the missiles located underneath.

U.S. Air Force's F-15 Eagles were reporting a fully mission capable (FMC) rate of 80.2 percent. At the one million flight hour mark, only 3.9 had been lost per 100,000 flight hours.

In 1987, the Air Force began taking deliveries of the F-15E, a long-range, two-seat, fighter-bomber based on the F-15D. The speed and maneuverability of the Eagle had made it the ideal airframe to adapt as the twenty-first century replacement for the aging F-111 fighter-bomber fleet. This plane had come about as an idea in 1983, when the Air Force expressed an interest in a new two-seat interdiction/strike (fighter bomber) aircraft to replace its aging fleet of F-111s. Long-range interdiction is an air-to-ground mission designed to prevent an invading force from sustaining an attack by knocking out bridges, roads, railways, and airfields that could be used to transport supplies and

troop reinforcements. McDonnell Douglas incorporated many of the basics for such a mission into the F-15 originally, so the aircraft was an excellent candidate to be adapted for this role. The Air Force announced plans to purchase 392 of these aircraft under the designation F-15E.

The F-15E had the same dimensions as the earlier Eagles, but its maximum gross weight for take-off increased to 81,000 pounds from 68,000 pounds, and the stronger airframe had twice the fatigue life of previous F-15 variants. With this, it carries up to 24,500 pounds of bombs. The F-15E is powered by two Pratt & Whitney F100-PW-229 turbofan engines, each delivering 29,100 pounds of thrust. They fly nearly 40 percent farther on some missions because new conformal fuel tanks can carry additional fuel while keeping drag to a minimum.

The F-15E's central computer holds four times as much information as earlier Eagles and processes it three times faster. New electronics include the Hughes Aircraft Company APG-70 radar and the Martin Marietta LAN-TIRN (Low-Altitude Navigation and Targeting Infrared for Night) system. The LANTIRN system's navigation pod has a forward-looking infrared sensor. It creates daylight-quality video pictures that are displayed at night on a transparent screen at the pilot's eye level. The pod also

The McDonnell Douglas F-15 Eagle first flew in July 1972 and entered squadron service four years later. It was designed to replace the Phantom II as the Air Force's first-line fighter.

contains a terrain-following radar system for low-level, high-speed flying. A second LANTIRN pod, used for targeting, contains a high resolution infrared system and a laser designator. It aids the crew in identifying targets and aiming weapons at ranges previously impossible for tactical aircraft.

Israeli F-15s were first involved in combat in 1982, and U.S. Air Force Eagles first saw action during the Gulf War. When Iraq invaded Kuwait in August 1990, the United States responded immediately by deploying air and airborne forces to Kuwait under Operation Desert Shield. The first to go were 48 McDonnell Douglas F-15C and F-15D fighters of the 1st Tactical Fighter Wing from Langley AFB, Virginia. These fighters joined the McDonnell Douglas F-15s of the Royal Saudi Air Force that were already on station.

When Desert Shield became Desert Storm in January 1991, F-15Cs went to work in their air superiority role, flying combat air patrol (CAP) cover missions for strike packages of Coalition bombers. The Coalition bomber force included 48 F-15Es of the 4th Tactical Fighter Wing.

On the first night of the war, U.S. Air Force F-15Cs shot down six Iraqi interceptors in air-to-air combat and two days later, a Saudi F-15 pilot downed two Iraqi aircraft. Subsequent action was sporadic because Iraq's air force chose to run or hide, but at war's end, F-15Cs accounted for 31 of the 34 Iraqi fixed-wing aircraft shot down in the war. Two additional victories came in March 1991 as the Eagles were helping to enforce the postwar "no-fly" zones. The Iraqis had not been able to shoot down a single Coalition aircraft in aerial combat. During the Gulf War, the F-15 Eagles had maintained a 95.9 percent average mission-capable rate, the highest of any fighter in the war.

After the war, F-15Cs remained in the Middle East as part of the Operation Southern Watch enforcement of the no-fly zones, while others flew CAP missions in support of American and NATO forces deployed to Bosnia in 1995–1996.

FOUR DECADES AFTER it was first deployed, the KC-135 Stratotanker, the first jet aerial refueling airplane, was still the world's most widely used aerial tanker and likely to remain with that distinction to the half-century mark.

The Air Force had several types of jet bombers in service and needed a fast jet to refuel them. The converted piston-engined aircraft were too slow. The Boeing KC-97 tankers (based on the Boeing 377 Stratocruiser propliner) couldn't keep pace with the new B-52s, but the Boeing model 367-80, called the "Dash-Eighty," could and the Air Force ordered some 732 of them under the KC-135 designation. The Air Force also ordered nearly a hundred 367-80s, as C-135 cargo planes, EC-135 electronic warfare aircraft, and RC-135 reconnaissance aircraft.

The KC-135 has a wingspan of 130 feet 10 inches and a length of 136 feet 3 inches, which is 2 feet longer than the C-135. The first Stratotankers were delivered with four Pratt & Whitney J57-P turbojets, each delivering 13,700 pounds of thrust.

Beginning in 1982, much of the Stratotanker fleet was re-engined with more efficient General Electric/SNECMA F108-CF-100 (CFM56) high-bypass turbofan engines, each delivering 22,224 pounds of thrust. The retrofitted aircraft were redesignated as KC-135R and KC-135T.

While the KC-135 is the most well known and the most common, the Boeing Model 367-80, or Dash-Eighty, airframe has been used for a myriad of services other than aerial refueling, such as the EC-135 and RC-135 special reconnaissance aircraft. The NKC-135 seen here is used for testing various systems that may be used in other KC-135s.

The original gross weight rating of the KC-135A was 297,000 pounds, but the strengthened and re-engined KC-135R and KC-135T have a gross weight rating of 322,000 pounds. The service ceiling was also increased from 40,000 to 50,000 feet. The Stratotanker typically carries 120,000 pounds of transfer fuel and has a range of 2,128 miles when loaded. Empty, the KC-135 has a range of 11,192 miles.

Because its highest priority role was refueling long-range bombers, the entire KC-135 fleet was assigned to the SAC and remained so until the SAC was merged into the ACC in 1992. At that time, the U.S. Air Force moved the refueling squadrons under the umbrella of Air Mobility Command (AMC). The KC-135 entered service with the SAC in 1957 and has been continuously active around the world since, refueling aircraft assigned to all U.S. Air Force Commands as well as the U.S. Navy and air arms of allied countries.

The EC-135 and RC-135 special duty aircraft have essentially the same specifications as the KC-135s; most are actually converted KC-135s. EC-135s have long been used as airborne command posts for the various Air Force commands. The SAC operated one group of EC-135s, code-named Looking Glass, that were in the air continuously for three decades during the Cold War. If the SAC's control center on the ground in Omaha was destroyed, the high-level team aboard Looking Glass would have picked up the task of managing the command's global assets and counter-strike. To aid the long-duration missions, EC-135s retained the refueling capability that they had as KC-135s so that Looking Glass aircraft could refuel each other or other aircraft.

Over 250 KC-135s—more than any other American aircraft type—participated in Operation Desert Storm. They were organized into nine provisional air refueling wings and were based at every major base in the region that hosted Coalition aircraft. Meanwhile, much of the remaining Stratotanker fleet was active in supporting aircraft flying from the United States. They made it possible for combat and transport aircraft to fly to the Middle East nonstop.

Many Stratotankers have been rebuilt, strengthened, and re-engined with the F108-CF-100 (CFM56) turbofans. Designated as KC-135R and KC-135T, they are scheduled to remain as an integral part of U.S. Air Force operations until 2020 or beyond.

(Above) *This is the view of the KC-135 as seen by the pilot of the aircraft being refueled. The boom is operated and directed by a boom operator, or "boomer," who lies on his stomach and looks out the small window forward of the root of the boom.* (Left) *The U.S. Air Force's fleet of Boeing KC-135A Stratotankers entered service in 1956 and remained in production for a decade. The majority of the airframes still exist but have been upgraded, re-engined, and redesignated as KC-135E and KC-135R.*

THE C-5 GALAXY WAS born in that optimistic era of the 1960s, when aircraft were making enormous leaps in performance, flying higher and farther, and becoming faster and bigger. For 17 years, the Galaxy was the biggest airplane in the world until the Soviet Union's Antonov An-124 made its debut in 1985. The An-124's tail cone was 5 feet longer than the Galaxy's.

While the Galaxy was conceived in a time of optimism, it was born amid controversy over the cost and performance. Boeing, Douglas, and Lockheed each submitted proposals to the U.S. Air Force, and Lockheed's was selected. In a certain sense, however, Boeing was the ultimate winner, because that firm adapted its proposal to become the 747 "jumbo" jetliner and sold over 1,000 aircraft, while Lockheed manufactured only 131 Galaxies.

When the Galaxy made its first flight in 1968, it was the largest USAF aircraft to date. The C-5A had a wingspan of 222 feet 9 inches, a length of 247 feet 10 inches, and a gross weight of 769,000 pounds. It had a service ceiling of 35,750 feet and an unrefueled range of up to 3,000 miles loaded. It was powered by four General Electric TF39-GE-1C high-bypass turbofan engines, each delivering 43,000 pounds of thrust, giving it a top speed of 571 miles per hour.

In the meantime, Lockheed's original low-price estimates on the project proved costly for the company; delays and cost overruns resulted in Congress funding only 81 of the original 115 C-5As. These aircraft were delivered between December 1969 and May 1973, and they reached Military Airlift Command (MAC) squadrons in time for limited service during the Vietnam War. By the end of the 1970s, the C-5A had performed

A Lockheed C-5A Galaxy lifts off. For 17 years after its debut in 1968, the Galaxy was the biggest airplane in the world. They were first used by the Military Airlift Command (MAC) during the Vietnam War, and they've been used in every major U.S. Air Force overseas operation ever since.

Lockheed delivered 50 C-5B Galaxy transports to the U.S. Air Force between 1986 and 1989. These planes were the same size as the C-5A of two decades before, but they were capable of lifting heavier loads.

such feats as having parachute-dropped 80 tons of cargo in a single mission and carrying a Minuteman ICBM. The entire fleet had logged 400,000 hours and had hauled four billion tons of cargo.

The Galaxy's gargantuan cargo bay has room for two lanes of traffic, one going in each direction. This can accommodate 16 army trucks or over two dozen compact cars. Two 60-ton Abrams tanks could fit here comfortably—and frequently do. Six Apache attack helicopters could also be carried, as could 10 Pershing missiles. A large number of passengers can be accommodated along with the cargo. The aft passenger compartment alone can carry as many as a small jetliner. From the floor of the cargo bay to the flight deck is the equivalent of a three-story building. The flight deck itself is, in turn, like a small apartment. There is a galley and dining area more reminiscent of a Pullman car than a C-130, and there are enough bunks for an extra flight crew and a rest area for 15.

A decade after the Galaxy went into service, the Air Force identified a serious shortfall in its mandated ability to provide strategic airlift services for the U.S. Army and others in the event of an emergency. In 1982, with this in mind, Congress approved the Air Force's request to acquire another 50 Galaxies. Designated C-5B, the new aircraft are similar in appearance to the C-5As but have stronger wings, bigger engines, and improved avionics. The first C-5B, painted in its gray-green European One camouflage scheme, joined the MAC in 1986, and the 50th was delivered in 1989.

In 1990, during the Desert Shield deployment to Saudi Arabia, the entire C-5A/C-5B fleet was placed into service carrying men and materiel overseas. The Galaxies alone carried tonnage equivalent to the entire Berlin Airlift in just the first 21 days. The Galaxy fleet carried 47 percent of all air cargo delivered to the Gulf area during Desert Shield and the subsequent Desert Storm.

When the Military Airlift Command (MAC) was absorbed by the new Air Mobility Command (AMC), the C-5A/C-5B fleet was transferred as well. Since Desert Storm and the AMC transfer, Galaxies were used in the 1993 deployment to Somalia and in support of NATO and United States forces in Bosnia. Based on the attacks made on transport aircraft in Bosnia, some Galaxies were equipped with Tracor ALE-40 flare dispensers and the Honeywell AAR-47 missile warning system.

NO OTHER AIRCRAFT has ever had the distinction of having been the fastest operational aircraft in the world from the day it entered service until the day it was retired. The phrase "faster than a speeding bullet" was literally true for the Blackbird. Of all aircraft ever manufactured, only the experimental X-15—which didn't take off under its own power—was clocked at faster speeds. In 1976, an SR-71 set a world's absolute speed record of 2,193.167 miles per hour, but its actual top speed is much faster. Even after its temporary retirement in 1990, the Blackbird's top speed remained secret. Officially, it is rated at "Mach 3+" but the emphasis is always on the plus.

The SR-71 evolved from the Mach 3 YF-12 interceptor, which had itself evolved from a Central Intelligence Agency (CIA) spy aircraft. The mysterious Model A-12 reconnaissance airplane was developed in the early 1960s for clandestine missions behind the Iron Curtain where withering speed and extreme altitude were required for secrecy and safety. The A-12 first flew in 1962, a product of Lockheed's secret "Skunk Works" laboratory.

In the meantime, Skunk Works director Clarence "Kelly" Johnson suggested that the Air Force consider a Mach 3 interceptor version for its Air Defense Command (ADC). A new

As the last rays of the setting sun tint the tops of the afternoon thunderheads, a Lockheed SR-71 strategic reconnaissance aircraft skims the cloud tops, heading out on a mission. The SR-71 was capable of flying above any weather disturbance.

(Above left) *Seen here is a heavily guarded flock of Blackbirds on the tarmac of their cold war-era home port at Beale AFB, California. The aircraft in the middle is the SR-71B dual-control operational training aircraft.* (Above right) *An SR-71 pilot, known in the vernacular as a "sled driver," prepares for a mission at Beale AFB in California. The Blackbird crews wear space suits similar to those worn by Space Shuttle astronauts.* (Below) *The mandate given to Lockheed's Skunk Works in the late 1950s was to build an aircraft that was faster than any other aircraft before it. Little did the designers realize that the SR-71 would remain as the fastest operational aircraft in the world for half a century.*

generation of supersonic bombers was predicted to be taking shape in the Soviet Union, and an aircraft such as the YF-12, which could cruise comfortably at three times the speed of sound, was seen as desirable. The YF-12 was the fastest interceptor ever flown, before or since, although the Soviet MiG-25, which entered service a decade later, was close.

The SAC saw the A-12/YF-12 capability as desirable for a new "reconnaissance/strike" airplane, and they ordered such an aircraft under the designation RS-71. Its designation was later transposed to SR-71 for "strategic reconnaissance." The YF-12 went into mothballs because the Secretary of Defense decided that the Soviets didn't have any bombers fast enough to

pose any real challenge to it, and the A-12's role was subsumed by the SR-71.

From its design and engineering to the fuel that it burned in its engines, the Blackbird's family was like no other. The materials used in the construction of these airplanes were experimental at the time, and the overall design and the shape of their fuselage to provide most of the lift, was an engineering breakthrough. Fewer than 80 of the YF-12/SR-71 series were built.

The SR-71 had a wingspan of 55 feet 7 inches, a length of 107 feet 5 inches, and a gross weight of 172,000 pounds. It had a service ceiling of "over 80,000 feet," but that, like its "Mach 3+" speed, was a conservative underestimate. The two

The Lockheed SR-71 Blackbird reconnaissance aircraft has the mysterious look of a strange vehicle from the future, but it was designed in the early 1960s.

JT11D-20B continuous-bleed turbo-ramjet engines, which were designed specially for these aircraft by Pratt & Whitney, delivered 23,000 pounds of thrust, or 34,000 pounds with afterburner. The SR-71 was the only airplane in the world known to burn JP-7 fuel, which is so non-volatile that it cannot be lighted with a match. It takes a chemical reaction to get the engines started.

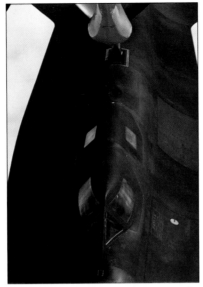

This Lockheed SR-71 Blackbird is refueled from a U.S. Air Force KC-135Q, which is the only refueling aircraft designed to carry the SR-71's unusual JP-7 fuel.

Internal bays were designed to contain the Blackbird's optical, digital, and electronic reconnaissance equipment. The two-man crew wear space suits similar to those worn by astronauts. The pilot and the reconnaissance systems operator manage the hardware secreted behind removable panels that are spread across the belly of the Blackbird.

The Blackbird was "high-nineties technology" that we were lucky to have in the sixties. Ironically, the Air Force announced in 1989 that the Blackbird would be retired, and it actually flew what was scheduled to be its last operational flight in 1990.

The SR-71's reconnaissance capabilities were missed during Operation Desert Storm and an effort was made to reactivate part of the fleet. This was ultimately successful, and several of the world's fastest operational airplanes went back into service in 1995.

CLARENCE "KELLY" JOHNSON

One of the greatest airplane designers of all time, Kelly Johnson grew up around Ishpeming, Michigan. He graduated from the University of Michigan in 1932 with a degree in aeronautical engineering. The following year, he began his career as a designer at the Lockheed Aircraft Company, working under the legendary chief engineer Hall Hibbard.

In 1943, when Lockheed was assigned the task of building what was to be America's first operational jet fighter, Johnson and a handpicked team were told to design and build a prototype in 180 days. This was the beginning of the Lockheed Advanced Development Projects (ADP) office, which continues to be known as "Skunk Works." Johnson's Skunk Works had the prototype XP-80 jet fighter ready for engine tests in 139 days, and two years later it was the standard fighter in the USAAF.

After World War II, Johnson's Skunk Works designed a series of high-performance aircraft, including the F-94 Starfire interceptor and the remarkable Mach 2 F-104 Starfighter. The latter earned him the Collier Trophy. The Skunk Works team also designed an extremely long-range, high-altitude "spy plane" used for flights over the Soviet Union—better known as the U-2.

After the U-2, the Skunk Works produced the amazing family of reconnaissance aircraft that included the A-12, YF-12, and SR-71. This series, especially the SR-71, was Johnson's masterpiece. The Collier Trophy that he received was a small measure of recognition for such a design feat.

In 1969, Johnson became a senior vice president at Lockheed, and he remained active until 1975 when he took partial retirement to care for his ailing wife.

BEFORE IT WAS OFFICIALLY revealed in November 1988, the Lockheed F-117 had been the subject of intense speculation for nearly a decade. Nobody knew what it looked like or even what it was called. In more ways than one, it was an invisible airplane. During the 1980 presidential campaign, it had been revealed that the U.S. Air Force was working on a super-secret technology called "stealth" that would absorb or deflect radar so as to render an aircraft invisible.

The F-117 and stealth technology were developed at Lockheed's Advanced Developments Projects office, known informally as the Skunk Works, and presided over by the late Ben Rich. The Skunk Works had been responsible for aircraft ranging from the P-80 Shooting Star to the U-2 "spy plane" to the SR-71 Blackbird. Kelly Johnson, who with men such as Ben Rich and others, had started working on stealth technology in the 1970s. Rich had proven the concept with the top secret Have Blue demonstrator aircraft.

It was discovered that a faceted fuselage would provide the lowest possible radar cross-section, and by building an aircraft with a surface containing no right angles and was composed entirely of triangular and trapezoidal surfaces, its radar "signature" could be virtually eliminated. Beyond this, radar could be absorbed by coating the aircraft's surface with a fibrous boron-polymer resin material called fibaloy.

The first of 59 F-117 aircraft delivered to the U.S. Air Force made its first flight in June 1981, and the first F-117 unit, the TAC's 37th Tactical Fighter Wing, based in the highly secret Nellis AFB range near Tonopah, Nevada, became operational in 1983. The F-117 is painted flat black to absorb both light and radar. It has a wingspan of 43 feet 4 inches, a length of 65 feet 11 inches, and a gross weight of 52,500 pounds. It is powered by two non-afterburning General Electric F404-GE-F1D2 turbofan engines delivering 10,800 pounds of thrust and giving it a top speed of 645 miles per hour. The engine exhausts are narrow slots in which hot exhaust gasses are mixed with cool air to reduce the aircraft's thermal signature in the same way that stealth technology reduces its radar signature.

The Nighthawk is powered by two nonafterburning General Electric F404-GE-F1D2 turbofan engines. The exhausts are actually narrow slots in which hot exhaust gasses are mixed with cool air to reduce the aircraft's thermal signature.

(Above) *A pair of Lockheed F-117 Nighthawks fly during a low-level mission over the vast U.S. Air Force test range in southern Nevada that includes the mysterious Area 51. All the F-117s were originally assigned to the 37th Tactical Fighter Wing, based near Tonopah, Nevada.* (Left) *An F-117 touches down at dawn after a night flight. Nighttime training operations are essential in order to maximize its stealth characteristics. The Nighthawk usually flies its strike missions in the dark.*

(Above) *A group of Nighthawks depart at sundown. During Operation Desert Storm, F-117s flew 1,270 missions without ever being tracked on enemy radar. The Iraqis never found or hit an F-117.*
(Right) *The smooth lines of the Lockheed F-117 are undisturbed by the weapons that hang from other tactical aircraft. All the Nighthawk's ordnance are carried internally.*

The F-117's weapons—all carried internally to avoid providing a radar return—include GBU-10 and GBU-24 Paveway laser-guided bombs, AGM-65 Maverick air-to-ground missiles, AGM-88 HARM antiradar missiles, or AIM-9 Sidewinder air-to-air missiles. Its Forward-Looking Infrared (FLIR) nighttime viewing system has been augmented with Downward-Looking Infrared (DLIR) in a steerable turret with a boresight laser designator and autotracker to insure precise targeting. The F-117's unrefueled combat radius with 5,000 pounds of weapons is 656 miles.

Composed entirely of triangles and trapezoids, the surface of the F-117 has no right angles and radar cannot detect it. Radar is also absorbed by the plane's coating of fibrous boron-polymer resin material called fibaloy.

The 37th Tactical Fighter Wing flew their F-117s in complete secrecy—and only at night—for five years, earning the plane the nickname "Nighthawk" (though for its color, the F-117 is often known simply as "the Black Jet"). It was difficult for new pilots to learn to fly at night and in turn to fly *only* at night. The nighttime operations took their toll, with three crashes ocurring during the 1980s. Finally, in 1988, the aircraft's existence was officially revealed and daytime missions became possible.

The Nighthawk's first combat action came in December 1989 during Operation Just Cause, when two F-117s flew non-stop—with aerial refueling—from the United States to Panama to bomb a Panamanian Defense Force base. When one of the bombs missed the target due to incorrect targeting data, it was suggested that the long-secret stealth aircraft was a paper tiger.

In 1990, after the Iraqi invasion of Kuwait prompted the Desert Shield buildup in preparation for the liberation of Kuwait, 40 F-117s were sent to Khamis Mushait Air Base in Saudi Arabia. It was in the hangars on this base that a strange and interesting demonstration of stealth technology occurred. Bats that lived in the hangers, when flying out at night, would hit the F-117s' tailplanes. The bats' sonar, sensitive enough to locate insects in flight, couldn't "see" the Nighthawks.

When Operation Desert Storm started on January 17, 1991, the F-117s were the first manned aircraft to fly into Baghdad's heavily defended air space. Their mission was to attack and destroy extremely high-priority command and control centers, fortified bunkers, and bridges, targeting highly sensitive areas where absolute precision was a must. Although the Iraqis put up a withering barrage of anti-aircraft fire, they never found or hit an F-117.

In 1992, after the TAC was absorbed into the new Air Combat Command, the F-117s were transferred to the 49th Fighter Wing and moved to Holloman AFB adjacent to the White Sands Missile Range in New Mexico.

Since Desert Storm, the F-117 has continued to be upgraded. For example, a Pilot-Activated Automatic Recovery System that will allow a pilot to recover a tumbling aircraft has been retrofitted. Proposals to build additional F-117s are occasionally discussed.

KNOWN SIMPLY as "the stealth bomber" for years before it was officially unveiled in 1988, the B-2 is one of the most remarkable aircraft ever conceived. In the 1980s, the project was known formally as the Advanced Technology Bomber (ATB), but it was well known that the "advanced technology" was called "stealth." For eight years after the existence of the ATB was first leaked in the press, no details—not even its shape—had ever been officially announced, but its price tag was correctly rumored to be such that it was the most expensive airplane in history.

A capable "bomb truck" for all its futuristic styling, the Northrop B-2 can carry a variety of air-to-ground munitions including 20 B61 nuclear bombs, 16 B63 nuclear bombs or conventional gravity bombs, and precision-guided "smart" bombs.

The cornerstone of the aircraft's design is a once-mysterious technology called "stealth," which could render it invisible to radar. To create an airplane that was invisible to radar, a design team would first have to examine the nature of radar. Radar does not perceive size, only contour, shape, and surfaces. A glossy, light-colored surface reflects light and also reflects radar back to its receiver, so designers would paint the airplane with a dark, flat, radar-absorbing paint.

Until the 1970s, when advances in nonmetallic structural materials made new techniques possible, it wasn't possible to build such an aircraft. Conversely, if not for advances in radar and radar-guided antiaircraft missile technology during the same period, it would not have been necessary.

Metallic surfaces also reflect radar, so the use of a non-metallic plastic material like Kevlar would go a long way toward reducing radar detectability. Jet engines, especially when they are hanging under a wing on pylons are very easy for radar to spot, so the designers would certainly conceal them entirely within the wing or fuselage. Even the difference between the way the engine turbine blades were concealed within the Rockwell B-1B, which was introduced in 1986, reduced its radar visibility by up to 90 percent when compared to the B-1A, which dated back to 1974.

A large portion of an airplane's radar signature is in its fuselage. However, an airplane doesn't need a fuselage to fly, it only needs a wing, so a wing can be made thicker (radar doesn't discern size, only contour), and the crew, the engines, and the weapons can be put inside the wing. The result is a "flying wing." Experiments conducted by John Northrop in the 1940s proved the validity of the flying wing design. It was out of these that Northrop developed the U.S. Air Force's flying wing strategic bombers—the YB-35 and YB-49—in the late 1940s and early 1950s. These great airplanes, which had a wingspan roughly the same as the B-2, were never ordered into production because of control problems, but by early 1983, control was much easier to achieve with the "fly-by-wire" controls than it had been with the hydraulics in the 1940s. When it was announced in 1983 that Northrop was building the stealthy Advanced Technology Bomber, many people began to suspect that it too would be a flying wing.

(Above) *The Northrop B-2 Spirit is the most technologically advanced — and expensive — bomber ever built. It has the potential to slip through enemy defenses unnoticed and untouched. (Left) The Northrop B-2 is a "flying wing" with a design that dates back to the experimental aircraft built by Jack Northrop in the 1940s. The B-2 recalls Northrop's giant flying wing strategic bombers, which were the YB-35 and YB-49.*

Hard edges and sharp angles are always very radar visible, so every effort was made to smooth out corners and edges. Even the B-1A had ten percent the cross section of the B-52 because it had the engines partially blended into the fuselage and there was a smoother contour between the fuselage and wings. The confluence of wing and fuselage and the multitude of sharp and even right angles in an airplane's tail would present a final and unique challenge to a stealth designer, yet one which easily could be solved just by getting rid of it. Because of fly-by-wire control, the B-2 needs no tail. Moving surfaces in the trailing edge of the wing function as aileron, elevator, and rudder.

In 1987, it was announced that the Air Force would be buying 132 ATBs, which would be built at the highly secure factory complex at Palmdale in the California high desert. The number was slashed to 75 before the first flight and finally to a mere 21, enough for two squadrons and a few test aircraft.

The first flight of a B-2 took place on July 17, 1989, and the second aircraft made its debut in 1990 as the slow production process geared up to build only 21 of the most advanced technology aircraft in production.

The Spirit has a wingspan of 172 feet, a length of 69 feet, and a gross weight of 376,000 pounds. It has a service ceiling of

(Above) *The prototype B-2 touches down on the runway at Edwards AFB in the California high desert after its July 1989 first flight. The first operational B-2 aircraft was delivered to Whiteman AFB in Missouri four years later. (Right) A trio of B-2s are shown on the factory floor at Air Force Plant 42 at Palmdale, California. The factory was designed and built with a production run of 132 aircraft in mind. However, by the time of the delivery of the first production aircraft, the total number procured was reduced to a mere 21.*

A Northrop B-2 lifts off on a training mission. These big aircraft are equipped with the Hughes APQ-181 multimode, phased-array radar and a Global Positioning System (GPS)-aided targeting system.

50,000 feet and an unrefueled range exceeding 11,000 miles. It is powered by four General Electric F118-GE-100 turbofan engines, each delivering over 19,000 pounds of thrust. The engines are concealed by scalloped overwing intake ducts and have shielded overwing, trailing edge nozzles.

The B-2 can carry a variety of air-to-ground munitions including 20 B61 nuclear bombs, 16 B63 nuclear bombs or conventional gravity bombs, and precision-guided "smart" bombs. The B-2's bomb bays can be equipped with either racks or rotary launchers, and in addition to bombs, it can carry AGM-69 SRAM or AGM-131 SRAM II Short Range Attack Missiles. Under the United States Single Integrated Operational Plan (SIOP), the B-2 would carry 25,000 pounds of nuclear weapons, although it has a total payload capacity of 40,000 pounds.

The B-2 is equipped with an Inertial Navigation System (INS) as well as a Hughes APQ-181 multimode, phased array radar system and a Global Positioning System (GPS)-aided targeting system for precision bombing.

Six B-2s were delivered for avionics and operational testing between 1989 and 1993, and the first operational B-2 was delivered to the 509th Bomb Wing at Whiteman Air Force Base in Missouri in December 1993. The 509th's first B-2 squadron, the 393rd Bomb Squadron, became fully operational in 1997, and a second B-2 squadron, the 715th Bomb Squadron, was formed.

The Spirit is designed officially to provide the U.S. Air Force Air Combat Command with a highly survivable supplement to its B-1 and B-52 fleet, although the probability that it will replace that fleet is slim.

THE JET AGE INTO SPACE

THE HALF CENTURY that followed World War II, from 1945 to 1997, contained many monumental years for aviation. The first two decades after the war were years of dramatic advances in aircraft performance. In 1945, the fastest fighter aircraft had top speeds of less than 500 miles per hour. By 1947, the Bell X-1 had broken the sound barrier and had rocketed to almost 900 miles per hour. Only three years later, the speed record was 1,241 miles per hour, and there were supersonic fighters in service. And by the tenth anniversary of supersonic flight, the speed record was 2,094 miles per hour, and supersonic fighters were standard.

In 1960, technology had advanced to the point of developing a rocket plane such as the X-15 that set new records almost at will. With the X-15, the absolute speed record hit 2,196 miles per hour in 1960; 4,093 miles per hour in 1961; 4,104 miles per hour in

(Above) *The Distinguished Service Medal is awarded by the National Aeronautics & Space Administration to astronauts with distinguished records of service.* (Opposite) *Terry Wofford's painting* Spirit of Discovery *is a dramatic image of the Space Shuttle Orbiter* Discovery *ready for launch from the Pad 39 complex at Kennedy Space Center.*

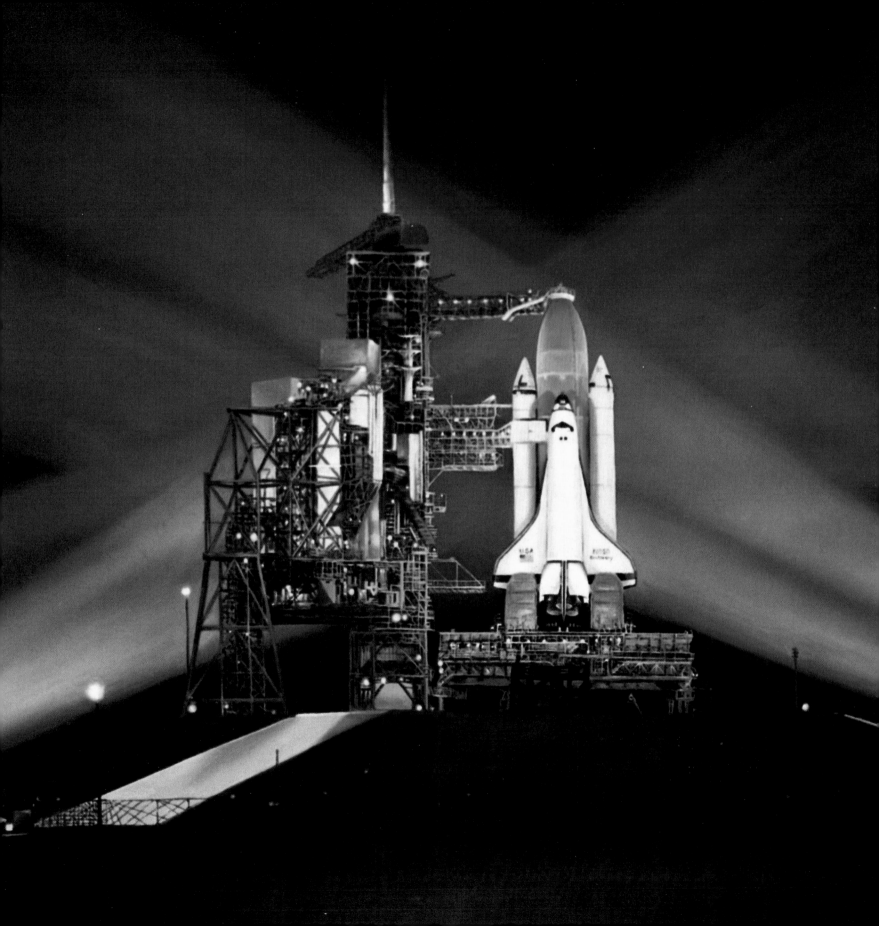

1962; 4,250 miles per hour in 1966, and 4,534 miles per hour in 1967.

What the X-15 did for the record books, the new generation of jetliners developed in the late 1950s did for the average air traveler. Planes like the Boeing 707, the Douglas DC-8, and the Convair 880 not only took twice as many passengers to their destinations twice as fast as the earlier generation of piston-engined, propeller-driven airliners, or propliners, but they were also quieter. Because they could fly higher—above the weather—they also gave the passengers a smoother ride.

With the introduction of a new class of "jumbo jets" in the 1970s, commercial aviation expanded even more. The Boeing 747, McDonnell Douglas DC-10, and Lockheed L-1011 carried double or more the passenger load of the first generation jetliners. While this fact meant little to the average passenger, people appreciated the fact that the bigger planes also flew farther still. The first jetliners had roughly dou-ble the range of the propliners, but the jumbo jetliners had roughly double the range of the earlier jets.

The advances in commercial flying were also reflected by the fast and efficient short-range jetliners such as the Boeing 727, 737, and 757 and the McDonnell Douglas DC-9, MD-80, and MD-90. From the 1970s through the 1990s and beyond, airlines bought thousands of these aircraft and others like them. Several airlines offered jetliner flights every hour on routes such as New York to Washington, Chicago to Dallas/Fort Worth, London to Amsterdam, or San Francisco to Los Angeles. By the mid-1970s, the British Aerospace/Aérospatiale Concorde made it possible for people to fly between Europe and North America in less than four hours.

In the field of general aviation, the postwar years were a boom. Tens of thousands of Americans took up flying as companies such as Beechcraft and Cessna created the airplanes that made it possible. Over the coming decade, tens of thousands of light planes would be sold around the world, including well over 10,000 Beechcraft Bonanzas and more than 30,000 Cessna 172s.

The NASA "worm" insignia was introduced in the post-Apollo mid-1970s. It was phased out in 1994 in favor of a return to the original blue circular insignia dating back to 1958.

As for space, that was the dream of the 1950s, the reality of the 1960s, and the routine of subsequent decades. In the 1950s, people thought above and beyond "the sky's the limit." Just as speed records tripled in less than two decades, so did altitude records. At the end of the 1940s, the world altitude record—held by the X-1—was 71,900 feet; at the end of the 1950s, the limit was pushed to 125,907 feet. During the 1960s, however, spaceflight had been achieved, and people had flown above and beyond the sky.

By the 1960s, the X-15 pushed the altitude record for winged craft taking off in level flight to 354,200 feet, and nine Apollo spacecraft flew to the moon. In the 1980s, the American Space Shuttle was in service, and space travel matured. This winged space vehicle accomplished two things: It made spaceflight routine, and it put wings into space. For the first time, there were winged vehicles touching down on runways, returning from outer space. The Space Shuttle put the "flight" into spaceflight.

Once upon a time—in the 1903 to 1910 era—airplanes existed simply to demonstrate that flight was viable. In the 1920s, flight became practical. It was routinely possible for a person in one place to climb aboard an aircraft as a passenger and fly to another place. In the 1960s, spacecraft existed to demonstrate that spaceflight was imaginable. Since the 1990s, thanks to this winged spacecraft, it is routinely possible for a person in one place—on earth—to climb aboard an aircraft as a passenger and fly to another place—in space.

Douglas DC-6

EVEN BEFORE THE DC-3 made its maiden flight in 1935, Douglas was thinking bigger, and bigger meant a four-engine airliner designated DC-4 that had twice the passenger capacity and twice the range of the DC-3. Sharing the same thought processes with Douglas were a number of airlines anxious to go the next step. The airlines were interested in buying and flying an airliner that routinely flew 2,500 miles without a refueling stop; this meant routine, if

Designed for the transatlantic route, the DC-7C was potentially the ultimate Douglas propliner, but its troublesome R-3350 engines prevented it from being a great propliner.

ney R-2000 Twin Wasp engines that gave it a cruising speed of 227 miles per hour. Its range was 2,500 miles.

The DC-4s were nearing completion when the United States entered World War II. While the war years were good for aviation in general because of the government-sponsored leaps in technology, they arrested the development of commercial aviation. Commercial DC-4s were supposed to be flying the airways in 1942, but the U.S. Army Air

not nonstop, flights across the once-formidable North Atlantic. Among the airlines interested in the DC-4 were American, Eastern, Pan American, TWA, and United.

Meanwhile, Lockheed was also developing a triple-tailed, four-engine airliner called the Constellation. Both Pan American and TWA switched to the Constellation, but the other three airline companies placed orders for a total of 50 production models of the DC-4. The Constellation carried varying numbers of passengers, from 44 to 86, depending on its internal arrangement, and provided more than double the capacity of the DC-3. It had a wingspan of 117 feet 6 inches and a length of 93 feet 10 inches. It weighed 73,000 pounds fully loaded and fueled and had a service ceiling of 22,300 feet. It was powered by four 1,450-horsepower, air-cooled, 14-cylinder Pratt & Whit-

Force (USAAF) recognized their value as military transports and commandeered all 50 off the assembly line to turn them into C-54s. Douglas didn't mind, however, when the USAAF ordered another 1,100 C-54s.

When the war ended in 1945, Douglas attempted to go back to where things had left off in 1941. Deliveries began on over 70 commercial DC-4s, but it was time to start thinking of a major improvement on the design—not as radical a jump as from the DC-3 but a major step forward.

The initial catalyst for the DC-6 was actually a wartime request from the USAAF for an enlarged C-54 to be produced under the designation C-118. By the time that the XC-112 prototype was completed in 1946 (by enlarging a C-54 airframe), the war was over, so there were no immediate production orders.

(Above) *Douglas produced the DC-6 airframe as the "Liftmaster" military transport in the late 1940s and early 1950s under the designation C-118 for the U.S. Air Force and R6D for the U.S. Navy. The DC-6 prototype was a modified DC-4 ordered by the Air Force as XC-112.* (Left) *The Douglas DC-6B, seen here in the markings of Northwest Airlines, was one of the most successful of the Douglas propliners. The DC-6B made its debut in February 1951.*

The successful Douglas DC-6 transports were equipped with four powerful and reliable Pratt & Whitney R-2800 radial engines. The later model DC-7 had the more powerful but less reliable Wright R-3350s.

However, the experience of producing the prototype gave Douglas a head start on the DC-6, and by March, the first commercial DC-6s were in the hands of American Airlines and United Air Lines.

At first glance, the DC-6 was similar in appearance to the DC-4, but it was larger and faster, and it had a longer range. The DC-6 carried more passengers than the DC-4. The DC-6 also epitomized postwar engineering. Unlike the DC-4, it had a pressurized cabin, so it had the ability to fly above the weather, giving passengers a smooth and comfortable ride. Eventually, Douglas built 600 commercial DC-6s, more than any other DC propliner except the DC-3.

The standard production model was the DC-6B, which carried varying numbers of passengers, from 50 to 100, depending on its internal arrangement. It had a wingspan of 117 feet

6 inches (the same as the DC-4) and a length of 105 feet 7 inches. It weighed 107,000 pounds fully loaded and fueled and had a service ceiling of 25,000 feet. It was powered by four 2,400-horsepower, air-cooled, 18-cylinder Pratt & Whitney R-2800-CB16 Double Wasp engines that gave it a cruising speed of 315 miles per hour. Its range was 3,005 miles, which was sufficient for flying coast-to-coast without fueling stops.

During the Korean War, the military took a second look at the DC-6 because of the need for long-range transports. After an all-DC-6 airframe was delivered as the YC-118 (in contrast to the XC-112, which was a converted DC-4), the U.S. Air Force bought 101 under the designation C-118, and the U.S. Navy bought 65 as R5Ds.

When the Korean War ended, the United States was in the midst of the greatest burst of prosperity in history. Air travel became part of everyday life. People who a generation before would have taken the train now took the plane without a second thought. A vacation in Hawaii or a trip to Europe, which were until recently a once-in-a-lifetime event for a handful of people, had become plausible for anyone in a rapidly expanding middle class. With this in mind, the airlines were clamoring for newer and bigger airliners.

The early 1950s were a critical time in the evolution of airliners. The Douglas DC-6 and the Lockheed Constellation were selling extremely well, and they were pleasing their customers. Boeing's Stratocruiser wasn't doing terribly well nor were most of the European liners of the era. In England, de Havilland took a chance on the Comet, the world's first jetliner. A series of spectacular Comet crashes convinced much of the world that jetliners weren't safe. Boeing wasn't convinced and started working on a jetliner. Douglas and Lockheed stuck with that at which they were successful. In 1953 and 1954, Douglas and Lockheed each brought out a much improved version of their most successful products: the Douglas DC-7 and the Lockheed Super Constellation.

The DC-7 first flew in May 1953, and the program culminated with the DC-7C, which was introduced in 1955 and nicknamed "Seven Seas," more for its 4,605-mile global range than for the pun value of the name. The DC-7C carried varying numbers of passengers, from 60 to 105, depending on its internal arrangement. It had a wingspan of 127 feet 6 inches and a length

Seen here in the Douglas corporate livery, this DC-6A carries the nickname "Liftmaster." This was the official name of the C-118 military version, but the name never caught on among civilian customers.

of 112 feet 3 inches. It weighed 143,000 pounds fully loaded and fueled and had a service ceiling of 21,700 feet.

The DC-7C was powered by four 3,400-horsepower, air-cooled, 18-cylinder Wright R-3350-18EA Turbo-compound engines that gave it a cruising speed of 355 miles per hour. It was the engines that illustrated the shortcomings of the Seven Seas. They were far more complex and far less reliable than earlier piston engines—and they were piston engines. Boeing was right about jetliners. Had Douglas invested its technical and financial resources on a jetliner, instead of sinking itself into the DC-7, it would not have had to play catch-up when Boeing brought out the 707—and aviation history might have been dramatically altered.

OFTEN OVERLOOKED in the history books in favor of larger, faster, and more glamorous airplanes are the light personal planes belonging to the genre generally known as general aviation. Of these, a handful stand out as classics, and high on this short list is the Beechcraft Bonanza.

In 1932, Walter Beech and his wife, Olive Ann Beech, founded Beech Aircraft Company (later known as Beechcraft), and his popular Staggerwing enclosed-cabin biplane was used in a flight around the world. In 1938, Beechcraft introduced the Beech Model 18, a small, eight-passenger airliner designed for short "feeder" airlines. Mildly successful in the commercial market, it was used extensively by the USAAF under the designations AT-7 and C-45 during World War II, and it remained in production as an executive aircraft until 1957.

As World War II came to a close, there was a lot of talk in the aviation industry about "private planes for everyone," with an airplane in almost every garage. There were over 300,000 licensed pilots in the United States, with over half of the pilots being former military pilots with commercial ratings. Beechcraft was planning ahead and was ready with the distinctive, low-winged, V-tailed Model 35 Bonanza. Initially powered

In service for decades, the reliable Beechcraft Bonanza had a comfortable interior and airliner-style soundproofing. It was one of the most successful personal aircraft in the history of flight.

by a 165-horsepower Continental in-line engine, it had tricycle landing gear and provided all the equipment necessary for a cross-country flight or night flying.

The Bonanza featured a comfortable interior that was padded with deep all-wool fabric and provided ample room for four people. It was one of the first private planes to offer airliner-style soundproofing. It first flew in December 1945 and went into production in 1947 with a price tag of about $7,000. Sales of the Bonanza were a bonanza for Beechcraft. The company sold 1,500 Model 35s, followed by 710 Model A35s, which were introduced in 1949.

By 1950, when the B35 Bonanza was introduced, Bonanzas accounted for 53 percent of the general aviation market in the United States. Beechcraft went on to produce a new model Bonanza every year through 1966—just as automobile companies released new model cars. Each model represented a subtle, or occasionally major, change. With the E35 Bonanza in 1954, Beechcraft upgraded to the 225-horsepower Continental E-225-8 engine.

The 5,000th Bonanza, an H35, was delivered in March 1957. The V35 series was introduced in 1965. The Bonanza V35B had a wingspan of 33 feet 6 inches and a length of 26 feet

An impressive array of timeless greats are shown on the field at Wichita. In the foreground are Beechcraft V35 Bonanzas, while the back row showcases the great Beech Model 18, a small, eight-person airliner that also served as a military aircraft during World War II.

5 inches. It weighed 3,400 pounds fully loaded and fueled. It was powered by a 285-horsepower, liquid-cooled, six-cylinder Continental IO-520-BA engine that gave it a top speed of 200 miles per hour. It had a range of just over 1,000 miles.

Two straight-tailed Bonanzas adapted from the V35B were introduced in 1968 and 1971, respectively. These were the six-seat 36 Bonanza and the four-seat F33 Bonanza, which also had roots in the Beechcraft Model 33 Debonair of the 1950s.

The Model 36 Bonanza had the same dimensions and gross weight as the V35B. It was powered by the same 285-horse-

power, liquid-cooled, six-cylinder Continental IO-520-BA engine as its V-tailed sister. Beechcraft 36 Bonanzas were acquired by the U.S. Air Force in 1971 under the designation QU-22 for the Pave Eagle data-gathering program.

The completion of the 10,000th V-tailed Beechcraft Bonanza, a V35B, took place in February 1977, and the 2,000th straight-tailed Bonanza 36 was delivered in 1981. The V-tailed Bonanza is no longer in production, but the others strongly continued in production into the 1990s, with their numbers having topped 5,000 each.

THE REALM OF SUPER-sonic speed was once regarded by pilots as a strange and dangerous place. It was assumed that any aircraft that reached the speed of sound (about 760 miles per hour at sea level or 700 miles per hour at 45,000 feet, though it varies with temperature and altitude) or passed the elusive "sound barrier" would be torn apart by the shock wave.

Even before World War II, high-speed aircraft were experiencing the compressibility phenomena of high subsonic flight, so American and German engineers began to study the feasibility of designing a supersonic aircraft. The war interrupted German studies, but in the United States a project was undertaken jointly by the USAAF and the National Advisory Committee for Aeronautics (NACA, the predecessor to NASA). The U.S. Navy conducted its own parallel project.

The NACA/USAAF project took place at Wright Field in Ohio and was directed by Dr. Theodore von Kármán, with Dr. Ezra Kotcher as the key engineer. NACA worked out the design studies, and then a manufacturer was sought to actually build the aircraft. Most of the major planemakers were heavily committed to war work, so a smaller firm, Bell Aircraft Company, was selected. Development began at the end of 1944 to produce what was to be the world's first supersonic vehicle. Originally designated as XS-1 (Experimental, Supersonic, first), the Army Air Forces contracted three of these aircraft in Febru-

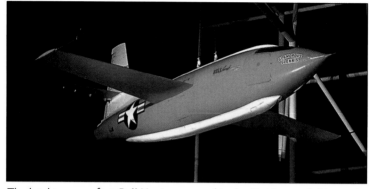

The bright orange first Bell X-1 is preserved in the Smithsonian's National Air and Space Museum in Washington, D.C. Chuck Yeager named it Glamorous Glennis *after his wife. The P-51s he flew during World War II were also named* Glamorous Glennis.

ary 1945. The XS-1 was later named the X-1.

The X-1 had a wingspan of 28 feet, a length of 30 feet 11 inches, and a gross weight of up to 14,751 pounds. It was powered by a four-chamber Reaction Motors XLR-11-RM-3 (Model 6062/6063) or XLR-11-RM-5 (Model 6000C4) rocket engine, delivering 1,500 pounds of thrust from each chamber and giving it a duration at top power of five minutes.

The X-1 was shaped like a bullet because the best aerodynamic data on objects moving at supersonic speeds was the data on bullets. Because of the fuel required for takeoff and the climb to altitude, the X-1 was carried aloft by a larger airplane and air launched.

The first of three X-1 aircraft was completed at the end of 1945, and it made its first flight in January 1946, having been carried aloft from Pinecastle Army Air Field near Orlando, Florida, by a B-29 "mother ship." Bell test pilot Jack Woolams made ten unpowered, subsonic glide flights in the X-1 before the project was moved to Muroc Army Air Field (later Edwards Air Force Base) in the California high desert.

In December 1946, after four glide tests in the second X-1, Bell test pilot Chalmers Goodlin made the first powered flight of the X-1 program, flying at Mach .75 (550 miles per hour), or three quarters of the speed of sound. Goodlin made a number of powered test flights through the winter, mainly designed to study

(Above) The first aircraft to officially break the sound barrier, the
Bell X-1 was painted bright orange
for high visibility so that observers
could track it in flight and search
and rescue teams could easily
locate it if it crashed in the desert.
(Left) The Bell X-1A is seen here
at Edwards AFB, shortly after
Chuck Yeager used it to set a
speed record of 1,650 miles per
hour in the aircraft's 11th flight on
December 12, 1953.

the "transonic" environment near the sound barrier prior to an attempt to actually "break" the barrier.

In June 1947, USAAF (U.S. Air Force after September 1947) test pilot Captain Charles "Chuck" Yeager took over from Goodlin. On October 14, 1947, after 12 subsonic X-1 flights, Yeager flew through the sound barrier and into aviation history. He achieved Mach 1.06 at 45,000 feet in the 50th flight of the X-1 program.

The X-1 flights continued over the coming weeks and months, designed to continue to explore transonic and supersonic stability and flight characteristics in aircraft. Yeager made the X-1's second supersonic flight on November 6, 1947, achieving a top speed of Mach 1.35, which was about 900 miles per hour at an altitude of 48,600 feet. It was also the second fastest speed ever timed in the X-1. Yeager achieved the fastest speed in the 77th flight of the X-1 program on March 26, 1948. He managed to hit a top speed of Mach 1.45, or 957 miles per hour at an altitude of 50,000 feet.

The highest altitude achieved by the X-1 was 71,902 feet— a world's absolute altitude record—accomplished by Major Frank Everest on August 8, 1949, in the 124th program flight. This made the X-1 both the fastest and highest flying aircraft in

JACQUELINE "JACKIE" COCHRAN

Jackie Cochran earned her pilot's license in 1932, and from that moment on, she became known as a woman of many "firsts" in aviation. In 1933, she became the first woman to fly in the Bendix Trophy Race. In 1938, she won the Bendix Trophy, flying 2,042 miles in 8 hours 10 minutes 31 seconds, beating out a field of men.

During World War II, there was a shortage of qualified male pilots to serve in the USAAF, so she organized the Women's Airforce Service Pilots (WASP) to fly noncombat missions. For her work in organizing the WASPs, Cochran was awarded the Distinguished Service Medal and later was given a lieutenant colonel's commission in the Air Force Reserve. In 1950, she received the Harmon Trophy as the Aviatrix of the Decade.

By 1953, Cochran was back in the cockpit for another record. After several weeks of coaching from Chuck Yeager, she became the first woman to pilot an aircraft faster than the speed of sound, breaking the sound barrier in an F-86E and hitting 652.5 miles per hour.

By 1961, she held over 200 aviation records—more than any person alive. In 1963, and again in 1964, she beat her own women's speed record, setting a Mach 2 speed record of 1,429.2 miles per hour in a Lockheed F-104G.

When NASA announced its corps of male astronauts for what seemed, in 1958, to be a promising future flying spacecraft, Cochran lobbied for a corps of women astronauts. The space agency insisted that women didn't have the stamina. Despite all of Cochran's efforts, NASA won that round.

Sadly, Cochran died two years before the first American woman—Sally Ride—flew in space in 1983. During the next two decades, dozens of American women flew in space, and in 1996, a woman named Shannon Lucid set the record for longest duration of *any* American in space. Ironically, Shannon Lucid was about the same age Jackie Cochran had been when she was told that women didn't have the stamina for spaceflight.

the world. Previously in 1946, Everest had reached 69,000 feet, but the aircraft suffered a severe loss of cabin pressure. However, thanks to his partial pressure suit, Everest survived.

The X-1 test program ended on October 23, 1951, after 157 flights, most of them flown under power and about a third above Mach 1. The first two X-1 aircraft were used equally during the test program. The third one, delivered in the summer of 1951, was destroyed after making one glide flight.

The X-1 proved that human flight above Mach 1 was possible, and it paved the way for a whole generation of supersonic aircraft. Its direct successor was the Bell X-1A/X-1B program, which was developed under the auspices of NACA and the U.S. Air Force to explore the environment above Mach 2 and up to 90,000 feet.

The Bell X-1A made its first flight on February 21, 1953, piloted by Jean Ziegler, and Chuck Yeager exceeded Mach 2 for the first time in the aircraft on December 12, 1953. His speed of Mach 2.44 (1,650 miles per hour) would not be exceeded in future program flights, and there would be only one more flight to exceed Mach 2. The program ended in January 1958 after 54 flights and a peak altitude of 90,440 feet.

The last X-1-derived test project involved the X-1E, which was actually the second X-1 aircraft heavily modified. The X-1E was flown by Joe Walker on 26 test flights between December 1955 and November 1958. During that time, the plane reached a top speed of Mach 2.1 and an altitude of 73,000 feet, both well below that achieved by the X-1A. However the X-1E did prove that high supersonic flight could be achieved with a thin airfoil. The Reaction Motors engine, with its low-pressure turbopump, was also a step forward that permitted development of even more reliable research aircraft in the 1960s.

CHARLES "CHUCK" ELWOOD YEAGER

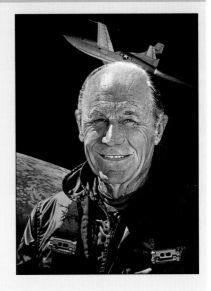

The archetype of the jaunty, self-confident air-man, Chuck Yeager was a World War II fighter pilot turned test pilot who made history as the first person to break the sound barrier. Yeager started his aviation career in 1941 as a mechanic in the USAAF and earned his wings two years later. During World War II, he went overseas to the European Theater and flew with the 8th Air Force. He named his P-51D Mustang *Glamorous Glennis* for his wife. In combat, Yeager claimed ten and a half aerial victories against Germany's Luftwaffe, including five in a single day!

After World War II, Yeager was assigned as a test pilot at Muroc Army Air Field in California's high desert. In June 1947, he was assigned to the program using the Bell XS-1 rocket plane to break the sound barrier for the first time. On October 14, 1947, after 12 subsonic XS-1 flights, Yeager achieved Mach 1.06 at 45,000 feet to become the first person to travel faster than the speed of sound.

Yeager went on to make nearly 30 flights in the XS-1, many of them at supersonic speeds. He was then assigned to the X-1A program, where he became the first person to fly at Mach 2 (twice the speed of sound) in a December 12, 1953, flight. For his record-setting flights, Yeager was awarded the Collier, Harmon, and MacKay trophies.

After serving as a test pilot for seven years, Yeager continued his aviation career, retiring as a brigadier general in 1975. He published his autobiography, *Yeager*, in 1985.

URING THE LATE 1950S, William Powell Lear, Sr., started working on the idea of a personal jet aircraft for business travelers that would equal the performance of commercial jetliners. He was impressed with the Swiss fighter known as the P-16 and set up a team of engineers in Switzerland to design what later became the Learjet 23 aircraft, the first in a series of highly successful business jets. Lear established his company in Wichita, Kansas, in 1962, and the Learjet 23 first flew on October 7, 1963—nine months to the day after work commenced in the Wichita plant.

In 1966, the Learjet 23 was succeeded by the similar but improved Learjet 24, which firmly established the Learjet tradition. It had a wingspan of 35 feet 7 inches and was 43 feet 3 inches long. It had a gross weight of 13,500 pounds and carried six passengers at a cruising speed of 534 miles per hour. It was powered by two General Electric CJ610-6 turbojets, each delivering 2,950 pounds of thrust. In 1967, Lear sold the company to Gates Rubber Company in Denver, and the name was changed to Gates Learjet Corporation. Since 1990 the company has been owned by Bombardier Inc. of Montreal, Canada, and operates under the name of Learjet Inc.

By that time, the Learjet "family" included the successful Learjet 31A lightjet and the Learjet 60 midsize jet, the leader in the midsize business jet category. In 1989, initial design studies

The Gates Learjet family tree included the Model 25 (top) that dates back to the 1960s, the Learjet 35 and Learjet 36 series, as well as the Learjet Longhorn 50 of 1979 (foreground).

for the advanced Learjet 45 aircraft were launched with what was perhaps the most extensive market research effort ever conducted for a new business aircraft.

Based on this research, Learjet decided to establish the aircraft cabin configuration first before the performance parameters and the rest of the aircraft configuration. In the final configuration, the cabin was 2 inches wider and 7 inches taller than those of previous light jets, necessitat-

First flown in 1987, the Lear Jet 31 was similar to the earlier Learjet 35A and 36A, but winglets were added at the tip of each wing for improved lift and fuel efficiency.

ing an entirely new fuselage design with a noncircular cross section developed to provide greater headroom and shoulderroom. Cabin length was set at slightly more than 19 feet, longer than the cabins of a number of mid-size jets, so as to permit individual seats for eight passengers.

Taking advantage of the fact that the Learjet 45 was to be a 100 percent new aircraft, Learjet decided to design it entirely on computer and build it largely with the use of computer-automated manufacturing equipment. Using three-dimensional, "solid-modeling" techniques, engineers could, in essence, put the aircraft together on-screen, allowing them to check fit and identify any interferences. Problems were thus identified early, in the "digital preassembly" phase, rather than on a hand-built mock-up or prototype aircraft.

In June 1995, the first completed Learjet 45 aircraft was turned over to Learjet's experimental flight test organization for installation of flight test equipment and for final checks. The Learjet 45 made its first flight in October 1995, powered by two Allied Signal TFE 731-20 turbofan engines.

As the Learjet 45 entered service in 1997, over 1,800 Learjet aircraft, notably the Learjet 24 and Learjet 31, were delivered to customers in the United States and 40 countries since 1964. Most of the Learjets were standard business transports, but the aircraft were also used for such diverse military, as well as civilian, operations as electronic warfare simulation, aerial photography, airways calibration, air ambulance, target towing, radar training, fire-control radar, and electronic countermeasures operations.

SINCE THE DAWN of the jet age in the 1940s, the two most important commercial jets—referred to as jetliners—have been the Boeing 707 and 747. The 707 was important because it was the first successful jetliner. The 747 was important because it was the first "jumbo" jetliner and the first airplane capable of carrying more than 300 passengers. Even more remarkable, it was first flown in 1969 yet it is still in production, current models still sell in significant numbers, and it is still the largest jetliner in the world.

The world of commercial flying was quite a different place in the early 1950s when the 707 was born. The airways were dominated by piston-engined, propeller-driven airliners, or propliners, primarily the Douglas DC-6 and DC-7 and the Lockheed Constellation family. Boeing had introduced the Model 377 Stratocruiser—based on the Model 367 military transport—but it was not as successful as the Douglas and Lockheed propliners. In 1952, British Overseas Airways put the British-made de Havilland Comet into service. The world's first jetliner, the Comet was the fastest commercial aircraft in the world. The three American propliner-makers considered making a jetliner of their own, but when the Comet suffered a series of headline-grabbing crashes, the public expressed horror at the new technology.

Douglas and Lockheed decided not to proceed with their jetliners—at least for the moment—but Boeing went forward. Because the Stratocruiser had not been successful, Boeing had nothing to lose. The prototype Boeing jetliner was the Model 367-80, known familiarly as the "Dash-Eighty." Although it was an all-new aircraft, Boeing used the "367" designation to camouflage the project from the competition.

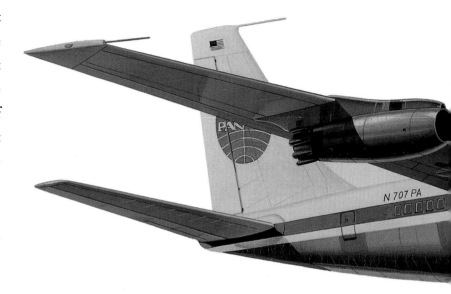

The 367-80 had a wingspan of 130 feet, a length of 128 feet, and a gross weight of 160,000 pounds. It was powered by four Pratt & Whitney JT3P turbojet engines, each delivering 11,000 pounds of thrust and giving it a cruising speed of 600 miles per hour, double that of the propliners. It had a service ceiling of 42,000 feet and a range of 2,000 miles. The Dash-Eighty made its first flight in July 1954. Ironically, the first orders for this ground-breaking new aircraft were from the U.S. Air Force, who wanted an aerial tanker version. The Air Force's tankers at the time were all piston-engined aircraft, and they were on the edge of being too slow to safely refuel the new jet bombers.

As the new Boeing jet went into production, the jetliner carried the Boeing model number 707, while the Air Force tanker version was designated KC-135, or simply C-135 if it was configured simply as a transport and not equipped with refueling equipment.

Pan American World Airways inaugurated the first scheduled service with the 707 jetliner in October 1958 on its high-profile route between New York and London.

The Boeing 707 served airlines flying international routes for many years. Some carriers, such as Braniff and Ecuatoriana (seen here), were notably unique with their color schemes.

(Above left) *Boeing technicians scan a data printout from a test flight of the Model 367-80, known familiarly as the "Dash-Eighty." The airline logos on the fuselage represent future customers for production 707s.* (Right) *An American Airlines 707 takes off from Chicago's O'Hare Airport, the busiest airport in the world. The ultimate 707 was the 707-320, which was powered by four Pratt & Whitney JT4A turbofan engines.*

Pan American was the first airline to offer regularly scheduled 707 passenger flights, with jetliner service beginning between New York and London in October 1958 and between New York and Miami in December. In January 1959, American Airlines was the first of several United States airlines to start offering 707 jetliner service between New York and the West Coast. In its first year, the Boeing 707 carried a million passengers for nearly a dozen airlines in Europe and the United States.

The 707-120 was similar to the Dash-Eighty, but it was 17 feet longer, had a gross weight of 248,000 pounds, and had a range of 3,000 miles, which was easily enough range for the North Atlantic and transcontinental routes. In 1960, Boeing introduced the 707-220, known as the 720, which was a short-range version of the 707 designed for routes such as those between San Francisco and Los Angeles or between New York and Chicago. The 720 was eight feet longer than the Dash-

Eighty and carried 167 passengers. Its life span was relatively short, for within a few years, it was replaced by Boeing's extremely successful 727 trijet.

The ultimate 707 was the 707-320, which was marketed as having "intercontinental" range. This translated as 4,200 miles, sufficient to bring Asia within range of Europe and to allow flights from the United States to cross the Pacific. The 707-320 had a wingspan of 142 feet 5 inches, a length of 152 feet 11 inches, and a gross weight of 316,000 pounds. It was powered by four Pratt & Whitney JT4A turbofan engines, each delivering 15,800 pounds of thrust and giving it a cruising speed of 600 miles per hour. The 707-420 was identical to the 707-320 but was powered by four Rolls-Royce Conway Mk.508 turbofan engines, delivering 17,500 pounds of thrust.

The 707 remained in production until 1992, with peak production centering on the late 1960s. A 707—designated

VC-137—served as *Air Force One*, the official airplane of the president of the United States from 1961 until 1990, when it was replaced by a Boeing 747-200 under the designation VC-25.

In the first decade that the 707 was in service, the market for jetliners mushroomed. Not only were they able to take passengers on flights across the United States and the North Atlantic in half the time of propliners, they were able to fly above the worst weather and to avoid the choppy turbulence that passengers disliked.

With the increase in traffic, it was only natural for airlines to start thinking about larger jetliners. Boeing forecasts in the 1960s showed that air traffic growth would be dramatic, and the company concluded that only a truly enormous 300-passenger jetliner could manage the expected passenger demand.

Development of the larger aircraft parallelled the development of much larger engines, the first generation of high-bypass turbofan engines, whose intakes were twice the diameter of any other jet engines in service. The jetliner itself was the Boeing 747, the largest ever built for commercial use, and whose size immediately led to the coining of the term "jumbo jet."

Thinking ahead to its future use as a cargo-carrier as well as a passenger jet, Boeing designed the 747 with the flight deck positioned above the passenger cabin so containers shipped on freighter and convertible versions could be loaded straight in through the nose, which swung upward on a hinge. The area behind the flight deck was initially used as a lounge and then for seating above the main passenger deck, creating the jetliner's characteristic hump.

The first Boeing 747 made its debut flight on February 9, 1969. It was painted in Boeing colors but was marked with the logos of the 28 airlines that had already placed orders for the revolutionary jumbo jet.

The first 747 flew on February 9, 1969, and it made a 5,100-mile demonstration flight to the Paris Air Show a month later. Pan American World Airways put the 747-100 into passenger-carrying service on the North Atlantic route in January 1970, and within a year, every major international carrier in the world had 747s in service or on order. The 747-100 had a wingspan of 195 feet 8 inches, a length of 231 feet 4 inches, and a gross weight of up to 735,000 pounds. It had a ser-

A modified Boeing 747-200 was chosen by NASA to carry its Space Shuttle Orbiters between Edwards AFB in California and the Kennedy Space Center in Florida. The Orbiter adds 148,000 pounds to the 747's 775,000-pound gross weight.

vice ceiling of 40,000 feet and carried 350 to 450 passengers, depending on configuration. It was powered by four high-bypass turbofan engines, and Boeing offered a choice of three types: the Pratt & Whitney JT9D, delivering 53,000 pounds of thrust; the General Electric CF6-50, delivering 52,500 pounds of thrust; and, originally for British Airways, the Rolls-Royce RB-211-524B, delivering 50,100 pounds of thrust.

In the mid-1970s, the 747-200 became the standard model. It was outwardly identical to the 747-100, but it had a gross weight rating of 775,000 pounds and a longer range. Where the 747-100 had a rated range of over 5,600 miles, the 747-200 had a range of 6,447 miles. Turbofan engines were offered from the same engine makers, but each was an improved variant with thrust in the 54,000-pound class. The higher gross weight 747-

200F freighter was also introduced, and it became the first aircraft to lift over a million pounds.

In 1975, Boeing introduced the 747SP (Special Performance) that offered greater range, albeit with a shorter fuselage and lesser passenger capacity. It was a trade-off that was attractive to foreign airlines with long, overwater routes. The 747SP was 47 feet shorter than other 747s but still had a capacity for 300 passengers. It was rated with a range of 7,000 miles, but in 1976, a Suid-Afrikaanse Lugdiens (South African Airways) 747SP made a flight of 10,290 miles.

In the 1980s, Boeing began development of an extended upper deck 747, which was designated 747-300 and in which the seating area behind the flight deck was elongated by 23 feet. The 747-300 was soon superseded by the 747-400, which also had the extended upper deck as well as six-foot "winglets" on each wing tip for improved lift.

Incorporating advances in aerodynamics, structural materials, avionics, and interior design, the 747-400 first flew on April 29, 1988. It had a wingspan of 211 feet 5 inches, a length of 231 feet 10 inches, and a gross weight of up to 735,000 pounds. It had a service ceiling of 40,000 feet and carried 350 to 450 passengers, depending on configuration.

The 747-400 was powered by four high-bypass turbofan engines, and, again, Boeing offered a choice of three types: the Pratt & Whitney PW4000, with 56,000 pounds of thrust; the General Electric CF6-80C2, delivering 57,900 pounds of thrust; and the Rolls-Royce RB211-524G, with 58,000 pounds of thrust. The 747-400 was rated with a maximum take-off weight of up to 870,000 pounds, and it provided accommodation for 398 to 550 passengers, depending on interior configuration. The maximum speed was 615 miles per hour, the cruising speed was 560 miles per hour at 35,000 feet, and the 747-400 had a range of 8,406 miles.

The 747-400F freighter carried 129 gross tons of cargo, which was a 5 percent increase in volume from the 747-200F. In addition to carrying more payload, the 747-400 freighter flew farther while consuming 16 percent less fuel than the earlier model.

In 1995, as the 747 celebrated a quarter century of passenger carrying service, there were 1,046 of them—including a growing number of 747-400s—in service with 83 airlines around the world.

The first Boeing 747 series 400 lines up on the runway at Payne Field, adjacent to Boeing's huge Everett, Washington, factory. The 747-400 first flew on April 29, 1988.

IT ACHIEVED ITS MILESTONES back in the 1960s, yet the remarkable North American Aviation X-15 remains the fastest and highest flying airplane ever manufactured. While the Space Shuttle Orbiting Vehicle achieves speeds of Mach 25 during reentry, it does not do so under its own power.

Though it was seen as just a step toward faster vehicles at the time, the X-15 is likely to remain the fastest and highest flying airplane ever manufactured well into the 21st century. Indeed, on the 50th anniversary of its record flights, there will still have been no faster airplane.

The X-15 program is a direct successor to the series of supersonic research aircraft that began with the X-1 in 1946. Indeed, the X-15 was conceived by the U.S. Air Force and NACA while the X-1 and X-1A projects were still underway. The idea was to build an aircraft that flew at Mach 6 (six times the speed of sound) and up to an altitude of 225,000 feet. The X-15 would be not just supersonic but *hyper*sonic (flying over five times the speed of sound). In the early 1950s, this projection was almost unimaginable. No conventional aircraft had yet come close to surpassing the X-1A, and the X-15 was intended to go three times as fast as the X-1A and more than twice as high.

In 1955, after having defined the parameters of the project, NACA and the Air Force picked North American Aviation as the prime contractor to build three X-15 aircraft, and Reaction Motors (who built the X-1 engines) to provide rocket motors for these aircraft.

The first X-15 was completed in late 1958, and after five months, it was ready for its first unpowered glide flight in March 1959, having been dropped from a B-52 "mother ship" over Edwards AFB, California. The first powered X-15 flight

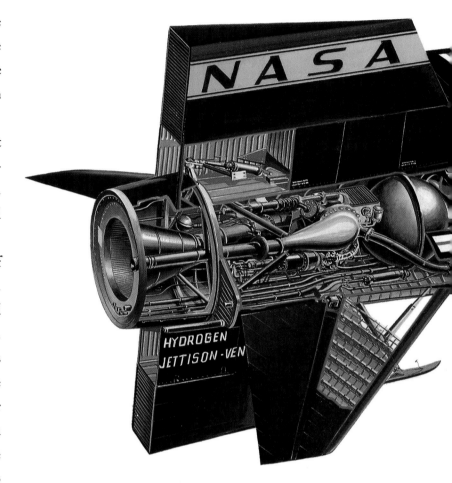

involved the second X-15, and it took place on September 17, 1959, with North American Aviation test pilot Scott Crossfield at the controls. It was an impressive first flight as he accomplished a speed of 1,393 miles per hour (Mach 2.11) and an altitude of 52,341 feet. On flight 18 in August 1960, test pilot Joe Walker set a world speed record of 2,196 miles per hour (Mach 3.31), and on the next flight Major Robert M. White took the aircraft to an altitude of 136,500 feet.

The X-15 had a wingspan of 22 feet 4 inches and a length of either 49 feet 10 inches or 50 feet 3 inches, depending on which

(Above) *This cutaway drawing shows the internal structure of the X-15, notably the titanium alloy framing, the 2024-T4 aluminum alloy cockpit pressure shell, and the Reaction Motors XLR-99 engine.* (Below) *The third of three X-15s, number 56-6672 (66672), made its first flight in December 1961 with Neil Armstrong at the controls. It was destroyed six years later in a crash that killed pilot Michael Adams, but a full-scale replica was later built with the same tail number.*

(Above left) *The North American Aviation X-15 research aircraft was carried aloft under the wing of a Boeing NB-52B and released at 38,000 feet to fly a mission profile that often included altitudes above 100,000 feet.* (Right) *This view shows the business end of the Reaction Motors XLR-11 ethyl alcohol rocket engines. The X-15s were powered by the XLR-11 or XLR-99, delivering 57,850 pounds of thrust at 100,000 feet for an hour.*

engine was installed. It had a gross weight of 31,275 pounds. The X-15 was powered by a Reaction Motors XLR-11-RM-5 (Model 6000C4) or XLR-99 ethyl alcohol rocket engine, delivering 57,850 pounds of thrust at 100,000 feet for a duration of 60 minutes. The initial 25 flights were made using the XLR-11, with the XLR-99 engine first used in the second X-15 in November 1960. The third X-15 made its first flight in December 1961 and was delivered with the XLR-99 installed.

Because it could be throttled, or speed controlled, the XLR-99 was a welcome addition to the X-15 program. On its second flight in November 1960, Crossfield stopped and restarted the XLR-99 in flight. Four months later, White became the first person to exceed Mach 4, and in June 1961, he surpassed Mach 5 for the first time. It was an important milestone to cross, for all but a handful of the remaining X-15 flights reached speeds in excess of Mach 4 and over half exceeded

Mach 5. In November 1961, White broke the Mach 6 barrier, the goal that was indicated in the X-15 design specifications.

In April 1962, Joe Walker made the first flight to top the design-specified 225,000 feet, reaching an altitude of 246,700 on the 52nd flight of the X-15 program. Three months later, White earned astronaut's wings for a flight above the earth's atmosphere to 314,750 feet. On August 22, 1963, Walker achieved the altitude record unequaled by any other aircraft, reaching 354,200 feet—67 miles above the earth's surface.

Meanwhile, the second X-15 suffered severe damage in a high gross-weight emergency landing in November 1962 and was completely rebuilt as the X-15A, with improved systems and a provision for removable external fuel tanks for longer flights. Its first flight in X-15A configuration came in June 1964.

The X-15 program set many speed records during 199 flights with three aircraft. Over half of them were above

Mach 5, and there were four above Mach 6. The fastest and still unsurpassed speed of 4,520 miles per hour (Mach 6.7) was flown by Pete Knight on October 3, 1967.

The 199th and last X-15 flight occurred a year later on October 24, 1968, with test pilot Bill Dana reaching a speed of 3,682 miles per hour at 250,000 feet. During the program, the X-15 set aircraft speed and altitude records that will survive into the 21st century. There were 13 flights in which X-15 pilots were awarded astronaut's wings for flights above the earth's atmosphere—that's more spaceflights than the Mercury or Gemini spacecraft or the Apollo spacecraft through the lunar landing program.

The X-15 program was successful in terms of exploring the nuances of hypersonic flight, in developing throttle rocket engines, in developing processing methods for metals and other materials for high-speed aircraft, in the development of pressure suits, in the development of structural components later used in spacecraft, and in studying the weightless environment of space.

Ironically, since the X-15 was retired in 1968, no other hypersonic aircraft are known to have entered development anywhere in the world. The two surviving X-15s are preserved at the Air Force Museum near Dayton, Ohio, and at the Smithsonian's National Air and Space Museum in Washington, D.C.

Rolled out at North American Aviation's Los Angeles facility in October 1958, the first X-15 was delivered with a long, striped nose probe used for pitch and yaw assessment. The probe was later deleted.

ALBERT SCOTT CROSSFIELD

One of the premier American test pilots of the postwar years, Scott Crossfield played an important role in an era when aviation and aeronautical technology advanced faster than it had before.

During World War II, Crossfield got a job with Boeing on the B-17 program. Joining the U.S. Navy, he served as a flight and gunnery instructor aboard the USS *Langley*. After the war, he attended the University of Washington, where he helped organize Naval Reserve Squadron 74 while earning his master's degree in aeronautical engineering.

In 1950, he became a research test pilot with NACA at Edwards AFB. At this time, both the U.S. Air Force and U.S. Navy had funded high-speed aircraft research projects, and Crossfield was one of the few test pilots to fly both. He flew the Navy's Douglas D-558 Skystreak and D-558-2 Skyrocket, and he became involved in the Air Force/NACA X-1 program in April 1951.

He left NACA to work with North American Aviation on the project leading to the design of the most important research aircraft of its era, the X-15. Crossfield helped to design the X-15, he directed production testing, and he flew most of its first two dozen flights, including all of the first eight. In the X-15, Crossfield made nine flights at more than twice the speed of sound. In 1960, he became the first person to exceed Mach 3—and live.

After North American turned the X-15 program over to NACA and Air Force test pilots in 1960, Crossfield became director of systems test at North American's Space & Information Systems Division. As director of Test & Quality Assurance for North American, he was involved in 13 major space launches through 1967.

URING THE 1960s, the aviation industry was in a unique place in its history. In a generation, aviation had gone from biplanes to jets. In two decades, technology had leapt from fear of the sound barrier to the X-15 rocket plane traveling at six times the speed of sound; air transport had gone from 24-passenger airliners grinding along at less than 200 miles per hour to 150-passenger jetliners cruising from continent to continent at 600 miles per hour. It was only natural to assume that it would all continue on the same curve. It was only natural to predict that supersonic jetliners would be standard equipment by the end of the 1970s.

In the early 1960s, all the major American planemakers were seriously working on the idea of a supersonic transport, and there was a great deal of discussion in the popular press where the acronym "SST" was casually adopted and put into common usage like the FBI or IRS. In Europe, British Aircraft Corporation (later British Aerospace) in England and Sud Aviation in France were also studying the SST concept. The Soviet Union's Tupolev design bureau also had an SST in the works, but the cloak of security that covered most things Soviet in the 1960s also made the Tupolev project much less visible than its Western counterparts.

Soon, the planemakers realized the technological leap from jetliner to SST was very costly, and government financial support for these projects involving "national prestige" was required. In Britain and France, neither government was willing to provide all the support necessary, and this led to the historic decision in 1962 to merge the two projects and produce a joint Anglo-French SST that would be called Concorde, a name coined by French president Charles de Gaulle.

In the United States, the government chose one of the competing SST proposals, and work began on the Boeing 2707. In the Soviet Union, where the government owned the design bureaus and factories in the first place, work continued on what was to become the Tu-144. In 1971, the United States Senate pulled the plug on the 2707, with the half-finished prototype still on the factory floor; the Soviets rushed the Tu-144 to completion with disastrous results.

The Tu-144 first flew on the last day of 1968 and first exceeded the sound barrier in June 1969. When the second prototype crashed at the Paris Air Show in 1973, the Tu-144 was taken out of service until the late 1970s, when it was used briefly on passenger flights between Moscow and the Soviet Far East.

Meanwhile, in the West, by 1969, over a dozen commercial airlines had placed orders for the 2707 and the Concorde, and there was serious interest in commercial SSTs. While the United States project was behind schedule, the Anglo-France joint effort moved ahead briskly. The first Aérospatiale-manufactured Concorde flew in

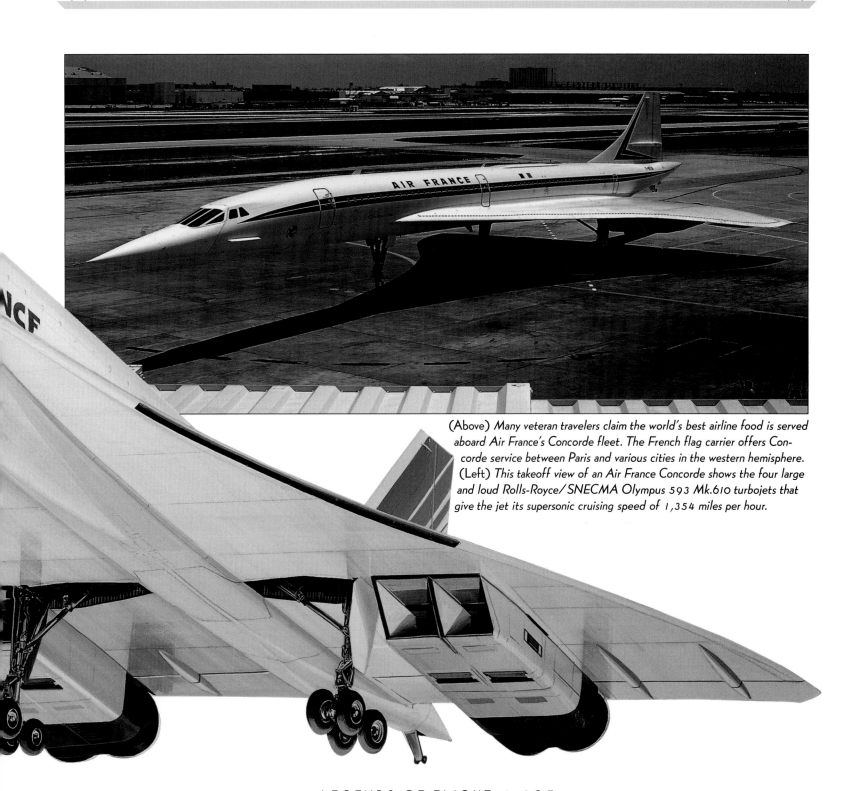

(Above) *Many veteran travelers claim the world's best airline food is served aboard Air France's Concorde fleet. The French flag carrier offers Concorde service between Paris and various cities in the western hemisphere.*
(Left) *This takeoff view of an Air France Concorde shows the four large and loud Rolls-Royce/SNECMA Olympus 593 Mk.610 turbojets that give the jet its supersonic cruising speed of 1,354 miles per hour.*

March 1969, and its British twin flew a month later. The Concorde had a wingspan of 83 feet 10 inches, a length of 203 feet 9 inches, and a gross weight of 407,994 pounds. It carried 144 passengers, and it had a service ceiling of 60,000 feet and a range of 3,870 miles.

The Concorde's four engines, also an Anglo-French collaboration, were Rolls-Royce/SNECMA Olympus 593 Mk.610 turbojets, each delivering 38,050 pounds of thrust and giving it a super-sonic cruising speed of 1,354 miles per hour (twice the speed of sound) at 51,300 feet.

The Concorde supersonic jetliner was a joint project of British Aerospace and Aérospatiale, and it flies only for British Airways (seen here) and Air France.

Although it was never actually built, the Boeing 2707, by contrast to the Concorde, was designed with a wingspan of 141 feet 8 inches, a length of 280 feet, and a gross weight of 635,000 pounds. It was designed to carry 234 passengers—nearly 100 more than the Concorde.

From the time of the first flights, the Concorde underwent over five years of flight testing and sales tours, but in those five years, dramatic changes occurred that affected the Concorde's future. The Concorde had a high rate of fuel consumption. The energy crisis of 1974 more than doubled the price of aviation fuel and threw off the financial projections that were made while it was in development. Another problem that was unanticipated

by the general public followed from the fact that there was a loud "sonic boom" when the Concorde broke the sound barrier. People living near airports didn't like that, so restrictions were placed on flying the Concorde at supersonic speeds over land.

The dozen airlines—including Pan American World Airways, Quantas, TransWorld, and Japan Airlines—who had once wanted an SST gradually withdrew their orders. By the mid-1970s, it cost more than twice as much to fill the Concorde's fuel tanks than it had when it was proposed. Further, if it couldn't fly at supersonic speeds over land, it made more sense to use a more economical conventional jetliner. As for overwater routes, the Concorde lacked the range to fly the Pacific, and the only route for which it had the range—and which also had the passenger density to justify the expense—was the North Atlantic.

Ultimately, the only two airlines that would buy the Concorde were the flag carriers of the two nations that built it: Air France and British Airways. Service on the routes for which the Concorde was primarily designed—Paris to New York and London to New York—was delayed by antinoise activists until 1977, but it has been continuous on those routes ever since. Meanwhile, regularly scheduled service on both airlines began in January 1976, with Air France flying to Rio de Janeiro and British Airways flying to Bahrain. Service to the United States began in May with simultaneous flights by both airlines to Washington, D.C.

On the North Atlantic, the most important overwater routes in the world, the Concorde completed the flight in less than four hours, or about half the time of a conventional jetliner. The jet's streamlined design demonstrated that the Concorde could withstand the stresses of supersonic flight. In one well-publicized demonstration, an Air France Concorde left Boston at the same time as an Air France 747 was leaving Paris for Boston. The Concorde flew to Paris, spent an hour on the ground, and returned to Boston, arriving only 11 minutes behind the 747.

By 1982, each airline had seven production Concordes in service, primarily on the New York run, although service to Washington D.C. was available as well. Air France offered flights from Paris to Mexico City and Rio de Janeiro, while British Airways offered its Bahrain and Singapore service for a time.

The huge, delta-winged Concorde has what can still be called a "futuristic" appearance, even after being in service with British Airways and Air France for over a quarter century.

THE FIRST AIRCRAFT in history designed specifically for a single successful nonstop flight around the world, the *Voyager* was the product of the talent and imagination of legendary aircraft designer Burt Rutan. The *Voyager* first flew on June 22, 1984, with Burt's brother Dick at the controls.

The *Voyager* was constructed mostly of Hercules Magnamite graphite fiber over a Hexcel Nomex paper honeycomb core, with some segments of DuPont Kevlar and glass fiber in an epoxy matrix. The wings, constructed of solid, oven-cured Magnamite, had a span of 111 feet and an area of 324 square feet. The craft weighed only 935 pounds empty, yet it carried 8,400 pounds of fuel in 17 tanks located throughout the aircraft. In flight, the fuel had to be drawn from the tanks symmetrically to avoid throwing the extremely light aircraft off balance.

Shaped like no other aircraft, the Rutan Voyager *was designed by Burt Rutan and constructed of Hercules Magnamite graphite fiber over a Hexcel Nomex paper honeycomb core, which made the aircraft lighter than its own fuel.*

Voyager was powered by two Teledyne Continental piston engines. The front engine was an air-cooled 130-horsepower O-240, and the engine driving the pusher prop was a 110-horsepower liquid-cooled IOL-200. The aircraft was capable of operating at an altitude of 30,000 feet, although its typical cruising altitude was between 7,000 and 11,000 feet. It had a range of 28,000 miles, greater than any aircraft ever.

In July 1986, after two years of flight testing, Dick Rutan and Jeana Yeager piloted *Voyager* on a 111-hour test flight up and down the California coast. They covered 11,593.68 miles, setting a new closed-course world distance record. This flight, which was less than half the distance and duration of a round-the-world flight, was the longest flight made in the aircraft before that epic voyage.

The round-the-world flight was repeatedly delayed, first from 1985 to the summer of 1986, and finally from September to December 1986. During the December 14 takeoff from Edwards AFB, California, *Voyager*'s wings, heavy with fuel, bounced against the runway, breaking off one of the aircraft's two winglets. Once airborne, however, observers in chase planes noted that *Voyager* seemed intact, and the flight continued.

It was intended that most of the flight be made using only the rear engine, but both were needed to climb around storms over the Indian Ocean, and this used up a great deal of fuel. When the flight ended on December 23 at Edwards AFB, there was only 18 gallons remaining of the initial 1,209.8 gallons.

The historic flight had taken 9 days 3 minutes 44 seconds. Dick Rutan, Jeana Yeager, and the *Voyager* had covered 24,986 miles. This was twice the unrefueled distance previously flown by any aircraft. The *Voyager* then made one more flight—the few miles back to Mojave, California, where the plane was originally built. There, the experimental aircraft was dismantled and was trucked to its new, permanent home at the Smithsonian Institution's National Air and Space Museum in Washington, D.C.

RICHARD "DICK" RUTAN, ELBERT "BURT" RUTAN, AND JEANA YEAGER

By the 1990s, it was generally assumed that the era of aviation triumphs was over. It seemed everything that could be done, with the resources available, had already been done. But actually, one space was still blank in the record book. While spacecraft could orbit the earth, no aircraft had flown around the world nonstop—without refueling in flight.

Burt Rutan was a brilliant aerodynamicist who took his degree from California State Polytechnic University and

Voyager *designer Burt Rutan (left) and pilots Jeana Yeager (center) and Dick Rutan (right).*

designed a series of revolutionary aircraft, including the immortal Beech Starship. Dick Rutan was a former fighter pilot who worked as chief test pilot for Rutan Aircraft in Mojave, California, the leading-edge aircraft development company founded by his brother.

Into Dick's life came Jeana Yeager, an engineering designer on Robert Truax's commercial space rocket project and a helicopter pilot. In 1981, Burt Rutan suggested they try to break the existing aircraft world distance record (set in 1962 by a B-52 bomber flying 12,532 miles). Not only was Burt sure he could design an airplane that could do that, he was sure he could design an aircraft that could fly *twice* that far, sufficient to fly around the world in a single flight.

The aircraft he designed for the distance record, the *Voyager*, was completed and first flown by Dick Rutan and Jeana Yeager in 1986. In July, Dick and Jeana made a 4.5-day, 11,600-mile flight and traveled in laps up and down the California coast, setting new world records for distance and endurance.

The flight test program continued into the fall, and on December 14, 1986, they took off from Edwards AFB and headed out over the Pacific. After 9 days 3 minutes 44 seconds, the triumphant crew landed near Edwards AFB, where 50,000 spectators turned out to watch them touch down.

BORN AT A TIME when it seemed as though humankind's manifest destiny was to fly routinely in space, the Space Shuttle Orbiting Vehicle is the only winged vehicle ever to fly into orbit and bring a crew back from orbit aerodynamically. In the United States Mercury, Gemini, and Apollo manned space programs, operational between 1961 and 1975, each mission required a dedicated capsule, which was used only once. The same is true with the Soviet, now Russian, Vostok and Soyuz space capsules that have been in use since 1961.

By the late 1960s, the National Aeronautics & Space Administration (NASA) decided that if spaceflight was going to be as routine as hoped for, then spacecraft would have to be reusable. It was also decided that it would be less costly if the spacecraft could return to earth as an "airplane" and simply land at an airport, rather than being plucked out of the ocean, as was the case with space capsules.

NASA's original idea was for a fleet of a dozen "space shuttles" to fly into space once or twice a week, taking people to and from a space station that would be fully operational in the late 1970s. With this in mind, NASA issued a request for proposals, reviewed suggestions from all of the leading American aircraft makers, and picked the one submitted by North American Rockwell (later Rockwell International and formerly North American Aviation).

This detailed cutaway drawing shows a Tracking & Data Relay Satellite (TDRS) being deployed from the 60-foot payload bay of the orbiter Discovery. *TDRS satellites serve as NASA's communications link, relaying the voices of the astronauts and data from space shuttles in orbit.*

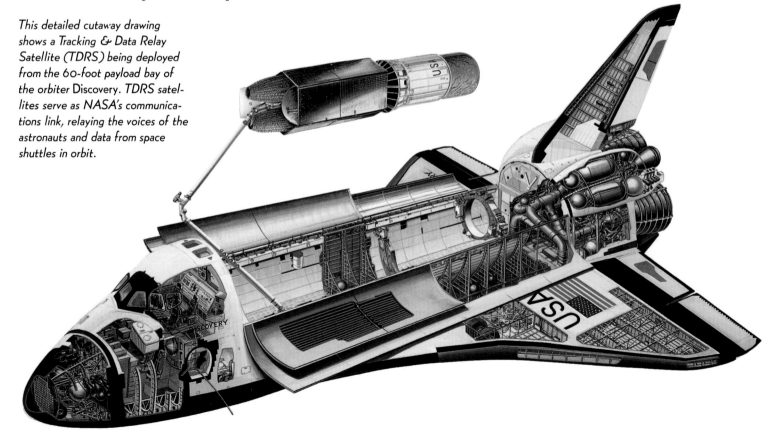

In 1972, Rockwell began work on the Space Transportation System (STS). The system consisted of a huge external tank for liquid rocket fuel, two "strap-on" solid rocket boosters, and the airplanelike Space Shuttle Orbiting Vehicle that carried the crew and the payload. The Space Shuttle Orbiting Vehicle, though it was just part of the Space Transportation System, was—and still is—known familiarly as the Space Shuttle.

The 148,000-pound Space Shuttle Orbiting Vehicle Columbia is seen here supported by a powerful gantry crane in NASA's Shuttle Processing Facility at the Kennedy Space Center in Florida.

The Space Shuttle Orbiting Vehicle had a wingspan of 78 feet, a length of 122.2 feet, and an internal payload bay 60 feet long with a 15-foot diameter. Its nose, wings, and surfaces susceptible to thermal heating during reentry were covered with over 27,000 ceramic thermal tiles for protection. The external fuel tank was 154.2 feet long and the solid rocket boosters 149.16 feet long. The overall Space Transportation System stood 184.2 feet high when fully assembled for launch.

The Space Shuttle Orbiting Vehicle weighed 148,000 pounds completely empty and 240,000 pounds fully loaded for launch. The overall system weighed 4.5 million pounds fully loaded and ready to launch. The Space Shuttle Orbiting Vehicle had three self-contained Rocketdyne rocket engines, each delivering 375,000 pounds of thrust at launch. The two solid rocket boosters each added 1.2 million pounds of thrust.

The original plan called for the Space Transportation System to make its initial flight in 1979 and to become operational with 22 flights in 1981. However, delays pushed the schedule back. The history-making first flight of a reusable spacecraft occurred on April 12, 1981, and the first airplanelike landing of the Space Shuttle Orbiting Vehicle Columbia took place at Edwards AFB two days later.

The primary mission of the Space Transportation System was seen as the launching of commercial—as well as government—satellites. The payload bay was configured to accommodate a half dozen, and if even three or four were launched, it was cheaper than doing it with expendable rockets; the Space Transportation System would actually make money. After four test flights involving Columbia in 1981 and 1982, the first operational, satellite-launching mission took place in April 1983 with the Space Shuttle Orbiting Vehicle Challenger.

FRANK BORMAN

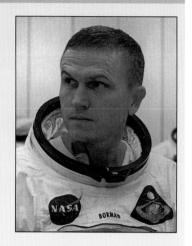

The first pilot to command a mission to the moon, Frank Borman graduated from the United States Military Academy at West Point and was commissioned as a second lieutenant in the U.S. Air Force in 1950.

In 1962, Borman was picked as part of the second group of NASA astronauts, the "Gemini class" who formed the backbone of crews for not only the two-man Gemini spacecraft but also the three-man Apollo missions that reached the moon. Borman was chosen to command the Gemini 7 mission flown between December 4 and December 18 in 1965. During this flight, he and Jim Lovell became the first crew to rendezvous in space with another manned spacecraft.

For the Apollo program, Borman was assigned as commander of Apollo 8, the second of the series to carry a crew. Apollo 8 was intended as an earth-orbit mission, but the decision was made to have the crew fly all the way to the moon. The crew would not actually land on the moon, but they would be the first to go there.

The 147-hour mission of Apollo 8 was launched on December 21, 1968, and reached lunar orbit on Christmas eve. The photographs of the earthrise over the lunar horizon taken by Borman, Jim Lovell, and William Anders remain as classic images of history and achievement.

After Apollo 8, Frank Borman made no more spaceflights. He left the Air Force to become a vice president at Eastern Airlines in 1970 and president and chief executive officer in 1975. He left Eastern to become director of Continental Airlines Holding, Inc., and later became chairman and chief executive officer of Paltex Corporation of Las Cruces, New Mexico.

Despite having wings, the Space Shuttle Orbiters were never intended for horizontal flight within the earth's atmosphere. For this reason, when an orbiter returns to Florida after its landing in California, it must be ferried over on top of a 747.

Over the next three years, the Space Transportation System seemed to be proving its worth. *Challenger* launched numerous satellites, and *Columbia* was flown with the Spacelab laboratory module. Two new Space Shuttle Orbiting Vehicles, *Discovery* and *Atlantis*, joined the fleet in 1984 and 1985, and they both began a busy satellite launch program. In the meantime, a number of programs were designed to take civilians into space; one of these was the Teacher In Space program. In early 1986, it seemed as though the Space Transportation System was destined for success.

The fortunes of the Space Transportation System suddenly turned sour on the 25th flight on January 28, 1986. The *Challenger* blew up 73 seconds after launch, killing the entire crew, including the Teacher In Space candidate Christa McAuliffe. The Space Transportation System fell into retrenchment. It was grounded for almost three years, and the launching of commercial satellites was banned.

The Space Transportation System finally returned to flight in September 1988, and although it will never realize the goals imagined in the 1970s, it has proven to be a reliable means of accessing space. The Hubble Space Telescope, the *Magellan* Venus Probe, and the *Galileo* Jupiter Probe were launched. *Columbia* continued to fly in the Spacelab configuration, and a fifth Space Shuttle Orbiting Vehicle, *Endeavour*, joined the fleet in 1992. By 1995, the Space Transportation System fulfilled the part of its original mission plan calling for rendezvous with space stations with a series of dockings and crew exchanges.

Through the middle of 1996, after more than 15 years in operation, the Space Transportation System had flown over 78 successful missions to one loss, with *Discovery* alone having chalked up more than 20 flights. Since the return to flight in 1988, between 40 and 50 people were flying in space annually aboard the Space Transportation System. The original one-week missions had been expanded to routine ten-day missions. The orbiter *Columbia* flew 16-day missions in October 1995 and February 1996, and the *Endeavour* made a 17-day flight in March 1995.

NEIL ALDEN ARMSTRONG, EDWIN "BUZZ" ALDRIN, AND MICHAEL COLLINS

The ultimate dream of a generation of American pilots was to be the first to get a craft on the moon. Neil Armstrong, Edwin "Buzz" Aldrin, and Michael Collins were the ones to do just that.

Armstrong joined the U.S. Navy as a pilot in 1949. He flew 78 combat missions in Korea before leaving the Navy in 1952 to work as a test pilot for NACA.

(Above left) *Neil Armstrong came to the space program by way of a career as a NASA test pilot and later became mission commander of Apollo 11.* (Right) *After walking on the moon's surface for 2 hours 20 minutes, Edwin "Buzz" Aldrin is back inside Apollo 11's Lunar Module.*

In 1960, two years after NACA became NASA, Armstrong was named as the second NASA test pilot to fly the X-15. Meanwhile, Aldrin was at the Gemini Target Office of the Air Force Space Systems Division in Los Angeles, and Collins was in training at the Experimental Flight Test Pilot School at Edwards AFB.

Armstrong was selected as a NASA astronaut in 1962,

Aldrin also served in Korea but with the U.S. Air Force. He flew 66 combat missions in Korea flying F-86s and shot down two MiG-15s. While Armstrong was flying for NACA, Aldrin was a gunnery instructor at Nellis Air Force Base in Nevada.

While Armstrong and Aldrin served in the Korean War, Collins attended the U.S. Military Academy. He graduated in June 1952 and then went into the air force. He earned his wings in December 1953 while he was at Nellis AFB.

and Aldrin and Collins joined the astronaut corps the following year. In 1966, Armstrong served as command pilot for the Gemini 8 mission; Collins became pilot of the Gemini 10 mission; and Aldrin flew as pilot of the Gemini 12 mission.

In 1969, the first moon landing was set for the Apollo 11 mission, with Armstrong, Aldrin, and Collins as the crew. On July 21, 1969, Armstrong and Aldrin made history as the first men on the moon while Collins circled the moon in the Command Module.

ALLEN, William McPherson (1900–1985) Once the Boeing Airplane Company corporate lawyer and, later, company president, Allen managed Boeing during its most productive era, from World War II through the development of the 747.

ANDREWS, Frank M. (1884–1943) World War I Army Air Service commander, Andrews helped establish independent General Headquarters Air Force. He served as commander of USAAF in the European Theater in 1943.

ARMSTRONG, Neil Alden (1930–) Test pilot, astronautical engineer, and Gemini 8 (1966) and Apollo 11 crew member, Armstrong was the first human to set foot on the moon on July 21, 1969.

ARNOLD, Henry Harley (1886–1950) The only airman to become a five-star general, Arnold helped establish and build the U.S. Army Air Forces into the largest air force in history during World War II.

ATWOOD, J. Leland (1904–) Atwood led North American Aviation in developing important aircraft such as the B-25 Mitchell Bomber, the F-86 Sabre Jet, and the Apollo Command Module.

BALCHEN, Bernt (1899–1973) Norwegian-born expert on arctic flight, Balchen was the chief pilot of Admiral Byrd's expedition to Antarctica, and he helped form Norwegian Airlines.

BALDWIN, Thomas Scott (1854–1923) A pioneer in ballooning during the late 19th century, Baldwin improved parachutes, and he designed and developed dirigibles in the first two decades of the 20th century.

BEACHEY, Lincoln (1887–1915) Perhaps the most talented flyer in the first decade of manned flight, aerobat Beachey was a daring exhibitionist. He died in a crash at the 1915 San Francisco World's Fair.

BEECH, Olive Ann (1903–1993) The "First Lady of Aviation," entrepreneur Beech cofounded Beech Aircraft Company with her husband, Walter, in 1932. She directed the company upon his death in 1950.

BEECH, Walter Herschel (1891–1950) Aviator Beech cofounded the Beech Aircraft Company with his wife, Olive Ann, in 1932, producing such aircraft as the Model 18 transport, the Staggerwing, and the Bonanza series.

BELL, Alexander Graham (1847–1922) Scottish-born engineer and telephone inventor, Bell researched principles of aviation and championed adequate test facilities. In 1907, he founded the Aerial Experiment Association.

BELL, Lawrence Dale (1894–1956) Bell founded the Bell Aircraft Corporation, which built the first U.S. jet airplane, the P-59 Airacomet, in 1942. He built the first aircraft to break the sound barrier, the X-1.

BELLANCA, Giuseppe Mario (1886–1960) Bellanca built the first parasol monoplane and the first aircraft with distinctive wing struts (Bellanca CF). He also designed the WB-1 and the "Miss Veedol," which completed the first nonstop Pacific crossing.

BENDIX, Vincent Hugo (1882–1945) Bendix, an entrepreneur, inventor, and founder of the Bendix Aviation Corporation, invented the pressure carburetor for aircraft engines.

BOEING, William Edward (1881–1956) Boeing was the founder of the Boeing Airplane Company in 1917, and he inaugurated mail and passenger service in the Northwest. The passenger service portion of the airplane company eventually became United Air Lines.

BONG, Richard I. (1920–1945) During World War II, Bong flew more than 200 missions and became America's all-time leading ace with 40 confirmed victories.

BORMAN, Frank (1928–) Borman commanded the Gemini 7 (1965) mission and the Apollo 8 (1968) mission, the first to orbit the moon. He served as chairman, president, and CEO of Eastern Airlines.

BOYD, Albert (1906–1976) Test-pilot Boyd set a world's speed record in 1947. He was the commander at Edwards Air Force Base during the days of pioneering research flights.

BRADLEY, Mark E. (1907–) Bradley, later a four-star general, was the USAAF project officer for the Curtiss P-40 program. He also helped improve the North American Aviation P-51 design that helped decimate the German Luftwaffe.

BROWN, George Scratchley (1918–1978) A USAAF aviator, Brown helped develop plans for U.S. defense after World War II. A four-star general, he served as chairman of the Joint Chiefs of Staff.

BRUKNER, Clayton J. (1896–1977) A pioneer in the design, development, and manufacture of biplanes, Brukner established the WACO Aircraft Company, the greatest producer of commercial aircraft in the early 1930s.

BYRD, Richard Evelyn (1888–1957) A naval aviator and explorer, Byrd pioneered the use of aircraft in polar exploration. He led expeditions to both the Arctic and Antarctic.

CESSNA, Clyde Vernon (1879–1954) An airplane designer and developer during the early days of manned flight, Cessna founded the Cessna Aircraft Company in 1927.

CHAMBERLIN, Clarence Duncan (1893–1976) Chamberlin was a barnstormer and entrepreneur in the 1920s and 1930s who set endurance and altitude flight records and promoted public flying.

CHANUTE, Octave (1832–1910) A civil engineer and a glider designer, Chanute built many successful glider designs, beginning in the 1890s. He became an advisor to the Wright brothers.

CHENNAULT, Claire Lee (1890–1958) A World War I aviator, Chennault organized the volunteer pilots' group "Flying Tigers." During World War II, the Tigers

and General Chennault joined the USAAF.

COCHRAN, Jacqueline (unknown–1980) Cochran founded the Women's Airforce Service Pilots (WASP), which ferried military aircraft during World War II. The first woman to achieve supersonic flight, she set numerous speed records.

COLLINS, Michael (1930–) Collins piloted the Gemini 10 mission (1966) and the Command Module of Apollo 11, the first lunar landing mission. He was founding director of the National Air and Space Museum.

COMBS, Harry B. (1913–) In 1929, 15-year-old Combs soloed in an OX-5-powered standard J-1. He later built the Combscraft, among other aircraft. In 1938, he cofounded Mountain States Aviation, which later became Combs Aircraft.

CONRAD, Charles, Jr. (1930–) A naval aviator and aeronautical engineer, Conrad was a member of the Gemini 5 crew and commander of Gemini 11 and the 1969 Apollo 12 lunar landing mission.

CRAWFORD, Frederick C. (1891–1994) Crawford was president of Thompson Products, which developed

the sodium-cooled valve used in Charles Lindbergh's *Spirit of St. Louis*. He established the Thompson Auto Album and Aviation Museum in Cleveland, Ohio.

CROSSFIELD, A. Scott (1921–) Crossfield, the first pilot of the North American Aviation X-15, helped develop advanced flight controls for that company's missile and space systems operation.

CUNNINGHAM, Alfred Austell (1882–1939) Cunningham was the first marine aviator to fly a landplane and the first to pilot an aircraft launched from a ship.

CURTISS, Glenn Hammond (1878–1930) A pioneer aircraft designer and inventor, Curtiss developed the U.S. Navy's first airplane and designed and developed the JN-4 "Jenny" used in World War I.

DARGUE, Herbert A. (1886–1941) Dargue made the first Army two-way air/ground radio communication with a set he designed. He was commander of the 1926 Pan-American Goodwill Flight and helped develop the Norden Bombsight.

DAVIS, Benjamin O., Jr. (1912–) A member of the Tuskegee Airmen, Davis was the first African-American

cadet to graduate from West Point in the 20th century and the first African American to earn his wings.

DE SEVERSKY, Alexander P. (1894–1974) de Seversky invented first gyroscopically stabilized bombsight and in-flight refueling method. He founded the Seversky Aircraft Corporation (later Republic Aviation) and authored *Victory Through Air Power*.

DOOLITTLE, James Harold (1896–1993) An aeronautical engineer and U.S. Army Air Corps/ USAAF pilot, Doolittle pioneered "blind flying." He earned the Medal of Honor for leading the first USAAF attack on Japan during World War II.

DOUGLAS, Donald Wills (1892–1981) An aircraft designer, Douglas formed the Douglas Aircraft Company in 1920. His company produced the Douglas World Cruisers, the "DC" series of commercial transports, and important military aircraft.

DRAPER, Charles Stark (1901–1987) Draper developed the Gyroscopic sight for antiaircraft guns. He led development of guidance systems for Trident missiles, NASA's Apollo lunar landings, the Skylab space station, and the Space Shuttle.

EAKER, Ira Clarence (1896–1987) Eaker piloted the *Question Mark,* which stayed aloft for 150 hours through aerial refueling (1929), and commanded the USAAF's 8th Air Force during World War II until December 1943.

EARHART, Amelia (1897–1937) The first recorded woman to fly solo nonstop across North America (1929) and solo across the Atlantic (1932), Earhart disappeared over the Pacific, attempting the first woman's flight around the world.

EIELSON, Carl Benjamin (1897–1929) Eielson was the first to fly commercial flights to Alaska, to fly over the Arctic Ocean and land there, and to fly over both polar regions.

ELLYSON, Theodore Gordon (1885–1928) The first naval officer assigned aviation duty, he flew the U.S. Navy's first seaplane.

ELY, Eugene Burton (1886–1911) Ely was an exhibition aviator who flew with Glenn Curtiss's exhibition team and became the first pilot to perform a shipboard landing and takeoff.

EVEREST, Frank K. (1920–) Everest was a pilot in World War II. As a test pilot, he set an unofficial

world altitude record of 73,000 feet and achieved the "Fastest Man Alive" award for his 1956 test flights in the Bell X-2 rocket plane.

FAIRCHILD, Sherman Mills (1896–1971) Fairchild developed precision aerial cameras, advanced commercial/military aircraft and engines, and space-related satellites and components. His surveys and photographs of the moon aided the Apollo landing missions.

FLEET, Reuben Hollis (1887–1975) Fleet helped direct World War I U.S. Army flight training, later developing "Fleet trainers." He formed Consolidated Aircraft Company, which built the PBY Catalina flying boat and the B-24 Liberator.

FOKKER, Anthony Herman Gerard (1890–1939) "The Flying Dutchman" built the top German fighters of World War I and designed the Fokker Trimotor. His planes helped establish airline routes throughout the world in the 1920s.

FORD, Henry (1863–1947) In addition to making automobiles, Ford produced Liberty aircraft engines during and after World War I. He built Ford Airport, the first modern airport, and introduced the Ford Trimotor aircraft.

FOSS, Joseph Jacob (1915–) The U.S. Marine Corps' leading ace during World War II, Foss helped organize the South Dakota Air National Guard. Two-term South Dakota governor, he also directed the Air Force Academy.

FOULOIS, Benjamin Delahauf (1879–1967) One of the first U.S. Army pilots and, later, a commander, Foulois flew dirigibles before airplanes. He designed the first airplane radio receiver and conducted the first airplane reconnaissance flights.

FRYE, William John (1904–1959) Holder of three transcontinental speed records, Frye founded the Aero Corporation, which formed Standard Airlines, an airmail transporter later consolidated to form Transcontinental & Western Air (TWA) then Trans World Airlines.

GABRESKI, Francis Stanley (1919–) A USAAF then USAF fighter pilot, Gabreski was an ace in World War II and the Korean War, a fighter squadron commander, and an executive with Grumman Aerospace Corporation.

GENTILE, Dominic Salvatore (1920–1951) Gentile, an American, flew with one of the Royal Air Force's leg-

endary Eagle squadrons in World War II, then the USAAF 336th Fighter Squadron. He was a decorated ace with 30 victories.

GILRUTH, Robert Rowe (1913–) An aeronautical engineer, Gilruth managed the National Advisory Committee for Aeronautics (NACA), which became NASA in 1958. He directed the Manned Spacecraft Center and the Apollo 11 program in 1969.

GLENN, John Herschel, Jr. (1921–) Glenn became the first U.S. astronaut to orbit the Earth in 1962 in the third Mercury spaceflight. In 1974, he was elected to the U.S. Senate from Ohio.

GODDARD, George William (1889–1987) Born in England, Goddard, an aerial photographer, created the first aerial mapping units, and he pioneered stereoscopic, high-altitude, and color photography.

GODDARD, Robert Hutchings (1882–1945) Physicist Goddard launched the first successful liquid-propellant rocket in 1926, developed the first gyroscopic stabilizing system, and was the first to fire a rocket faster than the speed of sound.

GODFREY, Arthur (1903–1983) A popular

radio and television personality, Godrey promoted aviation throughout his life. He was also a civilian pilot who participated in a round-the-world flight in a JetCommander business aircraft.

GOLDWATER, Barry Morris (1909–) As a U.S. Senator, he cosponsored legislation creating the Federal Aviation Administration and supported various space and aviation programs and the building of the National Air and Space Museum.

GRISSOM, Virgil I. (1926–1967) An Air Force fighter pilot in Korea, Grissom was an astronaut on the second Mercury mission and the first Gemini mission. He was one of three to die in the only fatal accident to occur during the Apollo missions.

GROSS, Robert Ellsworth (1897–1961) Gross purchased the Lockheed Aircraft Corporation in 1932. Under his leadership, the company built many important military aircraft. He expanded Lockheed, manufacturing missiles and commercial aircraft.

GRUMMAN, Leroy Randle (1895–1982) Grumman, a naval aviator and engineer, formed the Grumman Aircraft Corporation in 1929, which built naval aircraft and the Apollo lunar landing module.

GUGGENHEIM, Harry Frank (1890–1971) A naval aviator and aeronautics supporter, Guggenheim served in World Wars I and II. He also established funds and centers, such as the Jet Propulsion Research Center at Cal Tech.

HAUGHTON, Daniel J. (1911–1987) Haughton led Lockheed Aircraft Corporation in a number of high-level positions, ultimately serving as chairman for nine years.

HEGENBERGER, Albert Francis (1895–1983) An aviator and designer, Hegenberger made the first official solo "blind flight." He developed and tested flight instruments, especially in transpacific flights, and helped develop an atomic explosion detection system.

HEINEMANN, Edward Henry (1908–1991) Chief engineer at Douglas Aircraft Company, Heinemann designed numerous aircraft, including the A-4 Skyhawk attack bomber, the SBD Dauntless dive bomber, and the D-558 skyrocket.

HOOVER, Robert A. (1922–) A test pilot, Hoover was the first to fly the XFJ Fury jet and the U.S. Navy's T-28 trainer, and he holds several aviation records.

HUGHES, Howard Robard (1905–1976) Though later an eccentric recluse, Hughes was a gifted engineer who established Hughes Aircraft Company, set numerous speed and flight records, and developed TWA into a leading international airline.

INGALLS, David Sinton (1899–1985) The Navy's only ace during World War I, Ingalls cosponsored the Ohio Aviation Code, guided the Naval Aviation test and development program, and helped create the Naval Air Transport Service.

JAMES, Daniel, Jr. (1920–1978) A member of the Tuskegee Airmen, James also flew combat missions in the Korean War and Vietnam. He later commanded NORAD and was the first African-American USAF four-star general.

JEPPESEN, Elrey B. (1907–1996) An aviator and aerial cartographer, Jeppesen created the "Jepp Charts," the first navigational aid for pilots and now a standard guide for airplane navigation.

JOHNSON, Clarence Leonard (1910–1990) An aeronautical engineer at Lockheed Aircraft Corporation, he designed most of its greatest aircraft, including the P-38 Lightning, the F-80

Shooting Star, the U-2, and the SR-71 Blackbird.

JOHNSTON, Alvin M. (1914–) Johnston, a test pilot for Bell Aircraft Company, tested some of the most advanced aircraft. At Boeing, he was project test pilot for the first swept-wing bomber, the B-47 Stratojet.

JONES, Thomas V. (1920–) An aeronautical engineer with Northrop Corporation, Jones developed a number of systems that became state of the art in aviation technology.

KENNEY, George Churchill (1889–1977) World War I aviator and World War II commander Kenney pioneered the mounting of machine guns on warplane wings. He also developed low-altitude attack tactics and the parachute fragmentation bomb.

KETTERING, Charles Franklin (1876–1958) Kettering designed the ignition system for the Liberty aircraft engine during World War I and made the first synthetic aviation fuel. He helped form the Dayton-Wright Airplane Company.

KINDELBERGER, James Howard (1895–1962) Kindelberger was president of North American Aviation from 1935 to 1962, when the company produced numerous military aircraft, the Apollo spacecraft, and the second stage of the Saturn launcher.

KITTINGER, Joe W., Jr. (1928–) A decorated military test and fighter pilot, Kittinger is the holder of five world records in balloon research.

KNABENSHUE, A. Roy (1876–1960) Knabenshue piloted the first successful dirigible in the United States in 1904. He built and flew the first three-man dirigible. He later managed aviation exhibition teams for the Wright brothers.

KNIGHT, William J. (1929–) Air Force test pilot Knight flew the X-15 rocket to a record speed of 4,520 miles per hour (Mach 6.7).

LAHM, Frank Purdy (1877–1963) Lahm won the first international balloon races (1906) and became one of the Army's first dirigible and airplane pilots. He also organized training facilities for the Army Air Corps.

LANGLEY, Samuel Pierpont (1834–1906) An astronomer and designer, Langley studied air and space. In 1898, he constructed an "aerodrome," a model airplane powered by a gasoline engine.

LEAR, William Powell, Sr. (1902–1978) Lear developed an aircraft receiver of radio beacon navigation beams and the F-5 autopilot with a control for landing in "zero-zero" weather. In 1962, he established Lear Jet Industries.

LeMAY, Curtis Emerson (1906–1990) General LeMay planned the B-29 raids that brought victory over Japan. He built the Strategic Air Command into the world's most formidable strategic force.

LeVIER, Anthony William (1913–) With Lockheed, LeVier flight-tested the P-38 Lightning, the Saturn airliner, and the F-80 jet fighter, among others. He conceived improved jet intercoms, ignitions, and automatic wing stores release systems.

LINDBERGH, Anne Morrow (1906–) An author and glider pilot, Lindbergh assisted husband Charles in surveying and mapping air routes to Asia and transatlantic routes to Europe. She has written several books on aviation.

LINDBERGH, Charles Augustus (1902–1974) In May 1927, Lindbergh made the first solo transatlantic flight in the *Spirit of St. Louis*. With his wife, he made surveys for commercial air routes to Europe and Asia.

LINK, Edwin Albert (1904–1981) Link designed the "Link Trainer," a movable fuselage device that produced the motions and sensations of flying, and built advanced navigation and gunnery trainers and the first jet bomber simulator.

LOCKHEED, Allan H. (1889–1969) Lockheed built his first aircraft in 1916 with his brother Malcolm and made the first dual-pilot controlled flight. He helped found the Lockheed Aircraft Corporation in 1926, which produced the Vega, Explorer, and Air Express.

LOENING, Grover (1888–1976) Loening built the first monoplane flying boat and, with the Wright Company, the first short-hulled flying boat. He formed the Loening Aeronautical Engineering Corporation.

LUKE, Frank, Jr. (1897–1918) In World War I, this Arizona-cowboy-turned-Army-pursuit-pilot earned the nickname "Arizona Balloon Buster," developed new tactical combat maneuvers, and became America's second ranking ace.

MacCREADY, Paul B. (1925–) A pioneer of high-altitude wave soaring, MacCready was the first American to win the World Soaring Championship. He built the *Gossamer Condor*, the first controlled, human-powered airplane.

MACREADY, John Arthur (1887–1979) A pioneer test pilot, Macready set altitude and endurance records in the 1920s and completed the first nonstop transcontinental flight. He was also a pioneer in high altitude flight.

MARTIN, Glenn Luther (1886–1955) Martin formed the Glenn L. Martin Company and built the Army's first tractor-type trainer, the first multipassenger seaplane, the first twin-engine American bomber, and the B-10 bomber.

McCAMPBELL, David (1910–1996) McCampbell was the top-scoring naval fighter pilot of World War II with 34 victories during 1944. He received numerous honors and decorations, including the Medal of Honor.

McDONNELL, James Smith (1899–1980) McDonnell formed McDonnell Aircraft Corporation in 1939 and developed the FH-1 Phantom. McDonnell acquired Douglas Aircraft Company in 1967, creating the McDonnell Douglas Corporation.

MEYER, John C. (1919–1975) World War II

ace Meyer also served as commander in chief of the Strategic Air Command from 1972 to 1974.

MITCHELL, William (1879–1936) A U.S. Army Air Service aviator in World War I, Mitchell organized the first massive aerial attacks, demonstrating the concept of strategic bombing.

MITSCHER, Marc A. (1887–1947) A naval aviator and, later, admiral, Mitscher commanded the USS *Hornet* in World War II and became commander in chief of the United States Atlantic Fleet.

MONTGOMERY, John Joseph (1858–1911) Montgomery designed and built early gliders without flight control systems. He also made public demonstrations of gliders.

MOORER, Thomas H. (1912–) The first naval officer to serve as commander in chief of both Atlantic and Pacific Fleets, Moorer served in the Navy 45 years, retiring as two-term chairman of the Joint Chiefs of Staff.

MOSS, Sanford Alexander (1872–1946) Moss was an inventor who developed aircraft turbo-superchargers, enabling planes to attain higher altitudes. He built the first practical supercharger during World War I.

NEUMANN, Gerhard (1917–) As a mechanic at General Electric, Neumann developed the variable stator compressor system, which is standard in most jet engines. He led GE's development of the J79 jet engine.

NICHOLS, Ruth Rowland (1901–1960) Nichols was the first licensed woman seaplane pilot. The only woman to hold three maximum international records, she was "First Woman" in nearly 30 record categories.

NORDEN, Carl Lukas (1880–1965) Norden, an engineer, developed the Norden Bombsight during World War II, a system that allowed aircraft flying at high altitudes to bomb targets with more precision.

NORTHROP, John Knudsen (1895–1981) Founder of the Northrop Company, Northrop co-invented a process for making monocoque fuselages and designed the N-1M, the first successful flying wing, and the B-35 and B-49 Flying Wing bombers.

PANGBORN, Clyde Edward (1894–1958) A World War I Army pilot and, later, a barnstormer, Pangborn formed the famous Gates Flying Circus in 1922 and made the first nonstop flight across the Pacific Ocean.

PATTERSON, William Allan (1899–1980) A banker and entrepreneur, Patterson headed Boeing Air Transport and later United Air Lines. He introduced flight attendants, air express service, the flight kitchen, and United Air Lines sleeper service.

PIPER, William Thomas, Sr. (1881–1970) In 1930, Piper reorganized the Taylor Aircraft Corporation and developed, built, and marketed the Cub, a lightplane for general aviation use. He established the Piper Aircraft Corporation in 1937.

PITCAIRN, Harold Frederick (1897–1960) In 1925, Pitcairn formed Pitcairn Aviation (which became Eastern Airlines after he sold it) and designed and built the PA-5 Mailwing to carry mail from New York to Atlanta.

POST, Wiley Hardeman (1898–1935) Post made the first around-the-world solo flight in 1933. He designed and tested the first fully pressurized flying suit and helmet. In 1934, he discovered the jet streams.

READ, Albert Cushing (1887–1967) A naval aviator, Cushing participated in the first successful transatlantic flight in 1919. He later commanded several naval aviation training stations.

REEVE, Robert Campbell (1902–1980) Reeve was known as the "Glacier pilot" for making 2,000 glacier landings. His demonstration of the uses of the airplane influenced the economic, social, and cultural development of Alaska.

RENTSCHLER, Frederick Brant (1887–1956) Rentschler helped form Wright Aeronautical Corporation in 1919 and led its development of the Whirlwind engine. He also helped to establish Pratt & Whitney Aircraft Company.

RICHARDSON, Holden Chester (1878–1960) A naval aviator, Richardson helped develop a catapult to launch seaplanes. He helped develop the first Navy-built seaplane, the DN-1 Dirigible, the N-9 seaplane, and the NC Flying boats.

RICKENBACKER, Edward Vernon (1890–1973) Rickenbacker was America's leading ace in World War I. He assisted in the development of several major airlines, notably Eastern Airlines, which he headed for many years.

RODGERS, Calbraith Perry (1879–1912) An exhibition flier, Rodgers established his own airmail system. Demonstrating the feasibility of transcontinental flight, he piloted the *Vin Fiz* across the United States in 1911.

ROGERS, Will
(1879–1935) Popular humorist and entertainer during the 1920s and 1930s, Rogers was an aviation enthusiast and promoter of its development for defense and as a vital mode of transportation.

RUSHWORTH, Robert A. (1924–1993) A USAF test pilot and, later, general, Rushworth was responsible for major test programs, including the Northrop F-5, Republic A-10, McDonnell Douglas F-15, General Dynamics YF-16, and the Rockwell B-1.

RUTAN, Elbert Leander
(1943–) An inventor and aircraft designer, Rutan pioneered the use of nonmetallic materials in aircraft construction. He designed the *Voyager*, the first aircraft to fly nonstop around the world without refueling.

RYAN, T. Claude
(1898–1982) In 1925, Ryan formed Ryan Airlines, which produced the M-1 monoplane from which the *Spirit of St. Louis* evolved. He developed the radar-controlled system that enabled the lunar landing of the Apollo 11 *Eagle*.

SCHIRRA, Walter M., Jr.
(1923–) Schirra was the only astronaut to fly on the Mercury, Gemini, and Apollo missions: Mercury 8 (1962), Gemini 6A (1965), and Apollo 7 (1968).

SCHRIEVER, Bernard Adolf (1910–) Schriever oversaw the development and deployment of the U.S. Air Force Intercontinental Ballistic Missile fleet during the late 1950s and 1960s.

SELFRIDGE, Thomas Etholen (1882–1908) Selfridge became the first Army officer to pilot an airplane in 1908 and was the first casualty of flight when he died in a crash later that year.

SHEPARD, Alan Bartlett, Jr. (1923–) Shepard became the first U.S. astronaut launched into space. In 1971, he commanded the Apollo 14 mission and was the fifth man to walk on the moon.

SIKORSKY, Igor Ivan
(1889–1972) Sikorsky built a single-rotor helicopter in 1939. The company that bears his name—now part of United Technologies—has been one of the foremost builders of helicopters since World War II.

SIX, Robert Forman
(1907–1986) A pilot and entrepreneur, Six invested in Varney Speed Lines in 1936, became president in 1938, and transformed it into Continental Airlines, building Continental into a major international carrier.

SLAYTON, Donald K.
(1924–1993) A member of the original Mercury 7 astronauts, Slayton served as chief of the Astronaut Office and director of Flight Crew Operations.

SMITH, C. R. (1899–1990) In 1934, entrepreneur Smith became president of newly formed American Airlines and turned it into one of America's top airlines. He launched the first nonstop transcontinental air service.

SPAATZ, Carl Andrew
(1891–1974) Spaatz served in World War I, commanded the USAAF strategic forces in the European Theater during World War II, and later headed the USAAF. In 1947, he became the first USAF chief of staff.

SPERRY, Elmer Ambrose, Sr. (1860–1930) A prolific inventor, Sperry developed gyroscopic stabilizers for ships and, in 1909, for airplanes. He also invented the automatic pilot, the first guided missile, and the artificial horizon.

SPERRY, Lawrence Burst, Sr. (1892–1923) The son of Elmer Sperry, Lawrence Sperry pioneered the development of automatic flight stabilizers, new flight instruments, guided missiles, and innovative racing aircraft. He died in a 1923 crash.

STAFFORD, Thomas P.
(1930–) Stafford, a USAF Lt. General, was a test pilot and one of the second group of American astronauts.

STANLEY, Robert M.
(1912–1977) Stanley, an engineer and aviator, formed Stanley Aviation Corporation. He developed the U.S. Air Force's first downward ejection seats, the automatic release lap bolts, and the Yankee extraction escape system.

STAPP, John Paul (1910–) Biophysicist Stapp established preventive measures for high-altitude bends and dehydration. He demonstrated the safe use of ejection seats at supersonic speeds and the necessity of airplane safety belts.

STEARMAN, Lloyd C.
(1898–1975) A designer and engineer, Stearman formed the Stearman Aircraft Company. He was later an executive with Lockheed Aircraft Corporation, where he helped design and develop the Electra.

TAYLOR, Charles Edward
(1868–1956) Taylor, an engineer, assisted the Wright brothers and helped build the

first airplane and airplane engine. In 1911, he assisted Calbraith Rodgers in his famous transcontinental flight.

THOMAS, Lowell (1892–1981) A popular author and radio and television personality during the 1940s and 1950s, Thomas avidly promoted aviation.

TIBBETS, Paul W., Jr. (1915–) On August 6, 1945, Tibbets piloted the *Enola Gay*, which dropped the first atomic bomb on Hiroshima, Japan. He helped establish the National Military Command Center in the Pentagon.

TOWERS, John Henry (1885–1955) Director of naval aviation during World War I, Towers led the development of naval aircraft carriers in the 1920s. During World War II, he helped plan Pacific Theater strategy.

TRIPPE, Juan Terry (1899–1981) Trippe founded Pan American Airways in 1927. In 1936, Pan Am opened air routes across the Pacific; by 1947, routes were made around the world.

TURNER, Roscoe (1895–1970) A flamboyant air show and film star, Turner flew with a lion cub and won many speed races during the 1930s. He helped train pilots during World War II.

TWINING, Nathan Farragut (1897–1982) Twining commanded the USAAF 13th Air Force in the Southwest Pacific and the Mediterranean Allied Strategic Air Forces in the European Theater in World War II.

VANDENBERG, Hoyt S. (1899–1954) Commander of the USAAF 9th Air Force during World War II, Vandenberg helped plan the Normandy invasion. Between 1948 and 1953, he served as U.S. Air Force chief of staff.

VON BRAUN, Wernher (1912–1977) German-born von Braun helped build America's postwar missile program. He developed the Redstone, which was used to send astronauts to the moon.

VON KÁRMÁN, Theodore (1881–1963) In 1908, this Hungarian-born inventor discovered form drag and developed the theory of supersonic drag in flight. He founded the Jet Propulsion Laboratory and the Aerojet Engineering Company.

VON OHAIN, Hans P. (1911–) He was one of several scientists to conceive the idea for jet propulsion. He designed a liquid-fueled engine, which was successfully test-flown in 1939. He was the USAF Chief Scientist from 1947 to 1979.

VOUGHT, Chance M. (1890–1930) Vought formed the Lewis & Vought Corporation in 1917. He designed the Model V Wright Flyer, the VE-7, the Corsair observation plane, and the UO-1, the Navy's first catapult-launched aircraft.

WADE, Leigh (1896–1991) World War I aviator Wade participated in the first round-the-world flight in 1924, became chief test pilot for Consolidated Aircraft, then served as a USAAF commander during World War II.

WALDEN, Henry W. (1883–1964) In 1909, designer and balloon enthusiast Henry Walden designed, built, and flew the first monoplane built in the United States.

WELLS, Edward Curtis (1910–1986) Boeing Airplane Company engineer Wells directed design development of the B-17 Flying Fortress. He was vice president and general manager in the late 1950s when Boeing won important government contracts.

WILSON, Thornton Arnold (1921–) Boeing Airplane Company engineer Wilson helped develop the B-52; became president in 1968 and chairman in 1972; and directed Boeing in pro-

duction of the 707, 727, and 737 jetliners.

WOOLMAN, Collett Everman (1889–1966) A pilot and entrepreneur, Woolman ran the world's first aerial crop dusting company, which evolved into Delta Airlines.

WRIGHT, Orville (1871–1948) With his brother, Wright invented the first airplane to accomplish powered flight. Orville piloted the aircraft on its first such flight on December 17, 1903.

WRIGHT, Wilbur (1867–1912) Bicycle mechanics and aviation enthusiasts, the Wright brothers invented the first airplane to accomplish powered flight. The aircraft was piloted on its first such flight on December 17, 1903.

YEAGER, Charles Elwood (1923–) On October 14, 1947, in the Bell X-1, Yeager became the first pilot to attain supersonic flight, and in December 1953, he became the first to fly at twice the speed of sound.

YOUNG, John W. (1930–) Young was the first to fly in space on six separate missions: Gemini 3 (1965), Gemini 10 (1966), Apollo 10 (1969), Apollo 16 (1972), STS-1 (1981), and STS-9 (1983).

Note: Page references in italics indicate photographs and/or illustrations.

A6M Reisen Zero warplanes. *See* Mitsubishi aircraft
A7M Reppu. *See* Mitsubishi aircraft
A-36 Apache. *See* North American Aviation aircraft
Aces
  American, 48, 49, *49*, 98, 113, 117, 136, 146
  British, 36
  Canadian, 36, 46, 51
  French, 34, 46, 48
  German, 32, 38, 51, 53
Adams, Michael, 191
Advanced Technology Bomber. *See* B-2 Spirit; Northrop aircraft
Aerial Experiment Association, 24, 27
Aero Club (France), 17, 18
Aero Club (United States), 25, 26
Aerodrome plane, 19, *19*
Air Combat Command, 130, 141, 152, 163
Aircraft
  Cold War, 128–167
  early, 12–31
  Gulf War, 147, 148, 151, 154, 155
  interwar, 58–91
  Korean War, 133, 134, *135*, 136
  mail, 56, 71
  postwar, 128–167
  Vietnam War, 140, 142–147, 148, 154
  World War I, 32–57
  World War II, 92–127
Air Defense Command, 156
Air Force One, 187
Air France, 195, 197
Air Mobility Command, 152, 155
Air shows, 24, 26
Alcock, John, 61, 68
Aldrin, Edwin "Buzz," 203, *203*
Allen, Edmund T., 124
Allied Expeditionary Air Force, 137
Altair. *See* Lockheed aircraft
American Airlines, 49, 58, *59*, 60, 86, 88, *88*, 89, *89*, 90, 172, 174
American Expeditionary Force Air Service, 38, 44, 46, 48, 57
American Volunteer Group, 96, 97, 99
American Wright Company, 23
Anders, William, 6, 202
Apollo space program, 171, 200, 202
Archdeacon, Ernest, 17, 20

Archdeacon Prize, 18
Armaments, 32, 34, 36, 40, 46, 48, 52, 60, 61, 77, 99, 100, 102, 103, 106, 109, 111, 112, 114, 119, 121, 123, 124, 125, 128, 133, 136, 137, 148
Armstrong, Neil, 191, 203, *203*
Arnold, General Henry "Hap," 90, 108, *108*, 125, 127, *127*
Arnold, Lieutenant Leslie, 72, 75
Atlantic Aircraft Corporation, 55
A.V. Roe Company, 30
AVG. *See* American Volunteer Group
Avion Corporation, 65
Avro aircraft
  Avroplane, 30
  Roe I, 30
  Triplane II, 31, *31*
Awards
  Air Medal, 92, *92*
  Altitude Prize, 26
  Archdeacon Prize, 18
  Bennett Trophy, 24, 46
  Collier Trophy, 42, 89, 181
  Distinguished Flying Cross, 67, 146
  Distinguished Service Medal, 168, *168*, 180
  Guggenheim medal, 79
  Harmon Trophy, 180, 181
  Medal of Honor, 49, 83, 113, 117
  Navy Cross, 113
  Robert Collier Trophy, 27
  Schneider Cup, 39, 80, 81, 82, 83, 118
  Scientific American Silver Trophy, 27
  Thompson Trophy, 7, 83

B-2 Spirit (Stealth). *See* Northrop aircraft
B-17 Flying Fortress. *See* Boeing aircraft
B-26 Marauder. *See* Glenn Martin aircraft
B-29 Superfortress. *See* Boeing aircraft
B-35 bomber. *See* Northrop aircraft
B-49 bomber. *See* Northrop aircraft
B-52 Stratofortress. *See* Boeing aircraft
B-57 Canberra. *See* Glenn Martin aircraft
B-247 airliner. *See* Boeing aircraft
B-377 Stratocruiser. *See* Boeing aircraft
Balloons, hot-air, 9, *9*, 14, 32
Barnstorming, 56, 71

Bayerische Flugzeugwerke, 120
Beard, Henri, 80
Beech, Olive Ann, 176
Beech, Walter, 176
Beechcraft aircraft, 170
  Bonanza, 171, 176, *176*, 177, *177*
  Model 18, 176, 177, *177*
  Model 33 Debonair, 177
  Model 35, 176
Bell, Alexander Graham, 19, 24, 27
Bell aircraft, 124
  X-1, 10, 168, 171, 178, *178*, 179, *179*, 180, 181
Bell Aircraft Company, 178
Bell Rascal missile, 140
Bendix Trophy Race, 83, 180
Bennett, James Gordon, 24
Bennett Trophy, 24, 46
Bernardi, Major Mario de, 83
Bf109. *See* Messerschmitt aircraft
Birkigt, Marc, 48
Bishop, William, 36, 46
Black Jet. *See* Lockheed aircraft
Black-McKellar Act (1934), 79
Blanchard, Jean-Pierre, 12, 14
Blériot, Louis, 18, 23, 25, 26, 27, 28, 29, *29*, 48
Blériot aircraft
  Type XI, 28–29, *28–29*
  Type XII, 28
Blériot Type XI. *See* Blériot aircraft
Blériot Type XI. *See* Blériot aircraft
Bock's Car, 126
Boeing, William Edward, 78, 79
Boeing aircraft
  B-17 Flying Fortress, 104, *104–105*, 106–109, *106–109*, 141
  B-29 Superfortress, 124–126, *124–126*, 141
  B-52 Stratofortress, 138–141, *138–140*
  B-247 airliner, 78–79, *78–79*
  B-377 Stratocruiser, 152, 184
  Boeing 367–80, 152, 184, 186
  Boeing 707, 170, 184–186, *185–186*
  Boeing 720, 186
  Boeing 727, 170, 186
  Boeing 737, 170
  Boeing 747 jumbojet, 154, 170, 184, 187–189, *187–189*
  Boeing 757, 170
  C-135, 152, 184
  Dash-Eighty, 152, 184, 186, *186*
  EC-135, 152

Boeing aircraft (*continued*)
  Fortress I, 106
  KC-97, 152
  KC-135 Stratotanker, 131, 139, *139*, 144, 148, *148*, 152–153, *152–153*, 184
  NKC-135, 152, *152*
  P-26 Peashooter, 76–77, *76–77*
  XB-15, 104
  XB-29, 124
Boeing Air Transport System, 78
Boelke, Oswald, 34, 53
Bonanza. *See* Beechcraft aircraft
Bong, Richard Ira, 117, *117*
Borman, Frank, 6, *6*, 7, 202, *202*
Braniff Airlines, 88, 185, *185*
British Aerospace/Aérospatiale Concorde, 170, 194–197, *194–197*
British Airways, 184, 188, 197
Brown, Captain Roy, 32, *33*, 38, 53
Brown, Lieutenant Harold, 82

C-5 Galaxy. *See* Lockheed aircraft
C-32. *See* Douglas aircraft
C-47. *See* Douglas aircraft
C-53. *See* Douglas aircraft
C-54. *See* Douglas aircraft
C-112. *See* Douglas aircraft
C-118 Liftmaster. *See* Douglas aircraft
C-135. *See* Boeing aircraft
Canadair, 137
Canadian Aeroplanes, Ltd., 57
Caproni, Count Gianni, 35
Caproni Ca33 aircraft, 40
Cayley, Sir George, 8, 15
Central Intelligence Agency, 137, 156
Cessna aircraft, 170, 171
Chanute, Octave, 8, 16
Chennault, Claire, 96, 99, *99*
Cherokee. *See* Piper aircraft
China Air Task Force, 99
Chinese Civil Air Transport, 99
Christmas Bombings, 141
Churchill, Winston, 94
Cochran, Jacqueline, 11, 180, *180*
Cockburn, George, 25, 26
Cody, Samuel F., 30
Collier Trophy, 27, 42, 89, 181
Collins, Michael, 203
Collishaw, Major Raymond, 51
Comanche 400. *See* Piper aircraft
Consolidated Aircraft, 124
Constellation. *See* Lockheed aircraft
Coolidge, President Calvin, 71

CR-1 racer. *See* Curtiss aircraft
CR-3 racer. *See* Curtiss aircraft
Crossfield, Scott, 10, 190, 192–193, *193*
Cubs. *See* Piper aircraft
Cuddihy, Lieutenant George, 83
Cunningham, Lieutenant Randy "Duke," 146
Curtiss, Glenn, 19, 23–27, *25*, *27*, 56, 81
Curtiss Aeroplane & Motor Company, Ltd., 27
Curtiss aircraft
   CR-1 racer, 81, *81*
   CR-3 racer, 80, 81
   Golden Flyer, 24, 26, 27
   H-81-B Warhawk, 97, *97*
   Hudson Flyer, 27
   JN-4 Jenny, 27, 35, 56–57, *56–57*
   June Bug, 24, 27
   Kittyhawks, 98, 100
   Model J, 56
   Model N, 56
   NC-4, 27
   P-6 Hawk, 80
   P-36, 96
   P-40 Warhawk, 96–99, *96–98*, 114
   R3C racer, 82
   R-3 seaplane, *82*
   Reims Racer, 24–25, *24–25*
   75 Hawk, 96
   Tomahawks, 98
Curtiss-Wright Corporation, 27

D-558 Skystreak. *See* Douglas aircraft
Dakotas. *See* Douglas aircraft
Dana, Bill, 193
Danti, Giovanni Battista, 12
d'Arlandes, Marquis, 9, 14
da Vinci, Leonardo, 8, 12
Davis, Benjamin Jr., 103, *103*
Dayton-Wright Company, 44, 45
DC-3. *See* Douglas aircraft
DC-6. *See* Douglas aircraft
DC-7 Seven Seas. *See* Douglas aircraft
DC-8. *See* Douglas aircraft
DC-10. *See* McDonnell Douglas aircraft
Debonair 33. *See* Beechcraft aircraft
de Havilland, Geoffrey, 30
de Havilland aircraft
   Comet, 184
   DH-4, 35, 44–45, *44–45*
   DH-9, 45
Delage, Gustave, 46

DH-4. *See* de Havilland aircraft
DH-9. *See* de Havilland aircraft
Dole Derby race, 62
Doolittle, Jimmy, 7, 66, 82, 83, *83*
Douglas, Donald, 65, 91, *91*
Douglas aircraft
   C-32, 89
   C-39, 90
   C-41, 90
   C-42, 90
   C-47/R4D, 90–91, *90*, 130
   C-53, 91
   C-54, 172
   C-118, 172, 173, *173*
   D-558 Skystreak, 193
   Dakotas, 91
   DC-2, 86–90, *86–87*
   DC-3, 79, 86, 88–91, *88–91*
   DC-6, 172–174, *172–174*, 184
   DC-7, 175, 184
   DC-8, 170
   Gooney Birds, 91
   Skysleeper Transport (DST), 89–90, *89*
   Skytrain, 91
   Skytrooper, 91
   World Cruisers, 72–75, *72–75*
   YC-118, 174
Douglas Aircraft Company, 72–75, 86
Douglas World Cruisers. *See* Douglas aircraft.
Downward-Looking Infrared (DLIR), 163
Driscoll, Lieutenant Bill, 146

Earhart, Amelia, 61, 66–67, *67*
Eastern Airlines, 6, 49, 88–90, *89*, 172, 202
EC-135. *See* Boeing aircraft
Eielsen, Carl Ben, 62
Eindecker. *See* Fokker aircraft
Eisenhower, General Dwight, 91
Ely, Eugene, 27
Engines
   air-cooled, 27, 38, 46, 50, 109, 116, 124
   Allied Signal, 183
   Allison, 98–100, 102, 133
   Antoinette, 30
   Anzani, 28–29
   Bentley B.R.2, 39
   BMW, 55
   Clerget, 38
   Continental, 84–85, 176–177
   Curtiss, 80, 82–83

Engines (*continued*)
   Cyclone, 86, 89
   Daimler-Benz, 120–123
   de Havilland, 132
   Franklin, 84
   gasoline, 15, 19
   General Electric, 132, 136–137, 142, 145, 152, 154, 160, 167, 182, 188–189, Gnome A, 46
   Goblin, 132
   Griffon, 119
   Hispano-Suiza, 35–36, 48
   Hornet, 41
   in-line, 24, 35, 41, 83, 98, 118, 176
   internal combustion, 14, 19
   JAP, 30
   Junkers Jumo, 120
   Kestrel, 120
   Le Rhône, 38, 46, 51
   Liberty, 35, 40, 42, 45, 72
   Lycoming, 84–85
   Mercedes, 54–55
   Merlin, 98, 100, 102–103, 118–119
   Mitsubishi Kinsei, 117
   Nakajima, 114, 116
   Oberursel, 50
   Pratt & Whitney, 62–63, *63–64*, 77, 79, 111–113, 138, 140, 148, 150, 152, 159, 174, 184, 186, 188–189
   radial, 52, 66, 86–87, 96, 174
   Reaction Motors, 178, 181, 190–192
   REP, 28–29, rocket, 193, 201, Rolls-Royce, 35, 44, 45, 92, 98, 100, 102, 118–120, 186, 188–189, 195–196
   rotary, 35, 50
   steam, 14, 19
   supercharged, 98
   Teledyne Continental, 198
   Turbo-compound, 175
   turbofan, 140, 148, 150, 152–154, 160, 167, 183, 186, 188–189
   turbojet, 132–133, 136–138, 140, 142, 145, 182, 184, 196
   turbo-ramjet, 159
   Twin Wasp, 174
   Wasp, 62–63, *63–64*, 77, 79
   water-cooled, 22
   Whirlwind, 64, 68, 70, *70*
   Wolseley, 36–37, *37*
   Wright, 86–87, 90, 124–125, 174–175
Enola Gay, 126, *126*
Everest, Major Frank, 180–181

F2H Banshee. *See* McDonnell Douglas aircraft
F3H Demon. *See* McDonnell Douglas aircraft
F4F Wildcat. *See* Grumman aircraft
F-4 Phantom II. *See* McDonnell Douglas aircraft
F6F Hellcat. *See* Grumman aircraft
F8F Bearcat. *See* Grumman aircraft
F-15 Eagle. *See* McDonnell Douglas aircraft
F-80 Shooting Star. *See* Lockheed aircraft
F-86 Sabre Jet. *See* North American Aviation aircraft
F-89 Scorpion. *See* Northrop aircraft
F-94 Starfire. *See* Lockheed aircraft
F-104 Starfighter. *See* Lockheed aircraft
F-110. *See* McDonnell Douglas aircraft
F-111. *See* McDonnell Douglas aircraft
F-117 Nighthawk. *See* Lockheed aircraft
Farman, Henri, 18, 20, 36, 61
Feinstein, Captain Jeffrey, 147
Fibaloy, 160
Finnair, 60
FJ-Fury. *See* North American Aviation aircraft
Flying Circus, 38, 51–54, *52*, *54*
Flying Tigers, 96, 99
Flying wings, 65, 164–167
Fokker, Anthony, 34, 35, 39, 50, 55, *55*
Fokker aircraft, 10
   Dr.I, 34, 37, *37*, 39, 50–53, *52–53*, 55
   D.VII, 35, 53–55, *54*
   D.VIII, 55
   Eindecker E.III, 34, 50, *50*, 55
   F.VII, 55, *55*, 67
Fokker Aircraft Corporation, 49
Fokker Flugzeugwerke, 55
Fokker Scourge, 34, 36, 38, 46, 50–51, 55, *55*
Folding Fin Aerial Rockets (FFAR), 130, 137
Folland, H. P., 36
Fonck, Rene, 48
Forward-Looking Infrared (FLIR), 140, 163
Francis, Captain Roy N., 42, *42*
French Aviation Militaire, 48
Frost, Jack, 62
Frye, Jack, 86

Fw.159, 120
Fw.190, 119

Garros, Roland, 34
Gatty, Harold, 61, 64
Gemini space program, 200, 202–203
Glenn Martin aircraft, 124
    B-26 Marauder, 42
    B-57 Canberra, 42
    MB-1, 40–41, *40–41*, 43, *43*, 91
    MB-2/NBS-1, 41–42, *41*
    Model TT, 42
Gliders, 15, 18, *18*, 22, 29
Global Positioning System, 167
Gloster aircraft
    IIA racer, 82–83
    Meteor, 134
Golden Eagle. See Lockheed aircraft
Goodden, Frank, 36
Goodlin, Chalmers, 178, 180
Gooney Birds. See Douglas aircraft
Gordon, Louis, 67
Gotha aircraft, 35
Granville Gee Bee race, 83
"Great Marianas Turkey Shoot," 110, 113
Grumman aircraft
    F4F Wildcat, 110, 114
    F6F Hellcat, 110–113, *110–112*, 116
    F8F Bearcat, 113
    Hellcat II, 112–113
    Martlet I, 110
Gulf War, 130, 131, 141, 147, 151
    Operation Desert Shield, 151, 155, 163
    Operation Desert Storm, 151, 153, 159, 162–163
    Operation Southern Watch, 151
Guynemer, Georges, 46, 48

Hall, F.C., 64
Hamilton, Charles, 26
Handley-Page aircraft, 35, 40
Harding, Lieutenant John, 72, 73, 75
Harmon Trophy, 180–181
Harris, Commander Cecil, 113
Harvey, Sergeant Alva, 72
Hauptman, Bruno, 71
Hawker, Harry, 39
Hawker Engineering Company, 39
Hawker Hurricane, 119
Hawker Siddeley Group, 39
Heinkel He112 aircraft, 120

Hellcat II. *See* Grumman aircraft
Henson, William Samuel, 15
Hibbard, Hall, 159
High Velocity Aerial Rockets (HVAR), 128, 133
Horkoshi, Jiro, 114, 115
Hughes Aircraft Company, 151

Immelman, Max, 34
Imperial German Army, 53
Imperial Japanese Navy, 114, 117
Inertial Navigation System, 167
Irvine, Lieutenant Rutledge, 82
Italian Air Force, 48

Jagdgeschwer No.1, 51
James, Daniel "Chappie," 146, *146*
Jennies. See Curtiss aircraft
Johnson, Amy, 61
Johnson, Clarence "Kelly," 156, 159, *159*, 160
Johnson, President Lyndon, 3

Kármán, Dr. Theodore von, 178
KC-97 tanker. *See* Boeing aircraft
KC-135 Stratotanker. *See* Boeing aircraft
Kelly, Oakley, 61
Kenney, General George, 117
Kenworthy, J., 36
Keys, Clement, 27
Ki43 Oscar aircraft, 117
Kill Devil Hills (North Carolina), 9, 16, 18, *18*, 22
Kirkham, Charles, 27
Kitty Hawk (North Carolina), 16
Kittyhawk warplanes. See Curtiss aircraft
Knight, Pete, 193
Korean War, 103, 113, 126, 130–131, 133, 146, 174
Kotcher, Dr. Ezra, 178

L-1011. *See* Lockheed aircraft
Lafayette Escadrille, 47, *47*
La Grande Semaine d'Aviation, 24, 25
Lahm, Lieutenant Frank, 20, 21
Langley, Samuel Pierpont, 15, 19, *19*, 22, 27
Lear, William Powell, 182
Learjets, 182–183, *182–183*
LeMay, General Curtis E., 125–126, 141, *141*
Lilienthal, Otto, 8, 15, 22
Lindbergh, Anne Morrow, 6, 71, *71*

Lindbergh, Charles, 6, 10, 61, 66–71, *71*
Lockheed aircraft
    Altair, 66
    Black Jet, 163
    C-5 Galaxy, 154–155, *154–155*
    Constellation, 172, 175, 184
    Electra, 67
    F-80 Shooting Star, 132–133, 160
    F-94 Starfire, 159
    F-104 Starfighter, 159
    F-117 Nighthawk, 160–163, *160–163*
    Golden Eagle, 62
    L-1011, 170
    Model 4 Air Express, 66
    Orion, 66
    P-80 Shooting Star, 117, 132–134, *132–133*
    Sirius, 66
    SR-71 Blackbird, 156–159, *156–159*
    Super Constellation, 175
    T-33 T-Bird, 133
    U-2, 131, 159–160
    Vega, 62, *62–63*, 64, *64*, 66–67, *66*
    Winnie Mae, 62–63, 63–64
Lockheed Aircraft Company, 62, 65
Looking Glass, 152–153
Loughead, Allan and Malcolm, 62, 65
Lovell, James, 6, 202
Low-Altitude Navigation and Targeting Infrared Air Force Night system (LANTIRN), 151
Low-Light Television (LLTV), 140
Lucid, Shannon, 180
Luebbe, Heinrich, 34, 50, 55
Lufthansa, 60
Luftwaffe, 34, 120–122
    Fighter Group II, 122
Luke, Frank, 48
Lulu Belle. See Lockheed aircraft

M-1 mailplane. *See* Ryan aircraft
MacArthur, General Douglas, 117
McAuliffe, Christa, 202
McCampbell, Captain David, 113, *113*
Macchi M.33 aircraft, 82, 83
McConnell, Captain Joe, 136
McDonnell aircraft, 91
MD-90, 170
MacKay trophy, 181
McKinley, President William, 19
McNeely, Bo, 67
MacReady, John, 61

MacRobertson races, 78, 88
Magee, Jr., John Gillespie, 11
Manly, Charles, 19
Mannock, Major Edward C., 36
Martin, Glenn L., 40, 42, *42*, 91
Martin, Major Frederick L., 72
Martin Marietta Company, 151
Mattern, Jimmie, 66
May, Lieutenant Wilfred, 32, *33*, 38
McDonnell Douglas aircraft
    DC-9, 170
    DC-10, 170
    F2H Banshee, 142
    F3H Demon, 142
    F-4 Phantom II, 142–147, *142–147*
    F-15 Eagle, 148–151, *148–151*
    F-100, 142
    F-111, 150
    MD-80, 170
MD-80. *See* McDonnell Douglas aircraft
Me262. *See* Messerschmitt aircraft
Memphis Belle, 108, *108*
Mercury space program, 200
Messerschmitt, Willy, 120
Messerschmitt AG, 120
Messerschmitt aircraft
    Bf109, 98, 120–123, *120–123*
    Emil, 123, *123*
    Gustav, 122–123, *123*
    Me262, 10, 132, 134
Mikoyan-Gurevich aircraft
    MiG-15, 128, *129*, 133, 135, *135*, *136*
    MiG-25, 158
Military Airlift Command, 154–155
Missiles
    AGM-65 Maverick, 130, 163
    AGM-69 Short Range Attack, 167
    AGM-86 Air-Launched Cruise Missile (ALCM), 141
    AGM-88 antiradar, 163
    AGM-129 Advanced Cruise Missile (ACM), 141
    AGN-131 Short Range Attack, 167
    AIM-4 Falcon, 130
    AIM-7 Sparrow, 130, 145, 148
    AIM-9 Sidewinder, 130, 145, 148
    AIM-120 Advanced Medium-Range, 130, 148
    air-intercept, 130
    air-to-air, 148
    air-to-ground, 137, 163
    air-to-surface, 140
    ballistic, 42

Missiles (*continued*)
 Bell Rascal, 140
 Bullpup, 137
 cruise, 130, 140
 Minuteman ICBM, 155
 North American Aviation Hound
  Dog, 140
 Short-Range Attack Missile, 141
 Titan, 42
 warning systems, 155
Mitchell, General William "Billy," 35,
 43, *43*, 104, 124
Mitchell, Reginald J., 118
Mitsubishi aircraft
 A5M, 114
 A6M Reisen Zero, 97, *97*, 113–117,
  114–116
 A7M Reppu, 117
Montgolfier, Jacques Etienne, 9, 14
Montgolfier, Joseph Michel, 9, 14
Moore-Brabazon, J.T.C., 30
Mouillard, Louis, 10
Mussolini, Benito, 83

N-156 Freedom Fighter. *See* Northrop
 aircraft
National Advisory Committee for
 Aeronautics, 23
National Aeronautics & Space
 Administration, 168, 200, 203
Nelson, Lieutenant Erik, 72, 75
Nichols, Ruth, 66
Nieuport aircraft, 35
 Nieuport 11 *Bébé*, 46, *46*, 53
 Nieuport 17, 46–47, *47*
 Nieuport-Macchi Ni11, 46
Noonan, Fred, 67
North American Air Defense
 Command (NORAD), 146
North American Aviation aircraft, 49
 A-36 Apache, 102
 F-86 Sabre Jet, 128, *129*, 133–137,
  134–136, 180
 P-51 Mustang, 100–103, *100–102*,
  113, 123, 134, 146
 X-15, 10, 156, 168, 190–193,
  191–193
North American Aviation Hound
 Dog missile, 140
Northrop, John, 62, 65, *65*, 164, 165
Northrop aircraft
 Alpha, 65
 B-2 Spirit (Stealth), 65, 164–167,
  164–167
 B-35 bomber, 65

Northrop aircraft (*continued*)
 B-49 bomber, 65
 Beta, 65
 Delta, 65
 F-5, 65
 F-89 Scorpion, 65
 FJ-Fury, 136
 Gamma, 65
 N-156 Freedom Fighter, 65
 P-61 Black Widow, 65
 Sabre Dog, 137
 SM-62 Snark cruise missile, 65
 T-38 trainer, 65
 XP-86, 134
Northwest Airlines, 60, 88, 173
Nungesser, Charles, 46, 48

Ogden, Lieutenant Henry, 74
Olds, Colonel Robin, 146
Orion. *See* Lockheed aircraft
Ornithopters, 8, 29
Orteig, Raymond, 71

P-6 Hawk. *See* Curtiss aircraft
P-26 Peashooter. *See* Boeing aircraft
P-36 warplane. *See* Curtiss aircraft
P-40 Warhawk. *See* Curtiss aircraft
P-51 Mustang. *See* North American
 Aviation aircraft
P-61 Black Widow. *See* Northrop
 aircraft
P-80 Shooting Star. *See* Lockheed
 aircraft
PA-6 Skysedan. *See* Piper aircraft
PA-28 Turbo Arrow. *See* Piper aircraft
Pan American World Airways, 60, 71,
 88, 172, 185–186, *185*, 188, 196
Pangborne, Clyde, 78
Paris Air Show (1969), 188
Paris Air Show (1973), 194
Pershing, General John J. "Blackjack,"
 49, 57, 82
Piedmont Airlines, *89*
Pilâtre de Rozier, J.F., 9, 14
Pilot-Activated Automatic Recovery
 System, 163
Piper, William T. Sr., 84
Piper aircraft
 Cherokee, 85
 Comanche, 85
 Cub, 84–85, *85*
 PA-6 Skysedan, 84, *84*
 PA-28 Turbo Arrow, 85, *85*
 Super Cub, 84–85, *85*
Post, Wiley, 61, 64, *64*, 66

Prevost, Maurice, 10
Pulitzer Race, 80–82
Putnam, George Palmer, 67

Quarles, Donald, 138
Quimby, Harriet, 28–29, *29*

R3C racer. *See* Curtiss aircraft
R-3 seaplane. *See* Curtiss aircraft
Radar, 95, 147, 149, 151, 160, 164
RC-135. *See* Boeing aircraft
Records
 altitude, 66, 127, 180, 190, 193
 distance, 10, 61, 64, 67, 71
 endurance, 22, 66–67
 speed, 10, 61, 64, 71, 88, 156, 168,
  180, 190, 193
Red Baron, 32, *33*, 38, 51, 53, *53*
Refueling, air-to-air, 74, 131, 140, 144,
 152–153, 163
Reno National Air Races, 113
Rethel, Walter, 120
Richthofen, Baron Manfred von, 32,
 33, 38, 51, 53, *53*
Rickenbacker, Captain Eddie, 6,
 48–49, *49*, 117, 132
Rickenbacker Motor Company, 49
Ride, Sally, 180
Ritchie, Captain Richard "Steve," 147
Rittenhouse, Lieutenant David, 80
Rockwell International aircraft
 Space Shuttle Orbiters, 200–203
 Space Transportation System,
  201–202
Rodgers, Calbraith, 21, *21*
Roe, Alliot Verdon, 23, 30
Rogers, Will, 64
Rolling Thunder campaign, 141
Roosevelt, President Franklin, 89, 113
Royal Aircraft Factory aircraft
 F.E. pusher biplanes, 36
 S.E.5, 36–37, *36–37*
Royal Air Force (Belgium), 38
Royal Air Force (England), 39, 91, 94,
 96, 99, 100, 102, 106, 110, 118,
 119, 122
Royal Dutch Airlines (KLM), 55, *55*,
 60, 88
Royal Flying Corps (England), 32, 36,
 38
Royal Navy Air Service (England), 38
Royal Navy (England), 110, 118
Royal Netherlands Air Force, 55
Royce, Henry, 118
Rutan, Burt, 198–199, *199*

Rutan, Dick, 10, 198–199, *199*
Ryan, Claude, 68, 71
Ryan aircraft
 M-1 mailplane, 68
 NYP. *See Spirit of St. Louis*

Sabre Dog. *See* North American
 Aviation aircraft
Santos-Dumont, Alberto, 18
Savoia S.13 racer, 80
Schneider, Jacques, 80
Schneider Cup, 39, 80–83, 118
Selfridge, Lieutenant Thomas, 21, 24
75 Hawk. *See* Curtiss aircraft
Short-Range Attack Missile, 141
Sikorsky, Igor, 35
Simms Station (Ohio), 16, 18, *18*, 22
Sirius. *See* Lockheed aircraft
Skunk Works, 156–157, 159–160
Skysleeper Transport. *See* Douglas
 aircraft
Skytrain. *See* Douglas aircraft
Skytrooper. *See* Douglas aircraft
SM-62 Snark cruise missile. *See*
 Northrop aircraft
Smith, C.R., 89
Smith, Herbert, 38
Smith, Lieutenant Lowell, 74, 75
Smithsonian Institution (Washington,
 D.C.), 19, 178, 193
 National Air & Space Museum,
  70
Snipe. *See* Sopwith Aviation Company
 aircraft
Société pour les Appareils
 Deperdussin (SPAD), 29
 A.2 fighter, 48
 SPAD VII, 48
 SPAD XIII, 34, 48–49, *49*, 54, 55
Sopwith, Sir Thomas Octave
 Murdoch, 38–39, *39*, 56
Sopwith Aviation Company aircraft
 Bat Boat, 39
 Camel, 32, *33*, 34, 38–39, *38–39*,
  51, 53
 Snipe, 38–39, 55
 Tabloid, 38–39
Space Shuttle Orbiter, 171, 188, *188*,
 190, 200–203
 Atlantis, 202
 Challenger, 201, 202
 Columbia, 201, *201*, 202, 203
 Discovery, 168, *169*, 200, *200*, 202,
  203
 Endeavour, 203

SPAD. *See* Société pour les Appareils Deperdussin (SPAD)
Spirit of St. Louis, 6, 68–71, *68–70*
SR-71 Blackbird. *See* Lockheed aircraft
Stearman PT-17 Kaydets, 109, *109*
Strategic Air Command (SAC), 124, 126, 130–131, 138, 141, 152, 158
Stutz, Wilmer, 67
Super Constellation. *See* Lockheed aircraft
Supermarine Seafire, 119
Supermarine Sea Lion II, 80, 83
Supermarine Spitfire, 92, *93*, 118–119, *118–119*
Swissair, 60

T-33 "T-Bird." *See* Lockheed aircraft
T-38 trainer. *See* Northrop aircraft
Tactical Air Command (TAC), 130, 163
37th Fighter Wing, 160–161
Taylor, C. Gilbert, 84
Taylor, Charles E., 16, 21
Thomas, B. Douglas, 56
Thompson Trophy, 7, 83
Tomahawks. *See* Curtiss aircraft
Transcontinental & Western Airlines, 60, 86
Trans-World Airlines (TWA), 60, 65, 90, 172, 196
Truax, Robert, 199
Truman, President Harry S, 43, 126
Turner, Roscoe, 66, 78, 83
Tuskegee Airmen, 103, 146

U-2 spy planes, 131, 159–160
United Aircraft & Transport Corporation, 78–79, 86
United Air Lines, 60, 79, *79*, 90, 172, 174
United States Air Force, 43, 65, 142
  1st Fighter Group, 134
  4th Fighter Group, 134, 151
  8th Air Force, 181
  49th Fighter Wing, 163
  393rd Bomb Squadron, 167
  509th Bomb Wing, 167
  715th Bomb Squadron, 167
  Air Defense Command, 156
  Air Mobility Command, 152, 155
  Pave Eagle data gathering program, 177
  Red Flag readiness exercise, 146
  Systems Command, 141

United States Air Service Reserve, 71
United States Army, 23, 40, 96
  1st Aero Squadron, 57
  9th Armored Division, 94
United States Army Air Force, 65, 84, 94, 96, 99, 127
  1st Bombardment Division, 107
  2nd Bombardment Group, 106
  5th Air Force, 103, 117
  8th Air Force, 83, 101, 103–104, 106, 108, *108*, 109, 9th Air Force, 94, 137
  10th Air Force, 103
  13th Air Force, 103
  14th Air Force, 96, *96*, 99, 103
  15th Air Force, 109
  20th Air Force, 125, 126
  23rd Fighter Group, 99, *99*
  27th Pursuit Squadron, 141
  94th Fighter Squadron (Hat in the Ring), 132
  322nd Fighter Group, 103
  332nd Fighter Group, 146
  357th Fighter Group, 103
  361st Fighter Group, 101
  401st Bombardment Group, 107
  447th Bombardment Group, 104
  VF–15 fighter squadron, 113
United States Army Air Service, 40, 42, 45, 72, 76–77, 83, 95
  10th Air Force, 32
United States Army Signal Corps, 20, 21, 49, 91
United States Marine Corps, 89, 110, 113, 136
United States Navy, 27, 40, 41, 43, 71, 74, 80, 83, 89, 96, 104, 113, 142, 193
  Task Force 58, 110
  VF-84 Squadron, 143
United States Single Integrated Operational Plan, 167
United States State Department, 74
United States War Department, 19
USS *Birmingham*, 27
USS *Essex*, 112–113
USS *Hornet*, 83
USS *Independence*, 111–112, 143
USS *Langley*, 193
USS *Ranger*, 113
USS *Wasp*, 113
USS *Yorktown*, 111–112

Valencia, Commander Eugene, 113
Vandenberg, Hoyt S., 137, *137*

Vega. *See* Lockheed aircraft
Vietnam War, 103, 130, 140, 142, 145, 147, 154
  Christmas Bombings, 141
  Operation Arc Light, 141
  Operation Bolo, 146
  Rolling Thunder campaign, 141
Voisin, Charles, 18
Voisin, Gabriel, 29
Voss, Werner, 51
Vought F4U Corsair aircraft, 113, 116
Voyager, 198, *198*, 199

Wade, Lieutenant Leigh, 74
Wagner, Lieutenant Boyd D., 98
Walcott, Dr. Charles, 19
Walker, Joe, 181, 190, 192
Welch, Lieutenant George, 98
Western Airlines, 66, 88
White, Major Robert M., 190, 192
Whitten-Brown, Arthur, 61, 68
Wilkins, Sir George Hubert, 62, 66
Williams, Lieutenant Alford, 82
Willys, John North, 27
Wilson, Charles, 137
Windham, W.G., 30
Winnie Mae. See Lockheed aircraft
Women's Airforce Service Pilots (WASP), 180
Woolams, Jack, 178
World War I, 10, 23, 27, 29, 34, 83
  American aircraft in, 40, 42, 56, 57
  British aircraft in, 38, 44–45
  French aircraft in, 46, 47, *47*
  German aircraft in, 50, 51, 52, *52*
World War II, 10, 71, 83, 92–127
  American aircraft in, 65, 84, 92, 96–113, 124–126
  Battle of Britain, 118–119, 121, 122
  Battle of Leyte Gulf, 113
  Battle of Midway, 116
  British aircraft in, 92, 118–119
  European Theater, 103, 106, 108–109, 113, 120–123, 127, 181
  German aircraft in, 94, 120–123
  "Great Marianas Turkey Shoot," 110, 113
  Japanese aircraft in, 94, 114–117
  Mediterranean Theater, 98, 103
  Normandy, 102, 137
  Operation Bodenplatte, 123
  Operation Overlord, 137
  Pacific Theater, 109, 110, 113, 114, 116, 117, 125, 126, 127
  Russian aircraft in, 92, 94, 122

Wright, Orville, 3, 8–10, 12, *12*, 16, 18, *18*, 20–23, *23*, 27, 44
Wright, Wilbur, 3, 8–10, 12, *13*, 16–18, *18*, 20–23, *22*, *23*, 27
Wright Aeronautical Laboratory, 23
Wright aircraft
  1908 Flyer, 20
  Flyer I, 10, 16–17, 22, 27
  Flyer II, 16, 22
  Flyer III, 16–17, 22–23
  Military Flyer, *16–17*, 20–21
  Model A, *16–17*, 20, *20*, 21, *21*
  Model EX, 21, *21*

X-1. *See* Bell aircraft
X-15. *See* North American Aviation aircraft
XB-15. *See* Boeing aircraft
XB-29. *See* Boeing aircraft
XP-86. *See* North American Aviation aircraft

YC-118. *See* Douglas aircraft
Yeager, Chuck, 8, 10, 178–181, *181*
Yeager, Jeana, 10, 198–199, *199*
Yom Kippur War, 143

Ziegler, Jean, 181